SPOR ... ᴊASICS

Sports Coaching: The Basics is an engaging and provocative introduction to sports coaching which combines coaches' views and experiences of their work with discussions and topical issues that feature in this fast-growing field. In doing so, coaches are placed at the centre of discussions relating to philosophical, historical, sociological, psychological and pedagogical interpretations of contemporary practice. Consequently, the book prompts questions such as:

- What is coaching?
- What does it mean to be a coach?
- How do coaches influence athletes/players?
- How do coaches learn?
- What is it like to be a coach?

In considering these questions, readers are encouraged to reflect upon their experiences of coaching and to start conversations with others about coaches' work. Therefore, the book is of use to coaches, those interested in studying sports coaching, and coach educators or facilitators of coach learning initiatives.

Laura Purdy is a Senior Lecturer in the Department of Sport and Physical Activity at Edge Hill University, UK. Her interest in the academic field of sports coaching was fostered by her involvement as a coach and coxswain in rowing programmes ranging from novice to elite levels, including junior, adaptive and veteran. This curiosity continues to be fuelled via contributions to coaches' Continuing Professional Development (CPD) in a range of sports and international settings. Laura's academic work focuses on performance sporting cultures and the experiences of coaches and athletes/players who operate in these contexts.

The Basics

For a full list of titles in this series, please visit www.routledge.com/The-Basics/book-series/B

SPORTS COACHING
THE BASICS

Laura Purdy

LONDON AND NEW YORK

First published 2018
by Routledge
2 Park Square, Milton Park, Abingdon, Oxon OX14 4RN

and by Routledge
711 Third Avenue, New York, NY 10017

Routledge is an imprint of the Taylor & Francis Group, an informa business

British Library Cataloguing-in-Publication Data
A catalogue record for this book is available from the British Library

Library of Congress Cataloging-in-Publication Data
Names: Purdy, Laura G., author.
Title: Sports coaching : the basics / Laura Purdy.
Description: Abingdon, Oxon ; New York, NY : Routledge, 2018. |
Includes bibliographical references and index.
Identifiers: LCCN 2017027285| ISBN 9781138890879 (hardback) |
ISBN 9781138890886 (pbk.) | ISBN 9781315709994 (ebook)
Subjects: LCSH: Coaching (Athletics). | Coaches (Athletics)--Training of.
Classification: LCC GV711 .P87 2018 | DDC 796.07/7--dc23
LC record available at https://lccn.loc.gov/2017027285

ISBN: 978-1-138-89087-9 (hbk)
ISBN: 978-1-138-89088-6 (pbk)
ISBN: 978-1-315-70999-4 (ebk)

Typeset in Bembo
by HWA Text and Data Management, London

This book is for Arben Krasniqi, Bob Mitchell, Diccon Lloyd-Smeath, Harri Mannonen, Karolis Čyžus and Paul Sparrowhawk.

CONTENTS

ACKNOWLEDGEMENTS

While there is only one name on the cover, this work was a team effort. Thanks to Simon, Cecily and Will at Routledge for initiating and supporting this project. Thank you to Dean Purdy for meticulously proofreading each chapter, to Bob Mitchell for being the 'test' coach, and to Jenn Purdy, Lisa Griffiths and ShuShu Chen for the constructive criticism and attention to detail. I am grateful for the support of subject specialists Mel Lang and Charlotte Kerner, and the contribution of Clodagh Glynn. I would like to recognise Chris Hughes who was always willing to converse, challenge and critique. And, I am indebted to Geoff Kohe without whom this project would not have been as coherent nor would the process have been as fun. Finally, to the coaches and athletes/players who have shared their experiences and insights, thank you for fuelling my curiosity and inspiring me to 'raise my game'. It has been a pleasure to work with you.

PREFACE

coachanon@sportsclub.com
Wednesday September 9
To: Laura Purdy

Hello Laura,

I hope you are keeping busy. Pre-season is going well – I've got a good group of players who are in reasonable shape so I've got something from which I can build. Given what I've seen of the players, we might actually be able to think about a top three finish in the league! Their physical training is under control, but I was wondering if you have come across any research on young athletes and the types of environments in which they can do well? Also, last season I think my coaching improved, but I know I need to learn a lot more about what I'm doing so that I can move up the ladder. I know there's no 'quick fix' to developing, but could you recommend a useful book that might give me some ideas of things to consider?

Thanks in advance

I often receive email messages from coaches who are looking for information to help 'fuel' their thinking. And, although there are numerous texts on the market, none seem to be entirely appropriate – either aimed at particular sports, written with disciplinary focuses, intended for academic audiences or too simplistic for a coach with several years of experience – I usually forward a few journal articles (to which there is usually no response!). More recently, I have replied by relating key findings from the literature to the coach's practice, and the reactions from the coaches have been positive. Of use then, would be a book that combines coaches' views and experiences of their work and some theoretical insights, issues and discussions that are prevalent in the academic literature. Therefore, when Routledge contacted me about the possibility of contributing to 'the basics' series, I responded with enthusiasm.

While my positive reaction was largely out of the prospect of creating a text that may be of interest or relevant to the coaches, coach educators or students with whom I have worked, in developing the book I would also have an opportunity to 'take stock' of the wider literature in the field. As scholarship focusing on sports coaches has expanded exponentially since I completed my doctoral studies, the book would enable me to see how the field has evolved and to engage with ideas outside of my 'academic comfort zone'.

Given its academic focus, this book is not centred on 'how to' coach; rather it offers readers a taste of the ideas and theoretical frameworks relating to sports coaches which have been the subject of scholarly interest. As the book is aimed at introducing 'the basics', there will be some overlap with other texts. Different to several other texts however, this book places the coach as *the* central focus. To clarify, although there will be implications on athletes/players, discussions largely focus around issues relating to coaches themselves. The content then, is aimed at encouraging readers to reflect upon their experiences as coaches and/or of coaches, and to start conversations about coaches' work.

In terms of structure, the book begins by 'setting the scene' regarding what coaching is and how it has been understood. The book then adopts a similar structure to Jones' (2005) resource guide which 'mapped' research and texts relating to sports coaching in light of 'parent' disciplines and sub-disciplines. Therefore, the first half of the book is structured around key themes or arguments within the literature which can be linked to 'parent' disciplines (i.e. philosophy, history, sociology and psychology). This approach was useful as each discipline has a particular framing of what a coach is, how a coach operates and why they do what they do. Also, a disciplinary base provided a helpful structure for arranging ideas and discussion points; however, it must be noted that these disciplinary (and sub-disciplinary) discussions are intertwined. It is also useful to highlight that Chapter 2 (The philosophical coach) provides the core arguments and discussions from which the subsequent content of this book is built. Hence, this chapter is structured differently and is slightly longer than the others.

Following the initial chapters, which are organised in light of disciplines, the second half of the book includes two chapters which are underpinned by the sub-discipline of pedagogy. These are: Chapter 6 (which covers athlete/player learning and coaches' methods); and, Chapter 7 (which covers coach learning initiatives). The final chapters move beyond sub-disciplinary-specific ideas to focus on prevalent and developing areas within the literature, specifically, Chapter 8 (which covers problematic coaching behaviours) and Chapter 9 (which covers the careers of performance coaches).

Given the size of the book, it has not been possible to include every topic and acknowledge every piece of literature. Therefore, the content has been largely influenced by my reading of the literature, with decisions on what to include and exclude largely based around key arguments or discussions within the field. Certainly, subject specialists may object to the inclusion or exclusion of particular words, viewpoints, or theories; however, a book of this size and nature cannot be, nor is it is intended to be, everything to everyone. Central to my thinking was that the content would not focus on issues that predominantly related to coaches in a small number of nations; rather, the arguments should resonate with a more global audience of coaches, coach educators and students. Additionally, where relevant, coaches' (and some athletes'/players') ideas, musings and comments are included. These data were largely drawn from semi-structured interviews with coaches and athletes in various sports, levels and nations. To protect coaches' identities, some data have been anonymised. Also, although these data mostly feature the voices of elite and professional (i.e. performance) coaches and athletes/players, this is not meant to suggest that these are the 'gold standard' in understanding coaching, rather, they have been included because many of their ideas may resonate with coaches or interest coaches at all levels and in various domains. Furthermore, while comments are included from Paralympic coaches, the book does not provide a 'domain' that specifically acknowledges adaptive sport. Instead, adaptive sport is encompassed within the domains of participation, development or performance (see Chapter 1 for a discussion of domains). Finally, in an effort to recognise the differences in terminology across nations and sports, as opposed to referring to all sports participants as athletes, where relevant, the term athlete/player is used.

In summary, *Sports Coaching: The Basics* provides a 'taster' of coaches' views and experiences of their work in light of (sub) disciplinary discussions and topical issues which feature in the fast-growing academic field. It is my hope that the book's content will ignite a curiosity in the reader to consider some of these ideas in their coaching practice or to explore the field further. Additionally, in generating this text, I've had the opportunity to 'take stock' of the field and appreciate areas beyond my academic 'comfort zone'. In a similar way, I hope this book helps readers to go beyond their 'comfort zones' regarding coaching and consider new possibilities.

WHAT IS SPORTS COACHING?

Traditionally sports coaches have focused on preparing athletes/ players for international competition or working with professional athletes/players in various leagues. However, coaches are increasingly moving beyond sports-specific positions to assisting with the delivery of school physical education or promoting social policy in the areas of health, youth engagement, social inclusion, lifelong learning and community regeneration. Given the range in coaches' roles and responsibilities, it is worth exploring how they interpret their work, that is, how they define sports coaching.

This chapter 'sets the scene' for the subsequent content of the book. It begins by drawing together coaches' definitions of sports coaching with those presented in the literature and considers the various domains in which coaches work. The discussion continues with a brief history of how coaching has been investigated, paying attention to models of coaching and notions of 'effective' and 'successful' coaching.

DEFINING SPORTS COACHING

To begin this section, two coaches working in elite sport contexts provided their views of sports coaching. The coaches stated:

> At the end of the day, it's their progression. It's getting somebody, I mean even though I work at an elite level, they athletes are not all going to make Olympics, but they might make Europeans or they might make Europa Cup. And it's really the joy of seeing somebody get from where they start and where I can get them to go. And, the

end result is not always the same because people are different talents
and have different abilities. So I suppose coaching is that; it's trying to
get somebody to perform to the best they can (elite athletics coach).

(Glynn, 2008)

Well, [the athletes] just want to win. Purely and simply, they just
want to go faster. Different ones require different things I guess, but
generally they just want your support to go quick (elite rowing coach).

(Purdy, 2006)

As articulated in the quotes, in considering their work, both coaches
highlighted their central purpose which was to improve athletes'/
players' sport performances. To do this, the coaches offered their
support through a range of different activities including: planning
and implementing training programmes, teaching skills and
providing technical and tactical advice. Given they were working in
the highest level of competition in light of their primary focus on
improving athletes'/players' sporting performances, these coaches
may view themselves as 'experts' who transfer their knowledge
to athletes/players in an effort to 'get performance out' of them.
However, this approach tends to position the athlete/player as a
performing machine or an inanimate object to be recorded and
ranked (Bale & Sang, 1996). For example, a professional basketball
player commented, '[The] coach makes the decisions … We are like
chess pieces and he's the chess player. We have to do what he wants
us to do' (Purdy, Kohe & Paulauskas, in review). For some coaches,
the advantage of adopting such a functional approach that privileges
the physical performance and treats athletes/players as machines is
that it enables the coach to simplify her/his work and focus attention
(and energy) on areas perceived to be of most impact. This may lead
the coach to feel as though s/he is better able to rationalise actions
that, if personalised, may be morally problematic (Ryall, 2016).
Additionally, being detached enables the coach to pursue her/his
goals (e.g. keep her/his job, get promoted), protect her/his interests
and make rational decisions.

Some coaches may have adopted a performance-focused approach
because it was what they had experienced as athletes/players, what they
were taught to do, or it was the dominant approach among coaches at

their sports club/organisation. However, coaches do not only act how they have been influenced to behave, they also have choice over their actions. For example, a novice volunteer rowing coach reflected upon her first season in which she was working with a junior girls' crew:

> I remember going to a training session and I was working on one athlete and saying 'Move your hands away, move your hands away', thinking about the technique I was trying to get and then I realised, okay, this is Ana. Why isn't Ana moving her hands properly? Maybe she doesn't understand what I'm saying or I'm saying it the wrong way, so I changed something or did it another way or whatever, but it immediately brought my focus onto the person and now I was dealing with Ana and Simona and Maria, rather than just a group of athletes to whom I was teaching a technique. And it just kind of struck me then 'Ah, this is the way you go about it. This makes it much more interesting'!

As the coach viewed herself as responsible for developing the athlete's technique, this quote highlights her change in thinking in terms of *how* this knowledge was translated to athletes. Initially it appears the coach had adopted the role of knowledge-provider (akin to the coaches' comments earlier in this chapter), but this changed as she began to appreciate that, for athletes to develop in a more meaningful way, she needed to recognise them as individuals and work *with* them. This approach is reflected in the International Council for Coaching Excellence's (ICCE) definition of sports coaching, which is: 'the *guided* improvement of sports participants in a single sport at identifiable stages of participant development' (2013, p. 14). Therefore, as opposed to positioning the coach as a trainer, the novice rowing coach hints at considering the coach as an educator, a position that requires an appreciation of how people learn and develop (to be discussed in Chapter 6). While some may argue that this approach is more appropriate when working with junior or young athletes/players, there are elite coaches (see Jones, Armour & Potrac, 2004) who also view themselves as educators or guides in developing athletes/players.

Whether focused on participation or performance, viewing a coach as an educator raises awareness to a more holistic approach to athlete/player development. A holistic approach to coaching places importance on recognising that 'each [athlete/player] is a unique individual and has their own idiosyncratic knowledge base, preferred ways of learning, personality, motivations, interest, values and social history' (Hallam & Ireson, 1999, p. 69). By acknowledging the life situations of the athletes and including them in the coaching process, coaches could better engage athletes/players and have an impact beyond the performative (i.e. relating to performance). An elite field hockey coach who had transitioned into coaching following her retirement as an elite player, stated:

> When I started coaching, I was focused on improving the team's performance, but as I gained more experience, I started to play with different ideas, strategies and tried different approaches in my sessions. I guess my early coaching was very 'by the book' because I was still finding my feet. It is so different to what I do now because my focus isn't fully on performing skills. I think about how I can involve the players in the process, this means I need to get to know them better, find out more about who they are, what they do outside of the sport and maybe how I can incorporate some of their interests in what we do as a team. I guess I'm thinking about more about them as people and how I could facilitate their development beyond sport.

The quote suggests that the coach's focus is on the development of players as performers and as people. This is echoed by Wayne Smith, former head coach of the All Blacks (New Zealand's men's rugby team) who stated, 'I believe coaching is all about trying to develop better people, not just better players' (Kidman, 2005, p. 26). One could draw upon Lyle and Cushion's (2017, p. 47) definition here as it positions sports coaching as the 'purposeful improvement of an individual or team's performance in sport'. This definition moves the emphasis of coaches' work beyond the development of sport-related skills (i.e. their sport performance) to consider the participant's wider development (i.e. their 'performance in sport'). Certainly, the wider development of a person may be the central focus of sports coaches who are operating in broader contexts with increasingly diverse populations. For example, a boxing coach who spent several years coaching elite and professional boxers changed her focus and began to work with youth at risk. She stated:

In the early days [as a coach], my priority was to train athletes to win things – it was my motivation ... but more recently it has changed ... I work with teenagers and youth at risk so sport is the medium in which we can talk anger issues and stuff like that. Sport enables me to make a connection with them ...

(Glynn, 2008)

Here, the coach views sport as the medium in which she can connect with young people to discuss wider issues. Accordingly, Kidman and Hanrahan's (2011) definition of sports coaching as 'striving to contribute to the success of each athlete' (p. 3) is useful because it considers wider interpretations of success and, by extension, what coaching is and who it might be for.

At this point, readers may wish to reflect upon the definitions provided by the coaches and academics featured in this section and consider their definition of sports coaching. In light of the section's content, how does the reader position the athlete/player? For example, the comments at the outset of the chapter positioned the coach as an 'expert' who was responsible for transferring knowledge to athletes/players 'to get them to perform to the best they can'. There was some acknowledgement from the elite rowing coach that 'different ones require different things ...' but ultimately the coach recognised that the rowers 'just want your support to go quick'. The novice rowing coach, in part, echoed this sentiment. Although her initial focus was on the junior rowers' performances of the skill, she soon realised that, for the rowers to develop in a more meaningful way, she needed to recognise their individuality and work *with* them. This shifts the focus from the athlete/player as a performer to the athlete/player as a person. Such a view was supported by the coaches who recognised their role in 'develop[ing] better people, not just better players' and was extended by the boxing coach, who used sport with young people as a way to open up a dialogue about wider issues. These definitions are useful as they can spark discussions that highlight that coaching and the coaching process are not only shaped by the coach, but also by the participant and the context. To illustrate how the sporting context and the participant's requirements impact upon the coach's practice, scholars (e.g. Lyle, 2002; Lyle & Cushion, 2017) have utilised the terminology 'coaching domains'.

COACHING DOMAINS

Coaching domains are organised around the commonalities in practices, assumptions and expectations that frame coaches' work – in particular, sporting contexts (Lyle, 2002; Lyle & Cushion, 2017). For example, while coaches working in community sport contexts might find themselves having to be 'everything to everyone' (Phillips, 2000, p. 129), in elite sport, the presence of assistant coaches, scouts, biomechanists, physiologists, psychologists, performance analysts, strength and conditioning coaches, nutritionists, physiotherapists, agents, lawyers and media specialists have modified the coach's roles and responsibilities. Recognition of the coaching domains then, allows for a degree of separation between the different skills and knowledge required by these different coaches in practice (Lyle, 2002; Lyle & Cushion, 2017). These distinctions would not only better recognise the differing emphases in coaches' work, but also have implications on their preparation and development.

Some scholars use the domains of participation, development and performance to differentiate coaches' work (e.g. Lyle, 1999; Lyle & Cushion, 2017). Participation coaching describes the contexts in which the goal is not competition success, while performance coaching involves preparing an athlete/player for competition. Lyle (2002) also suggests that participation coaches emphasise instructional, pedagogic and motivational skills while performance coaches focus on planning, monitoring, decision-making and management skills. It must be clarified that while participation coaching is more involved in the instructional episodic act of coaching, this does not mean that a performance coach does not prepare a session as thoroughly or the coach is not concerned about instruction! Additionally, not all coaches 'fit' within the categories of 'participation' and 'performance'; developmental coaches are a subset of performance coaching with a number of characteristics of participation coaching (Lyle, 2002).

Slightly different to Lyle's (2002), the European Framework for Coaching Competence and Qualifications' (EFCCQ) domains take the athlete's/player's age into consideration. That is, participation coaching is sub-divided into coaching children (under the age of 12) and adolescents and adults (age 18+). Performance coaching is separated into: coaching emerging athletes/players (i.e. focus on building technical, tactical, physical, cognitive, social and personal foundation needed for current performance and the next level of competition), coaching performance athletes/players (i.e. focus is on competition and the development of the capabilities that contribute to enhanced performance) and coaching high-performance athletes (i.e. athletes/players competing in world championships, major events, high-level leagues) (ICCE, 2013).

Although these discussions of coaching domains can be traced back to 2002 (and re-visited in 2017), the terminology has not been consistent in the literature. Instead, scholars (e.g. Trudel & Gilbert, 2006) have also elected to classify coaching contexts into recreational, development and elite. First, recreational sport coaching contexts are not specific to athletes/players in particular age ranges and the emphasis of the context is in participation and leisure. Second, developmental sport coaching contexts consist of more formal competitive structures and places emphasis on athlete/player development, which requires more commitment from athletes/players and coaches. Third, elite sport coaching contexts are characterised by intense preparation, public performance objectives, and demanding and restrictive selection criteria.

In addition to the terminology proposed by Lyle (2002; Lyle & Cushion, 2017) and Trudel and Gilbert (2006), some also adopt the term 'grassroots sport' to describe organised sport which is practised regularly by amateur sportspeople, and sport for all for health, educational or social purposes (European Commission, 2016). Additionally, Wharton and Rossi (2015) created further distinctions within the domains by employing the term 'interceptive sports coaching' to refer to coaches of sports that involve two opposing teams of interactive players.

While discussions of this terminology can be viewed as semantics or 'language games', it is a useful starting point as it highlights necessary contextual information (which is accompanied by expectations or assumptions) that impact upon coaches' work. Additionally, acknowledgement of domains enables coaches to better consider appropriate developmental opportunities. For example, an elite swimming coach stated:

> The desire of the coach and the ambition of the coach is really important. If your desire as a coach is to be an Olympic or international level coach, then there are things that you need to do to be at that

level, if your desire is to coach at the participation level, then there are things you need to do to work within that level. This is important as coaches are judged differently. Being a 'good' coach within one domain does not translate to being a 'good' coach in another.

As this coach highlights, these domains are not on a continuum. That is, a 'participation' or 'recreational' coach does not naturally evolve into an elite coach. However, coaches might not recognise this. There are examples of coaches working in grassroots or youth development contexts who have ambitions to work in elite contexts and approach their sessions in a similar way. As these behaviours are not aligned with the expectations within the context and different understandings, they may be viewed as inappropriate or problematic. Conversely, there are examples of coaches who are more familiar with elite or performance contexts and move into participation or development positions. A professional basketball coach recalled the difficulty in adjusting from a professional sports team to one in a lower league.

It was a mistake to take the job, because it was not the level which is normal for me. The players didn't want to play at a higher level; they were not interested in increasing the difficulty of their practices or doing anything differently. They were satisfied with what they had ... So, after couple weeks I saw that it wasn't for me and I resigned.

In another example, an elite athletics coach, who moved from working with the junior national team to the senior national team, reflected on how she had mistakenly assumed that some behaviours were transferrable across domains.

I think that's where I made a huge mistake in that what I thought was good practice at the higher levels was really much more suitable to new people – you know juniors and people who hadn't been involved in the sport very long. I gave a lot of information ... a lot of talk and tried to talk them through everything and you don't need to do that at the higher levels.

These two quotes are helpful to illustrate the differing expectations and assumptions for these domains. As these coaches have highlighted, a lack of appreciation of the differences in domains will not only impact upon coaches' experiences, but may also have consequences on obtaining and maintaining the respect of athletes without which coaches simply cannot operate (Potrac, Jones & Armour, 2002; Purdy & Jones, 2011).

INVESTIGATING COACHING

As an area of scholarly interest, sports coaching has experienced significant growth in the past decade. This expansion is not only evidenced in an annual increase in journal articles relating to the topic, but also in the development of several subject-specific journals. The subsequent content 'charts' the progression of ideas within the field.

Coaching has had a long history (to be discussed in Chapter 3); however, as an area of investigation it is relatively young. Early investigations were conducted on coaches who were also teachers; hence, rather than viewing coaching as a separate domain, it was considered an extension of research on physical education teachers and their behaviour. At this time, educational research was strongly influenced by Edward Thorndike, who was adamant that 'the subject matter of psychology was behaviour' (Carlson & Buskist, 1997, p. 16). Consequently, psychology became 'the foundational discipline for educational thought and research' (Doyle, 1992, p. 489), and, by extension, the 'parent' discipline of sports coaching (Jones, 2005).

With investigations in coaching emulating the early research that was occurring in physical education, the coaching literature was dominated by the sciences. Consequently, coaching veered away from the original view that it was related to teaching and became associated with 'training'. This connection encouraged coaches to privilege factual knowledge over interpretation by emphasising the role of the coach in providing technical direction. Therefore, work focused on coaches' behaviour, the impact on athletes/players and athletes'/players' preferences for particular coaching behaviours, with researchers drawing upon the physical sciences (e.g. psychology) to define precisely what must be done in order to develop athlete/players (Gilbert & Trudel, 2004). Here, research concentrated on identifying behaviours or characteristics of 'effective' coaches that could be developed and applied to all athletes/players. Consequently, researchers favoured behaviour assessment systems and leadership scales to observe and describe what coaches actually did in practice (e.g. the Coaching Behaviour Assessment System, the Multidimensional Model of Leadership, and the Leadership Scale for Sports). Hence, this scholarship was dominated by quantitative research.

Towards the end of the century, investigations evolved to recognise the complexities of coaching. This view was provoked by the trends in education which, rather than promoting the behaviourist orientation to learning, promoted social cognitivist and constructivist orientations (to be discussed in Chapter 6). Such approaches called for increased focus on the social world of coaches and athletes/players and how they operated. In an effort to understand its complexity, some researchers (e.g. Cross, 1995; Lyle, 1999; Jones, Armour & Potrac, 2004) highlighted its dynamic nature by recognising coaching as a process as opposed to a set of predetermined behaviours or series of isolated events. Such a view accepted that each coaching context was dependent on situational, ideological, cultural, ethical and social pressures. As a result, the early 2000s saw an increase in scholarship that argued for sports coaching to be appreciated as a social activity. Such a view recognises that coaching involves a complex interaction between coach and athlete/ players which is played out within a socio-culturally defined set of sporting practices. In doing so, researchers increasingly drew upon qualitative methodologies and methods.

The growth of sports coaching as an academic field has been useful in stimulating debate about the multidisciplinary and/or interdisciplinary nature of coaching and complexities of coaches' work. Therefore, the subsequent chapters draw attention to some of the key ideas and discussions which relate to the disciplines of philosophy, history, sociology, psychology and the sub-discipline of pedagogy. Before discussing the disciplinary-specific work which comprises contemporary scholarship in sports coaching, it is worth looking at trends in early work in the field. which was dedicated to the coaching process and/or identify the behaviours of 'effective' and 'successful' coaches. The following sections focus on various models 'of' and 'for' coaching, and the notions of 'effective' and 'successful' coaching.

MODELS 'FOR' AND 'OF' COACHING

Researchers and coach educators have adapted and developed a number of models to help 'capture' the coaching process. This work reflects the trends in scholarship which suggested 'whenever a domain is rationalised [structured] it becomes easier to measure performance in it and therefore to recognise promising talent' (Csikszentmihalyi, Whalen, Wong & Rathunde, 1993, p. 29). Models are viewed as useful as they can provide coaches with principles or a series of sequential and interrelated steps from which coaches can base their behaviours.

Within the scholarly community, academics debated (and continue to question) whether the unique nature of coaches' practice can be 'captured' by a model. Some have argued that there are patterns of behaviour that can be charted; consequently, they have developed models or part-models of key behaviours. These models can largely be organised into two categories, those 'of' and 'for' the coaching process. Models 'for' the coaching process are idealistic representations that have been developed based on a set of assumptions about the process (Jones, 2005). For examples, see Franks, Sinclair, Thomson and Goodman (1986), Fairs (1987), Lyle (1999) and Abraham, Collins and Martindale (2006). Models 'of' coaching have been developed from empirical research which has investigated 'expert' and/or 'successful' coaching practice. These include works by MacLean and Chelladurai (1995), Côté, Salmela and Trudel (1995) and Sherman, Crassini, Maschette and Sands (1997).

Models 'for' and 'of' the coaching process have been useful to raise questions and/or start conversations about what coaches do and how. However, they have been the subject of much critique (e.g. Lyle, 2002; Cushion, Armour & Jones, 2006: Lyle & Cushion, 2017). Criticisms relate to the episodic nature of these models (i.e. divided into separate parts) which pay attention to one component (e.g. instructions), but in doing so, largely neglect to recognise the complexity of performance and the interpersonal nature of the coaching process. An important factor that has been overlooked by the designers of the models is that they do not differentiate between the domains in which coaches operate. That is, they assume coaching is the same in participation, development and performance contexts with coaching viewed as a series of sequential steps which are the same whether working with a beginner or an elite athlete/player. Further concerns have been raised at the lack of recognition of the different needs and characteristics of the athletes/players at the various stages of their development. Additionally, they fail to acknowledge the complex social and contextual factors within the coach–athlete/player relationships that also influence the coaching process. Finally, concerns have been raised that utilising the models as a method of inquiry has restricted the study of coaching to a limited number of coaches' behaviours.

To summarise, models have been criticised for being too simplistic resulting in a lack of acknowledgment of the complexity of coaching and not giving coaches the appreciation that is deserved. Furthermore, the suggestion that a definitive set of characteristics can be developed and applied to all athletes/coaches everywhere is problematic as coaching is not an activity that can be easily reduced to a generic set of rules or predictable processes. This was highlighted over twenty years ago when Cross (1995), in his investigation into coaching effectiveness in field hockey, concluded that there is no one model of coaching practice that will be useful in every situation and in every context; rather, behaviours may be appropriate at varying times and/or under different circumstances. This view has been gaining strength as coaching is increasingly recognised for its complex social and relational dimensions (Nash & Collins, 2006).

'EFFECTIVE' AND 'SUCCESSFUL' COACHING BEHAVIOURS

Models provide one approach to make sense of coaching. Comparably, some scholars have focused on organising coaching into lists of 'characteristics, competencies, cognitions, practice strategies and techniques, leadership styles or behavioural patterns that are most effective' (Horn, 2008, p. 240). Here, 'effective' behaviours relate to the observable, practical, technical and measurable (instrumental) characteristics of coaching. This suggests that coaches could be judged by athletes'/players' levels of achievement (win-loss percentage), or athletes'/players' personal attributes (satisfaction, enjoyment) (Horn, 2008). For example, in relation to a training session, 'effective coaching' may relate to sessions which athletes/players find enjoyable or satisfying because they are challenged physically and technically and the coach's instructional behaviours which help an athlete progress in the sport (leading to achievement in competition). An elite rowing coach reflected:

> I guess if you finish training saying it's a 'good' session, it must mean that it challenged the athletes and it was technically better than it was before or at least maintained what was before ... It would be that I felt that I helped the athletes and didn't hinder them, that my comments were effective and appropriate, not 'what's the coach talking about; we're not even working on that at the moment?' I guess another, a really big one which is a simple, but it took an awfully long time to actually put into practice, is not to overload the athlete with information. One or two points are enough to focus on, keep it simple ...

As this coach highlighted, and for many coaches, the notion of 'effective coaching' implies that coaches' behaviours have a positive impact upon athlete performance. However, in 1998, d'Arripe-Longueville, Fournier and Dubois published a landmark paper which focused on the interactions between expert French judo coaches and elite female athletes. The scholars identified that the coaches adopted an authoritarian interaction style which included stimulating interpersonal rivalry, verbally provoking athletes, displaying indifference, entering into direct conflict, developing a team cohesion intended to intimidate and exhibiting favouritism. These behaviours led to strong athlete performances. Thus, if 'effective' is defined in light of wins-losses, the coaches' behaviours were 'effective'; however, if 'effective' relates to athlete/player satisfaction or enjoyment, the coaches were not 'effective'.

The terms 'effective coaching' and 'coaching effectiveness' continue to be debated. Some scholars have challenged such terminology (e.g. Cassidy, Jones & Potrac, 2009; Lyle, 2002), arguing that it lacks clarity. Additionally, concerns have been raised that the categorisation of coaching into lists of 'effective' behaviours could lead to a recipe-approach to coaching practice, which will neglect the social realities of coaches' work (Jones et al., 2004). Finally, concerns have been raised that such an approach may encourage coaches, when reflecting upon their work, to consider a framework that looks in on itself (i.e. more 'in the box' thinking) (Lyle & Cushion, 2017) as opposed to looking 'outward' to new possibilities. The importance of 'looking outward' cannot be understated, as highlighted by one elite swimming coach, who said:

> One of the things I've learnt over the years ... I think this is maybe one of the things we don't do enough in sport is to get outside our sport, get outside sport altogether, look at what is going on in other areas, like business. We also need to get outside our country, look at what goes on in the world.

The quote reiterates a desire by some coaches to go beyond conventional practices and understandings and look to new ways to advance their work and thought. Underscoring such ideas is an inherent commitment for coaches to improve, which may be a synonym for 'become more effective'. Instead of the term 'effective', Cassidy et al. (2004, 2009) proposed the use of the notion of 'quality' to judge coaches and coaching. One of the reasons for such terminology is that it is already associated with judgement in other contexts (e.g. quality control). Furthermore, 'quality coaching' is viewed to be more amenable to a holistic view of coaching (Cassidy et al., 2004, 2009).

While the previous argument focused on 'effective' coaching, there has also been interest in the practices of 'successful' or 'winning' coaches in various sports. Indeed, numerous biographies and autobiographies of elite or professional coaches are purchased by the public on an annual basis (Cassidy et al., 2009). Within academic literature, scholars have focused on U.S. National Collegiate Athletic Association (NCAA) Division 1 men's and women's basketball coaches John Wooden and Pat Summitt, and American football coach Vince Lombardi (e.g. Becker & Wrisberg, 2008; Gallimore & Tharp, 2004; Tharp & Gallimore, 1976). While findings draw coaches' attention to particular behaviours (e.g. instruction, feedback), which arguably could lead to some improvements in our coaching practice, we cannot assume that such behaviours will ensure the success of the teams and athletes/players that we coach. That is, these behaviours are specific to the context in which they were observed. Additionally, replicating the work of another coach neglects to take account of the 'person' of the coach and how this is embedded in their craft (Jones, Bailey, Santos & Edwards, 2012). As football/soccer coach José Mourinho highlighted:

The same exercise on the pitch led by two different coaches is not the same exercise ... And the same words in a dressing room said by a coach and said by another one are not the same words ...

(Castles, 2010)

SUMMARY

Coaching is an increasingly diverse and demanding practice. In some nations, the volunteer coach comprises much of the coaching workforce with coaching only financially viable at the highest level, or in combination with other employment (Norman, 2008). With the expansion of the domains in which coaches operate and an improved understanding of the social nature of this position, the coach is becoming increasingly respected for being a subject-matter specialist and systematic method applier as well as for embracing the personal relationship and social context which comprise each coaching situation.

This chapter has provided a brief map of how research has been conducted and, in doing so, has aimed to provoke thinking about ways coaching is (and can be) understood. While early work focused on 'what' coaches do and 'how' they do their work, latter scholarship has expanded our understanding of 'why' coaches do what they do (i.e. the intentions behind their decisions), the expanding contexts in which coaches are working and, more recently, how the person of the coach or 'who' the coach is, influences this interaction. The exploration of ideas here is helpful as it sets up subsequent chapters that will look at how some different disciplines (and sub-disciplines) explain coaches' work.

While a multidisciplinary examination of coaching provides a useful foundation for knowledge, there is also a need and responsibility to consider where this knowledge might take us. As such, the future of coaching presents us with exciting and new challenges that are brought by the expanding contexts in which coaches work and the increasing technologies available. Technological developments raise new issues for sports organisations that may consider how they support coaches in the various contexts and how to aid coaches in the development or refining of digital literacy skills (i.e. skills for finding, assessing and creating information using various digital technologies) (Clark & Nash, 2015). Additionally, given the global reach of various technologies, the sports coach who operates in a different location to the athlete(s)/player(s) provides training programmes, analyses performance via recordings, and offers support through video chat and voice call services, is increasing, which impacts upon coaches' positioning and the related expectations. Finally, given the rapid development in eSports, questions can be raised about coaches' roles and identities therein. Readers may wish to ponder if it is within the possibility of eSports to destabilise 'traditional' notions about sport itself and what a coach does in relation to the performative and physical within sport. We can watch this 'e-space' with interest.

2

THE PHILOSOPHICAL COACH

The first philosophers were thinkers who were inspired by the world around them. Socrates, Plato and Aristotle, for example, sought answers to fundamental questions about the world rather than accepting the explanations provided by religion and custom. It is appropriate then, that the word 'philosopher' originates from the Greek term meaning 'love of wisdom'. In contrast to contemporary understandings of the word, this 'wisdom' was based on arguments, reasoning and asking questions (Warburton, 2011). Thus, modern-day philosophy depends upon conversation and dialogue (McGhee in Kenkmann, 2009, p. 23). Adopting a different approach to the other chapters in this book which highlight key discussions, this chapter foregrounds philosophical questions. As such, it provides the foundation for the content within this text as contemporary questions in the coaching literature invariably find their basis in philosophical questions.

Mary Midgley (1919–), an English philosopher, likened philosophy to plumbing: '[I]t is not grand, elegant and difficult, it is necessary' (1996, p. 1). She posited, like plumbing, philosophy comprises fairly complex 'systems' or networks of concepts and assumptions which underlie almost all of our thinking. These taken-for-granted 'systems' exist beneath the surface and usually go unnoticed until something goes wrong. Unlike plumbing however, the consequences of philosophical disruption or interruptions are unlikely to leak through ceilings or damage kitchen floors! Instead, they quietly distort and impede one's thinking (Midgley, 1996).

Although criticised for comparing philosophy to plumbing, Midgley was highlighting the importance of philosophy and its essential role in peoples' lives. While this comparison seems somewhat odd in a book about sports coaching, it is a useful way to draw attention to the underpinning concepts and assumptions which influence coaches' practice. For example, coaches may comment that their work with athletes/players or teams is not going as well as intended and might not be able to see why this is happening or what could be done about it. Here, early research identified that when training plans went awry or athletes/players underperformed, many coaches neglected to consider the problem as a unique case or sensitive occurrence, but addressed it more generally (Lyle, 2002). As it is easier to look for sources of trouble outside of themselves than within (Midgley, 1996), their attention might naturally focus on things external to their practice such as the athletes'/players' motivation or limited skills. However, the philosophy/plumbing comparison helps to remind coaches to 'look below the surface' of their coaching practice – that is, to turn their attention to reflect upon their practice critically and consider the underlying concepts and assumptions about their work that may have an impact upon their work with athletes/players. Such reflection may enable coaches to adopt alternative approaches that might lead to more productive coaching practices.

Philosophy (as a discipline and an activity) has much to offer coaches. At a minimum, philosophy provides a framework for coaches to ask questions about their assumptions relating to coaching (and sport). Furthermore, it asks coaches to identify (or better understand) what they stand for and consider why. This would also introduce the possibility that there is no logical necessity to continue with it! After all, it was Socrates who believed that life is only worth living if a person considers what they are doing.

There are numerous publications that hint at philosophical questions/thinking, or utilise the term 'coaching philosophy' to explain coaches' approaches to their work, however, scholarship relating to sports coaching which is explicitly positioned within the discipline of philosophy is relatively scarce. Some exceptions are work by Hardman, Jones and Jones' (2010), which argues for coaching to be recognised as a moral enterprise (i.e. the coach is central in constituting and regulating appropriate sporting behaviour) and Hardman and Jones' (2010) anthology regarding the ethics of sports coaching. Additionally, Simon's (2013) edited compilation entitled *The ethics of coaching sports: Moral, social and legal issues* must be recognised as well as several book chapters featured in various anthologies relating to sports coaching.

While the aim of this text is to highlight key messages in the area of sports coaching, this chapter is structured in light of the question 'How are we to coach?', which is a modified version of the popular philosophical question 'How are we to live?'. Specifically, it draws upon the following philosophical questions: what does it mean to be a coach? (ontology); what do coaches value? (axiology); how do coaches arrive at and justify their moral actions? (ethics); what is coaching knowledge? (epistemology) and; what is it like to be a coach? (phenomenology).

WHAT DOES IT MEAN TO BE A COACH?

Ontology (i.e. the study of being) is often viewed as the heart of philosophy as such questions relate to the meaning of life. While the relevance might seem somewhat odd to coaches, it is of use to consider the meaning they subscribe to their work. In particular, is coaching a meaningful practice? If so, how is it a meaningful practice? What is it about the position or role that people find meaningful?

Hardman and Jones (2013) argue that coaching can be viewed as a meaningful endeavour with its meaning found in its ability to enable people to engage in social practice. Social practices are activities through which individual and collective goals are realised and serve as a catalyst for social interaction. This interaction, when extended, provides a structure which underpins society (Hardman & Jones, 2013). Social practices are usually supported by formal mechanisms, such as organisations (National Governing Bodies), [coaching] associations, and institutions (universities) that ensure their well-being. However, for a social practice to be meaningful, people need to undertake a role. As such, people can find meaning in coaching in light of how they interpret their role, and, in fulfilling their role, people adopt behaviours that they perceive to be understandable or meaningful to themselves and to other group members (i.e. athletes/players, other coaches and administrators) (Mack & Gammage, 1998). To find out more about the meaning of coaching, we could look at what might attract a person to engage in coaching. For example, while training with her university athletics club, an athlete was given the opportunity to coach her fellow athletes/players in university competitions. Her involvement in coaching then extended to working with two local secondary schools that used the university's facilities and a programme for athletes/players with disabilities. The coach enjoyed her work because 'it was really exciting to see that ... what [I] did [as a coach] really paid off [in terms of athlete success]' (Purdy & Potrac, 2014, p. 785). Thus, for this coach, coaching had meaning as her contribution to athletes'/players' improved performances was a way to foster her own contentedness.

The above coach's sentiments echo work by Busser and Carruthers (2010) who identified that seeing participants improve and learn were key motives for volunteering in sport contexts. To this end, it appears that volunteer coaches may find meaning in feeling useful and needed through the relevance of their positions as coaches and through the acknowledgements of gratitude which they receive (Haas, 2011). In considering what it is about coaching that brings meaning, coaches would need to acknowledge who they are and how their values are enacted in particular contexts and situations. That is, the meaning that is ascribed to coaching reveals how people understand and value the interplay between themselves and society. However, coaching can also be viewed as *meaningful* in that it contributes to who they are. In the example above, coaching offered the athletics coach an avenue to develop her self-understanding and/or enhance her self-esteem (Hardman & Jones, 2013).

It would not be in keeping with philosophical thinking to accept the discussions within this chapter without debate. While the previous argument focused on coaching having meaning or being meaningful, it could also be said that coaching has no meaning. To consider this, we could draw upon the thinking of Albert Camus (1913–1960), a novelist and philosopher. Camus used the Greek myth of Sisyphus to explain the absurdity of human existence. Sisyphus, the cunning king of Corinth, was punished by Hades for tricking the gods. His punishment comprised rolling a large boulder to the top of a hill. However, every time Sisyphus, through great exertion and toil, attained the summit, the boulder would roll back down again! Using this story, Camus highlighted the conflict between what we want from life (i.e. meaning, order or reason) and what we find in life (i.e. chaos). Extending this argument to sport, this would suggest that we will never uncover the meaning that we want to find in coaching, but there is something within the struggle of 'rolling the rock up the mountain' that gives it meaning. Following Camus' reasoning, we could argue that coaching does not have any meaning, until we give it meaning.

Considering what it is about coaching that brings meaning (or not) or what is meaningful about coaching not only helps us to comprehend why people, particularly volunteers, get involved in coaching, but it could also help to make sense of why some people stop. For example, coaches have identified times in which what they are doing challenges their understanding of what it means to be a coach. A performance athletics coach noted:

> It's been a long time since I've had what I consider to be effective coaching from myself. Not [in this position], [I have not] done it or not consistently ... [As an assistant] my job seems to be just minding people rather than coaching them.

> (Purdy & Potrac, 2014, p. 789)

In this case, the coach's work was incongruent with her understanding of coaching, which created a tension as she struggled to find meaning in the activities she was undertaking. Feeling unfulfilled in her current work, but aware that coaching positions in performance sport were not plentiful, she contemplated whether she should find a more meaningful opportunity in another line of work.

In light of the aforementioned information, it may be of use for readers to reflect upon the following questions: is coaching a meaningful practice? What is it about the position or role that is meaningful? Here, consideration of meaning serves as a useful starting point in developing one's coaching 'system'.

WHAT DO COACHES VALUE?

During an interview with Gary Lineker on the BBC's *MOTD: The Premier League Show* (August, 2016), Jurgen Klopp, who at that time was the manager of the Premier League club Liverpool, was asked what he'd like to achieve before his contract at Liverpool ends. Klopp replied, 'The problem is I'm a Christian. That [in itself] is not a problem, but the problem is I think other people can have success too – it's not about me. But if you ask me about Liverpool I would like to celebrate something each season.' Klopp's comment helps to start conversations regarding what coaches value and what matters to them. Here, Klopp highlights how his Christian values, such as humility (i.e. 'having an accurate sense of oneself… an inclination to keep one's accomplishments, traits, and so on in unexaggerated perspective, even if stimulated to exaggerate' (Richards, 1992, p. 5) frame his view of sport and, consequently, influence his work.

The philosophical study of value or axiology centres on what is important and what matters. Therefore, values play a vital role in the decisions we make. However, some coaches make choices that are based on what they are feeling at that moment and may not consider what matters to them. This behaviour could raise questions as to whether the coach actually knows what they stand for, if they have direction and if they possess the fortitude to stand behind their commitments (Kretchmar, 2005). For coaches, a lack of awareness of their values (and how these are prioritised) can have devastating effects on their practice and/or careers.

A starting point would be to question what is valuable about sport. Is sport a way of achieving other things or is sport of value in itself? For some, sport is viewed as 'good' because it promotes positive values that contribute to society. An externalist would argue that sport is valuable because it is a way of expressing other values. That is, sport provides happiness, encourages friendship and promotes an active lifestyle (Ryall, 2016). Accordingly, sport could be viewed as 'good' because it leads to other things that are of value. For instance, excelling at sport could provide lucrative opportunities for athletes/ players, which can lead to other things that are of value (e.g. cars, property). In contrast, a coach may accept an internalist's argument and view sport as having value in and of itself and not a means to attain things that are of value (Ryall, 2016). While these values can be further divided into moral (i.e. relating to motives or personality traits such as honesty, fairness and respect) and non-moral (i.e. items that people want such as wealth, health, happiness), it is important to recognise that they are interrelated (Ryall, 2016). For example, a coach may value fairness and respect (moral values) because without these qualities, the game is not fun (non-moral value). The coach views fun as important because it motivates participants to develop skill (non-moral value) which may lead to more engagement in sport and physical activity which could be beneficial to health (non-moral value).

While the previous discussion has highlighted how values can be interconnected, they can also conflict. For example, if a coach values attitude and effort, s/he may feel frustrated if the club is promoting criteria for player selection that emphasises the player's physical performances. Additionally, coaches working in youth sport who are interested in positive youth development (i.e. character building, skill building and fun) may feel challenged by a club that promotes the outcome (i.e. winning) and is not concerned about the process (i.e. athlete development).

It is worth considering that sport is often promoted or positioned as a positive site for engagement; however, it does not always promote 'positive' values. Sport (particularly performance sport) has been criticised for excessive values: excess survivalism (i.e. extreme focus upon health, exercise addiction, an over-competitive attitude towards winning), runaway individualism (focus on the self rather than the community) and oppressive rationalism (obsession with breaking records and pushing the boundaries of human performance) (Kretchmar, 2005; Ryall, 2016).

Given the range of values that sport can promote, why do some coaches prioritise certain values over others? How do coaches decide which values matter? The following quotation from a male professional basketball coach draws attention to a decision which necessitated that the coach prioritised his values.

> When recruiting a player to my team, I tell them that if they play for my team, I will take care of them. They will get playing minutes, they will get their salary, I will not cut them and I am sincere. I mean it. I will protect them ... But there was one point in my career when one of my players was underperforming. I defended him and tried to protect him, but it got to the point when the management asked me to choose between myself and the player. I had promised to take care of the player and had been defending him [to the management] all season, but it was him or me. I had to stop the player's contract because I was scared that I would be fired.

This coach's comment highlights that various life circumstances warrant emphasis on different values (Kretchmar, 2005). Although the coach initially built a relationship with the player by treating him fairly and wanted to honour the promise to protect him (i.e. be honest), the coach was put into a position in which he had to consider what was of more value – the relationship with the player or his job. Here, the process of recognising and prioritising values is not simply personal preference (Ryall, 2016); rather, there is a rational basis. Baier (1958) suggests that people need to make at least two considerations when ranking values: surveying the facts and weighing the reasons. To do this, one must consider the characteristics and benefits of each value. This includes the benefits for others and ourselves and these benefits as ends in themselves or as means to other ends. Second, Baier (1958) proposes that in addition to considering the benefits, the rules of superiority involve evaluating the evidence in terms of their intrinsic value (i.e. intrinsic values are superior to extrinsic values), their ability to provide satisfaction (i.e. satisfaction that brings little/no harm in the world is preferred to satisfaction that brings harm) and those values which contribute to a coherent and *meaningful* life (Frankena, 1973; Kretchmar, 2005).

Understanding values is one of the most difficult tasks in philosophy as it is abstract, yet obvious; however, it is important to recognise their importance in directing coaches' priorities and influencing their actions (Ryall, 2016). While this section has provided a brief introduction to axiology, a useful starting point for readers could be to question: What values are important in your coaching practice? Do particular values matter more than others? How have they changed throughout your involvement as a coach?

HOW DO COACHES ARRIVE AT AND JUSTIFY THEIR MORAL ACTIONS?

> We discussed in the (coaches') box whether we would fake an injury ... But morally, I made the decision it wasn't the right thing to do ... In the spirit of the game, in the spirit of a World Cup semi-final, I didn't think that was the fairest or right thing.
>
> (Baldock, 2011)

This statement was made by Warren Gatland, who, at the time, was the rugby coach for Wales. The quote was in reference to Wales' World Cup semi-final defeat against France in 2011. Gatland's comment is useful as it enables us to go 'behind the scenes' regarding coaches' decisions relating to some of the moral dilemmas of performance sport – in particular, how the game 'should' be won, how the game 'should' be played or the 'right' way to play, and how people 'should' engage in the game. While in this chapter these have been referred to as moral dilemmas, many scholars use 'morals' and 'ethics' synonymously. To clarify, this is the sub-discipline of philosophy which is concerned with moral principles.

As mentioned in the previous section (i.e. axiology), moral values such as integrity, conscientiousness, courage and affection play a central role in coaching. Indeed, 'in every working moment, the [coach] is indirectly sending out a moral message' (Kristjánsson, 2006, p. 38). Morals frame coaches' practice (and vice versa). Indeed, this influence extends to actions that are encouraged or discouraged and qualities (e.g. character traits, dispositions such as integrity, fairness) that promote such practice and that of the participants (Hardman & Jones, 2013). While some clubs or sports organisations provide guidelines regarding the ethical conduct expected by coaches, athletes/players and other club members, it is worth understanding the moral standards that underwrite these clauses (McNamee, 2011). As such, coaches' ethics can be largely organised into three branches: deontology, utilitarianism/consequentialism and virtue.

Deontological ethics (i.e. duty-based ethics) is concerned with what people do (specifically 'rightness' or 'wrongness') and not with the consequences of their actions. Immanuel Kant (1724–1804), a German philosopher (considered to be central in the development of modern philosophy), made a significant contribution to deontological ethics. Kant believed that morality was about what a person does and why, not on the outcome that is achieved. And, the only way an act could be considered moral is if it emerges through reason and purpose (not emotion). Such reasoning involves consideration of the action to be performed. Consequently, one cannot judge the action or its type unless the intention is known. Deontologists consider morality to be a duty (i.e. one in which people do things which are 'right' and not do things that are 'wrong'). They believe people should be concerned with fulfilling these duties, not on bringing about the most good as, at times, focusing on the latter could violate a duty. Building on this, right and wrong are understood in terms of inherent qualities. For example, some coaches have clear beliefs that cheating is inherently wrong and honesty is inherently right. While Gatland's earlier words indicate that faking an injury is 'wrong', his words, 'in the spirit of the game, in the spirit of a World Cup semi-final, I didn't think that was the fairest or right thing', suggests that the context was important in decision making. That is, the significance of the event, the spirit of the sport appears to have had an impact upon the decision. This suggests that Gatland and colleagues used the basic 'code of sport' or 'sport ethic' as a guide. However, this may not be as straightforward as it may appear to be. For example, one could question why Gatland shared this information with the public – was he seeking to sway judgement of the team's performance and 'soften' the blow of the loss? By demonstrating that the team took the 'moral high ground', was he intentionally trying to portray the coaches in a more positive light (enabling them to keep their jobs)? Conversely, consider the public's reaction if the team had won and Gatland had highlighted that the coaching team had considered faking an injury. Additionally, what would happen if they had faked the injury and been caught? This 'thought experiment' moves our thinking beyond the 'rightness' and 'wrongness' (i.e. deontological ethics) of what the coach is doing and extends to the consequences of the actions. This would necessitate another view of ethics.

Utilitarianists (also known as consequentialists) focus on the consequences of the actions in determining the judgement. Accordingly, good and bad are distinguished based on their potential consequences and adopting the action which maximises good outcomes. Actions are good or 'right' if they increase overall goodness, pleasure or satisfaction, or decrease pain or suffering. Furthermore, actions are 'wrong' if they result in a decrease in good, pleasure or satisfaction, or increase pain and suffering (Hardman & Jones, 2013). Applying this view to Gatland's quote, the decision not to fake an injury was deemed to be in response to the spirit of the game and in recognition of the significance of the event. That is, to ensure that participation in that event was pleasurable and to protect its significance, Gatland and colleagues considered the basic 'code of sport' or 'sport ethic' and decided not to fake an injury. However, another coach in a similar situation might not make the same decision. Arguing that 'everyone else is doing it so I'm just making the game fair', 'the rules aren't fair' and/or 'we need to do this to keep our jobs' suggests the coach is focusing on the outcome (i.e. an 'even' playing field, 'unfair rules' or 'staying in employment') of which the good consequences (e.g. national pride, sponsorship agreements, etc.) outweigh, and morally justify, the action.

In contrast to emphasising duties or rules (deontology) or being concerned with the outcomes of the action (utilitarianism), a third branch of ethics, virtue ethics, places emphasis on virtues or moral characters. For coaches, virtue ethics are concerned with questions such as: What kind of person should a coach be? How should a coach act? and What values should be promoted in sport?

Aristotle deemed a virtuous person as someone who has 'ideal' character traits. Some of these traits include: kindness, courage, fairness and integrity, caring and nurturing (Baier, 1987; Hardman & Jones, 2013; MacIntyre, 1984). These virtues are ever present (as part of a person's character) and not employed as a 'duty' or to achieve an outcome. Therefore, when faced with a problem in coaching, a virtuous coach cannot consult a moral rulebook that provides guidance on what to do and what not to do (McNamee, 2008). In this situation, what the coach does is in light of what they conceive themselves to be: just, sensitive, trustworthy (McNamee, 2008). Linking back to Gatland, the virtue theorist might focus on his integrity (i.e. he chose not to fake an injury) as it would suggest he has good character.

The aforementioned content has highlighted how differing views of ethics influence coaches' practice. Consideration of deontological (i.e. duty-based ethics), utilitarian (i.e. focus on the consequences of the actions) and virtue ethics (i.e. relating to virtues or moral characters) helps coaches to appreciate how they (or others) arrive at and justify their moral actions. Perhaps a useful starting point for readers would be to consider, how we 'should' win in sports, how we 'should' play sports the 'right' way and how we 'should' engage in the game.

WHAT IS COACHING KNOWLEDGE?

> The knowledge you have as a coach in the science, the practical and the technical side is real important for every coach, but also important is the coach's ability to communicate … get the message across, what [s/he's] trying to do, to motivate and to bring the athlete to the level that the coach feels s/he can bring the athlete.
>
> (performance swimming coach)

As noted in this quote, coaches draw upon a varied knowledge base in their work, and how this knowledge is constructed, acquired and developed forms the foundation of coaches' thinking (Collins & Collins, 2015). Additionally, coaches who are concerned with athlete/player learning have an epistemological purpose – that is, supporting the development of knowledge and how that process can be facilitated (Schuh & Barab, 2007). Epistemology is a critical inquiry into the fundamental principles of knowledge, including its possibility and its justification (Crotty, 1998). Coaches encounter epistemological problems daily. However, what does knowledge look like for coaches? How is it acquired? What is it founded on? To answer these questions, we need to know more about where knowledge comes from and what it means to know something. While these questions use knowledge as the starting point, there are obvious connections to pedagogy. However, pedagogy is the application of philosophical concepts in an educational context. Therefore, to discuss pedagogy (see Chapters 6 and 7), one must consider its philosophical basis.

To begin, consider the following: In designing a session for the athletes/players with whom they are working, how do coaches know that the knowledge they are drawing upon in their practice is the 'best'? What is this knowledge based on? Is it possible that there is 'better' knowledge, but they have not considered it? Additionally, how do coaches know the components that comprise a session? A coach may respond to this question saying that their knowledge has been developed from their previous experience of a similar session (either as a coach or an athlete/player) or is based on something they learned on a coach education course. Perhaps this information was gleaned by observing others and the way they designed their sessions? However, how do coaches know that they have interpreted the information as it was intended? Does viewing other people do the same thing increase the likelihood that they think their beliefs are 'true'? Is their knowledge grounded in the acceptance of the claims of people they consider to be authorities on the subject? If so, are they choosing to believe what they tell them? These questions are important as a person's understanding of 'knowing' is based on the beliefs that they accept. However, it is worth considering that these beliefs can be false or mis-recalled. For example, someone might believe that Oxford won the boat race in 2015, but in recalling the race, they are remembering the events of 2014. Although Oxford were the victors in both years, it is not enough to justify the belief or mis-recollection as a mistake, rather true belief needs to be appropriately justified (Ryall, 2016). That is, 'truth' is a condition of knowledge as, without it, knowledge cannot be constituted.

Knowledge can be broken into different types: information that is true by definition (a priori) and that which is true by experience (a posterioiri). A priori knowledge requires no external verification (e.g. math, logic) while posteriori knowledge is learned empirically. A priori knowledge in coaching may include information such as anatomical and physiological understanding, principles of biomechanics, nutrition, fatigue, etc. In contrast, a posteriori knowledge in coaching refers to previous coaching experience, past interactions, social and cultural assumptions and beliefs that have emerged through informal and formal education and learning. Coach education programmes may reflect a varied combination of both knowledge types (arguably both are required for the holistic development of a coach); however, there has been a tendency for coach education programmes to privilege a priori knowledge (in particular, biomedical scientific principles). Recently, scholars have challenged such an approach and argued that, for coaches, a posteriori knowledge is essential because it cuts to the heart of the lived, sensed, felt, art of coaching practice, and, acknowledges that the coaching is constructed and that the specific experiences of the coach are central to their meaning making.

The potential difficulty coaches may face in understanding the ways in which their knowledge may come to bear (advantageously or otherwise) on their work stems from the element of romanticism and affectation that many coaches express toward to their roles and their sports. For example, in many instances, coaches have had long careers as players or coaches, been long-time fans, and/or are fully immersed in the sub-cultural nuances of the sport. Indeed, for some, coaching is/or becomes inseparable from who they are and the world in which they inhabit. Though this may naturally be a part of 'the game' or 'the role', and accepted as part the allure of working in the sport industry, it is clear that nostalgia for the sport may mask the way coaches construct their identities, read their contemporary situation, and reflect on their past practices and experiences (i.e. a posteriori knowledge). Nostalgia has been useful to explain an individual's (or a sports organisation's) emotional connections to sport and sporting cultures (Snyder, 1991), but is also demonstrated clearly in coaching. For example, consider coaches' use of past performances (those good and bad), an organisation's use of history and tradition to promote loyalty, allegiance and communal affiliation, and the ways in which (often long-serving) practices and beliefs become ingrained, unquestioned, entrenched and part of the very fabric of the team and its way of simply doing things. However, nostalgia becomes problematic for coaches because it relies on a selective (favourable) recalling of the past. This recalling requires coaches to select 'facts' (or a priori knowledge) that allow them to craft a particular (yet contestable) version of the past that suits them in the present (and ultimately may be used to justify and rationalise their coaching decision, behaviours and practices).

Coaches' knowledge has been a topical area of discussion since the 1980s, with research focusing on the origins and use of coaches' understanding and competencies in practice. As highlighted in this section, epistemological questions can be raised regarding the appropriateness of competency-based approaches to coaching that prevail in some sports organisations. For example, readers may consider how coaches' perceptions of knowledge construction, learning and sense of self have altered as a result of these formal learning experiences.

WHAT IS IT LIKE TO BE A COACH?

> I love it, I look forward to it every day and there's down times when I'm not doing things besides working on a computer, budget, planning and organising the season, I get really rambunctious and want to get back at it
>
> (Paralympic coach)

Phenomenology focuses on the structure of various types of experience – in particular, the way people experience things and the meanings these experiences have. Phenomenology has also been described as a way to understand one's own emotional and imaginative life in the manner in which it is meaningfully lived (Moran, 2000). Towards this end, it could be argued that only a true understanding of the human can emerge through a rich description of experience (Ryall, 2016). In relation to coaching, phenomenology enables us to focus on what it is like to be a coach and attempt to better understand the feelings, emotions and physical actions that this entails. Coaches have various types of experiences both passive (e.g. perception, thought, memory, imagination and emotion) and active (e.g. walking, throwing a ball) and it is these experiences which help us make sense of how they live, engage with others, and/or find meaning. A professional basketball coach described what it is like (for him) to be a coach.

> On game day, I feel that adrenalin. I played for such a long time at the highest level and every week it was like 'boom, boom, boom' [gestures to indicate the energy of game night]. I'm not playing anymore, but, as a coach, I still get that adrenalin. It is part of who I am.

The way in which the body responds and interacts with the world has interested philosophers for centuries. Notable within the above quote is the coach's emphasis on the sensations experienced when coaching. However, it is often difficult to verbally describe sensations due to the limits of language. Therefore, when considering what it is like to be a coach, it is worth acknowledging how language (or the absence of) may constrain our explanations of our experiences and their significance. Although metaphors rely upon language, good metaphors may serve a useful purpose to provide a platform to begin to articulate ideas and knowledge about coaching. A metaphor is a figure of speech which asserts an association between two things that are otherwise unrelated – for example, coaches and rollercoasters (to be explained later in this section). In relation to coaching, metaphors may be helpful to offer us a way to express ideas which we are unable to fully describe through literal language (i.e. emotions, sensations relating to coaching). To this end, metaphors can create strong images which aid to effectively and vividly communicate ideas (Hamilton, 2016). For example, as the professional coach highlighted earlier, coaching could be compared to a rollercoaster ride. Such a comparison might help to start a conversation about the sensations of coaching, and in highlighting the highs, lows and exhilaration or adrenalin, others may better appreciate what it is like (for him) to be a coach. Conversely, it may also be useful for readers to consider the thinking of Ludwig Wittgenstein (1889-1951), an Austrian-born British philosopher. Wittgenstein may argue that we will not fully 'capture' what it is like to be a coach simply because it is not 'capturable'!

Notwithstanding the difficulties in verbally expressing 'what it is like to be a coach', the sensations of coaching and those of the sport and the difficulty for coaches to express them are also highlighted by other coaches in the following quotes. Contrasting the previous example which focused on what the coach experienced during his work, the following statements highlight how some coaches focus their athletes/players on the sensations of the sport. In the first example, a rowing coach working in a development context focused her coaching on replicating a feeling she experienced when she was an athlete.

> When I first started coaching I was faced with questions about how I actually explain the technical side of the sport. I had to go back and think – how do you actually do this? What am I trying to get out of it? What am I actually trying to teach? Because it had been so engrained for me as an athlete so I was stuck thinking how do you articulate a feeling into a movement for someone else?

This notion of coaching a feeling was also identified by a performance athletics coach, who highlighted:

> I had a brilliant coach. Every session was just fantastic. You'd be in the zone all the time. There were very few sessions that weren't enjoyable. It's just that everything had disappeared around me and I was just one with the whole lot. I mean not that it happened very often, but I guess, for my athletes, now that's what I'm always looking for.
>
> (Purdy & Potrac, 2014, p. 784)

The phrase 'everything had disappeared around me and I was just one with the whole lot' may draw the interest of scholars who are familiar with the notion of 'flow'. Flow has been described as being completely involved in an activity for its own sake. The ego falls away. Time flies. Every action, movement, and thought follows inevitably from the previous one, like playing jazz. Your whole being is involved, and you're using your skills to the utmost.

(Geirland, 1996)

While psychologists refer to this phenomenon as 'flow', the underpinning concepts and ideas are philosophical. For example, Drew Leder used 'the absent body' to describe a similar state in which a person is completely engrossed within a situation that the body 'disappears' from one's attention. The athlete/player does not think about how to move the body (i.e. about locomotion); instead, their focus is on the accomplishment of a task. In this way, the body is that from which a person attends to the world (Leder, 1990). Relating this to the athletics coach's quote on the previous page, her focus on helping the athlete achieve a state in which they do not feel the body creates a paradox as her feedback and instructions on how to execute the skill bring attention back to the body, thereby breaking the 'flow'. Here, the coach could be viewed as guiding athletes through a journey of various points of 'absorption' and 'disruption' in an effort to, ironically, help the athlete more consistently achieve what Leder describes as an 'absent body'.

How do these passive and active experiences contribute to what coaching is like for other coaches? Considering 'what it is like' to be a coach can offer insights into the meaning it brings to coaches, the values that they deem to be important in their practice, and their actions within the sporting environment. However, such insights may challenge the focus of some traditional coach education programmes which focus on the 'what' and 'how' of coaching, but neglect to acknowledge what this experience is like and why. For readers, thinking about 'what it is like' to be a coach or the experience of coaching could be not only be useful in gaining a greater appreciation of coaching, what coaches do, how they do it and why; it could also impact upon their practice if they reflect on 'what it is like' to be an athlete/player that they are coaching (Hardman & Jones, 2013).

SUMMARY

As introduced in this chapter, philosophy is inescapable. It permeates every aspect of human life as it encompasses ideas and issues that feature in every domain of human existence. Every coach is guided by philosophical assumptions, even if they are not aware of them. As highlighted in this chapter, philosophical ideas can aid in conceptually analysing issues relating to the work of sports coaches, in particular the connections and messiness of how 'to be', 'to know' and 'to act'. Here, the chapter has focused on 'how are we to coach?' and, in doing so, it has sparked thinking regarding what it means to be a coach (ontology), what coaches value (axiology), how coaches arrive at and justify their moral actions (ethics), coaches' knowledge (epistemology) and what it is like to be a coach (phenomenology).

Although the process of questioning what one knows or believes can be difficult, posing philosophical questions is important in challenging coaches' thinking about their work. These questions are also important on a practical level as Loland (2011) suggests that a 'good' coach is one who not only searches for scientific knowledge, but also engages in a search for reflective and 'good' choices regarding the many dilemmas of their practice.

3

A HISTORY AND A HERSTORY OF
SPORTS COACHING

While people have been interested in the improvement of athletic performance since Ancient Greece, scholarly emphasis has largely been placed on the 'modern' coach, who emerged in the late nineteenth century in response to the modernisation of sport (e.g. Carter, 2010; Day, 2012; Day & Carpenter, 2015). At this time, the organisation of sport formalised the roles of those within the sport 'industry'. Coaches' roles, for example, were not only shaped by beliefs, assumptions and forces within the sport 'industry', but also by coaches themselves, as individual components of the historical context that influenced what coaching comprised, how it was used and who it was for. This is important as it recognises that people are living history who operate within complex cultures that contain language, traditions and practices that have been created over time (Corfield, 2008). An understanding of the past and present is, therefore, essential to provide context for everyday life. It also shows how context influences how coaching is, and has been, shaped in various times and spaces. Consequently, it is useful to consider the history of coaching in order to better understand, and potentially change, current practice.

Sports historians use a variety of sources to construct an understanding of the past. The coaching story that is constructed then, is based on surviving material, which, we assume, represents the dominant view of sport at the time (e.g. art, stonework, technical sports booklets written by coaches, athletes/players and medical professionals, training diaries, newspaper articles, and journalists' accounts of famous athletes/players). While these sources influence a telling of sports coaching, they are based on material that has been interpreted outside of the context in which it was developed. Therefore, they only represent a partial and subjective (i.e. based on beliefs) telling.

It is also useful to recognise that the coaching story will differ according to the reader's geographical and/or cultural milieu as distinctive coaching cultures have emerged in relation to each sport and by geographical context. In many contexts, these more recent 'stories' reflect government intervention, differing attitudes to the body, and varying levels of competition and commercialisation (Carter, 2010). Finally, it is important to acknowledge that gender, racial, class and sexual ideologies will be manifested differently in the histories that are told (Coakley & Pike, 2009).

Although some of the information used to construct this chapter focuses on sport in ancient times, the more current coaching histories primarily relate to the United Kingdom with some discussion of Australia, Canada and the United States of America. This is largely the result of the availability of peer reviewed scholarly activity which has pursued these lines of inquiry. Further, while there are significant repositories and sport museums, much of the archival information we have on sport and coaching remains scattered among the sporting community and is largely inaccessible to both scholars and the general public – including coaches who may have an interest in the past.

What follows, then, is a brief chronological history of coaching. As this history is male dominated, the second half of the chapter focuses on a *herstory* of coaching, which draws attention to the underrepresentation of women in the field, their marginalisation and empowerment.

A HISTORY

Throughout history, sports people have continuously passed on their skills to other interested participants with coaching traced to the first recorded Olympic Games in Greece (776 BC). However, it was not until 600–400 centuries BC when coaching was more formally developed. Sources suggest that, at this time, the training and preparation of athletes was the result of the physical education system and special preparation for Olympic competition (Mechikoff & Estes, 1998). The early coaches or trainers, to conform to the language of Ancient Greece, were *paidotribes*, which loosely translates to 'taskmaster of boys' (Köhne & Ewigleben, 2000). These trainers were valued for being technically competent specialists who were conversant with science and medicine. Nevertheless, their work was not always met with approval, as critics believed they did not have sufficient scientific training in the areas of physiotherapy and hygiene to help their athletes (Day, 2012). Additionally, the practices of some *paidotribes* were questioned with regard to their motives to further their own gain at the expense of athletes' reputations (Day, 2012). Although the modernisation of sport was centuries away, this marked one of the first efforts to recognise coaching as a legitimate profession. And, not unlike issues in contemporary sport, there were concerns relating to the *paidotribes'* malpractice, questionable ethics and corruption.

While gladiatorial combat was not invented by the Romans, Rome developed the essential features of the system (Köhne & Ewigleben, 2000). The initial gladiator combat comprised prisoners of war or slaves, but in the second and first centuries BC, these spectacles became more organised. Gladiatorial schools (*ludi*) were established and managed by a *lanista*, a private entrepreneur who recruited or purchased suitable men, trained them in martial arts and hired them out to interested parties (Köhne & Ewigleben, 2000). As gladiators represented a considerable investment to the trainer, they were well looked after. For example, the *lanistae* managed the gladiators, their training was entrusted to *doctors*, responsible for the weapons training of gladiators (Potter, 2011) and *magistri*, who were likely to be former gladiators (Köhne & Ewigleben, 2000). The careers of gladiators typically lasted five or six years and involved between ten and fifteen fights (Potter, 2011). Entering into combat was a timely process, as young gladiators (i.e. *novicuius*) were not immediately sent into battle; instead, their early development was a priority and they were provided with training so that their first defeats did not negatively impact their confidence (Potter, 2011). Although the staggered introduction to combat reflected interest in psychology, their preparation primarily focused on repetitive action and the effective reach of weapons (Potter, 2011).

The interest in gladiators changed with the development of a 'new Rome' (i.e. Byzantine Empire) in Constantinople (i.e. modern Istanbul). Shifts in religious and spiritual values, from multi-deity worship to Christianity, coupled with philosophical changes in how the body and exercise were viewed, altered perceptions and the acceptability of sporting activities. While gladiatorial combat was legitimised (i.e. given value) because it fulfilled pragmatic and cultural agendas, the finances that had supported sport had largely evaporated due to barbarian invasion, civil war, military catastrophe and a limited monetary policy (Potter, 2011). Consequently, most athletic games (e.g. the Olympics) and gladiatorial combat had ceased, with athletes limited to the role of entertainers in the circus. In contrast, chariot racing grew in popularity and demand. The charioteers were organised into four professional factions: Blue, Green, Red and White. Races occurred between groups who were responsible for the charioteers' needs including training, accommodation and subsistence (Giatsis, 2000). Training focused on mental and physical skill along with diet. Although chariot racing declined in the Byzantine world after the sixth century as the result of financial difficulties, a diminished form of chariot-racing continued until the eleventh century (Potter, 2011). As interest in chariot racing had lessened, the military preparation during this timeframe (sixth to eleventh centuries) would have required some formal training. It is likely this would have involved coaching; however, sport historians have largely shied away from this period due to the absence of reliable records or archival information.

In Great Britain, coaching has been traced to the twelfth century, when those who engaged in competitive activities which involved physical skill, strategy or chance, drew upon experts who aided in the preparation for such contests (Day, 2013). These experts included: fencers, riding professors, falconers, wrestling trainers and masters of arms (Day, 2013). Their knowledge then, in addition to increased entrepreneurial opportunities and regulation, provided a platform for the development coaching and training in the eighteenth century (Day, 2013). Furthermore, the gambling cultures of the eighteenth century which funded the professional livelihoods of athletes in rowing and pedestrian encouraged the use of professional trainers whose work involved assessing, planning, organising and monitoring the physical and psychological training (Day, 2013). It is interesting to note here that such practices (i.e. assessing, planning, organising and monitoring the physical and psychological training) still underpin much of contemporary coaching and many coach learning initiatives. While educational and technological development may have shifted why and how we coach, it appears that the 'fundamentals' have not changed!

Nineteenth-century Great Britain saw the introduction of the term 'coach', a colloquial expression for a private tutor who prepared candidates for exams. The term was adopted by sportsmen in public schools and in universities sports such as rowing and cricket (Carter, 2010). Conversely, the term 'trainer' was more popular in working-class sports (i.e. pedestrianism, wrestling, cycling and pugilism). In the present day, the terms may have become interchangeable, as have the terms 'coach' and 'manager' in football in Great Britain (Carter, 2010). Nevertheless, in some countries – for example, Australia – coaches and trainers were differentiated based on their role in the sporting context as opposed to social class. That is, trainers worked in the areas of conditioning athletes (including those who were injured) while coaches were responsible for the team management, tactics and skill development (Phillips, 2000). There was some blurring of boundaries; for example, in sports such as boxing, cycling and rowing, trainers also looked after skill development.

Returning to Great Britain, as coaches were central to success in boxing, cricket, pedestrianism and rowing (sculling), they were producing their own instructional manuals, which contained information about training methods, psychology, ergogenic aids and diet (Day, 2013). Notably excluded here was content relating to the practice of coaching as it was assumed that such knowledge could only be achieved through experience via observation and trial and error (Day, 2013). However, industrialisation and the emerging middle class ignited a cultural struggle between a commercialised sporting culture and the amateur ethos (MacLean & Pritchard, 2013). The loyalty to an amateur ethos resulted in a shift in attitude towards coaches who were viewed in an undesirable light (as it challenged the ethos of sport). Additional changes to the status of the coach were evident in the latter stages of the nineteenth century as a dominant professional middle class that comprised newly formed governing bodies of sport, rejected coaching and training, attacking working-class coaches for their lack of theoretical underpinning (Day, 2013). To ensure coaches were kept 'in their place', regulatory mechanisms were developed to exclude them (Day, 2013, p. 9). For example, the Amateur Swimming Association introduced a Professional Certificate to regulate their swimming teachers who, in contrast to coaches, were believed to be 'essential' for increasing participation (Day, 2013). The marginalisation vastly contrasted the treatment of swimming coaches in America, where career coaches were recognised as integral to the swimming environment (Day, 2012). However, by the late 1940s, national coaches had been introduced which had a significant impact upon the development of coaching and the sport (Lyle, 2002).

Following a similar timeline, in Australia, the second half of the nineteenth century marked a more formalised coaching as sport transitioned into a more organised and regulated activity (Phillips, 2000). The first sports to use coaches were the professional branches of boxing, rowing, pedestrianism and cricket (Phillips, 2000). Some of these coaches were full time, and as their livelihoods depended on success, they focused on their athletes' skill development and formulated complex training programmes. The presence of full-time coaches also resulted in attracting talented players (Philips, 2000).

In North America, the role of the coach developed quickly. The first 'real' coaches in the United States were associated with established schools and wealthy private athletic clubs in the New England states (Carter, 2010). Similar to Great Britain, Canada and the United States also experienced an amateurism-based rejection of coaching. However, in universities in the United States, the inter-varsity sporting rivalries and the related financial benefits from an increased institutional profile increased the need for teams to have a competitive advantage (MacLean & Pritchard, 2013). Sports such as athletics, rowing and later in the nineteenth century, football, became important in attracting students, increasing income as well as enhancing the contributions of alumni (Carter, 2010; MacLean & Pritchard, 2013). In the same way, in professional sport, leagues were governed by commercial considerations whose interests related to economic security or profitability (MacLean & Pritchard, 2013). Consequently, as soon as one team sought an advantage through the acquisition of professional staff, others swiftly followed (MacLean & Pritchard, 2013).

With the exception of American football, other team sports in the United States were not as quick to adopt coaches as individual sports. Prior to the appointment of official coaches, clubs spent income on trainers and used playing coaches in practices. In some teams, the captain fulfilled the roles of player and coach, the advantage being that playing coaches offered credibility among players for 'being able to do it' as well as providing the benefit of being in direct contact with the team throughout the entire match (Phillips, 2000). The position of player-coach became less popular as, in some sports, the role was perceived as too demanding (Phillips, 2000). In the present day, the player-coach role is not extinct. Likely to be found in non-performance sport, player-coaches are largely a consequence of a lack of resources to sustain a non-playing coach. There are exceptions as there have been instances where the role has been used in professional sport, albeit temporarily, in response to coach-turnover.

Additionally, in the late nineteenth and early twentieth centuries, in many Western nations, there were situations within tournaments in which individuals became ad hoc coaches or proxy coaches by default - for example, chaperones of touring Olympic teams, medical professionals charged with overseeing team management or athletes who did not have or could not pay for a coach (i.e. it may have contravened their amateur status) (Kohe, 2014a; Kohe, 2014b).

At this point, a more contemporary coaching story emerges. An account which moves beyond the focus of this chapter. This section has provided a brief outline of the prevailing historical narrative which has been generated by scholars and is largely based on a particular reading and interpretation of sources that have positioned coaching within the wider history and modernisation of sport. This has been compounded by a male orientated prevailing narrative, with women's involvement and 'voice' largely absent. Therefore, the following section attempts to provide some redress with a coaching herstory.

A HERSTORY

Historically and in more contemporary societies, coaching in western countries has largely been a domain for white heterosexual males. For example, in the UK in 2011, 69 per cent of the practising coaches were male, 97 per cent reported themselves as white and 45 per cent represented higher socio-economic groups (sports coach

UK, 2011). Similarly, in North America, male coaches outnumbered females, females rarely coached males and the proportion of female coaches decreased in higher levels (LaVoi & Dutove, 2012).

The underrepresentation of women in coaching positions raises concern in relation to supporting outdated stereotypes about women, leadership and sport in general. Furthermore, a lack of women represented in leadership roles can undermine women's aspirations to pursue careers in the same context (Hums, Bower & Grappendorf, 2007). Literature has recognised that women coaches can act as role models, motivating females to enter sport, continue participating and encourage them to seek coaching as a viable career (Demers, 2004; Werthner, 2005). Towards this end, LaVoi (2014) argues that if female athletes/players see women in positions of power (i.e. head coach), they are more likely to view and seek coaching as a viable career option. This is echoed by Gogol (2002), who found that female athletes/players with women head coaches are more interested in the field of coaching than those who have male head coaches. Perhaps more importantly, this literature has recognised the impact of women coaches on helping females feel more at ease in a sporting environment, which, as a consequence of its history, many still view as an exclusive male society (Sisley, Weiss, Barber & Ebbeck, 1990; Werthner, 2005).

The above argument is not exclusive to coaching, as women's participation in sport more generally has been marked by marginalisation and discrimination. Before presenting a herstory of coaching, it would be useful to provide some contextual information which helps to explain the current context in which women coaches operate. The following content offers some explanation of the social circumstances which have contributed to the underrepresentation of women coaches in the present day.

While the story of coaches begins in Ancient Greece, women's involvement in sport can be traced to the ancient Greek city of Sparta where women played ball games, wrestled, swam, drove chariots, hunted, danced and participated in athletic events and festivals (Kennard & Carter, 1994). More formally, women's participation in sport was celebrated at the Herean Games at Olympia (AD 175), which comprised foot races for maidens (Kennard & Carter, 1994). Beyond records of religious athleticism, female gladiators have been portrayed in stone work from Halicarnassus (first or second centuries AD), which extended the evidence of women's participation to combat sports (Köhne & Ewigleben, 2000). Notwithstanding the information available regarding women's engagement in sport in Ancient Greece, it is difficult to trace women's participation until the early Middle Ages. The literature resumes the story of women's participation in the twelfth century with the education of women of the nobility. These women were not only educated in reading and writing, but their training also involved hawking, chess, storytelling, singing, playing instruments and dancing (Kennard & Carter, 1994). Later, physical activity extended into equestrian, early forms of racquet sports, and lawn games.

Across seventeenth-century Europe, the social position of women declined. In German-speaking provinces, for example, women were beginning to be seen as a competing labour force and increasingly excluded from the workforce. In France, and not unlike elsewhere, patriarchal attitudes (fuelled by strong, yet inconsistently applied, religious doctrine) resulted in women experiencing increasing subjugation to their husbands (Park, 1994). While these practices and attitudes greatly restricted women's and girls' involvement in physical activity and sport, there was some participation, although far less than that of men and boys.

In the United Kingdom, the Victorian period (1837–1901) characterised men as naturally aggressive and competitive, with games played at public schools reflecting a dominant masculine identity in sport (Hargreaves, 1994; Williams, 2014). Conversely, women were considered to be emotional, passive and co-operative, rendering them to be unsuitable for strenuous physical activities and competitive sports (Hargreaves & Vertinsky, 2006). Additionally, there were those who believed that excessive exercise may have negative consequences on childbearing. This focus on the biological differences between men and women was one of the major justifications for limiting women's participation in sport and, because it was more common to see males playing sports (and not females), this confirmed to the Victorians that this was the 'natural' order of things (Park & Vertinsky, 2013). Consequently, emphasis was placed on their domestic virtues, which opposed sports participation. It is useful here for the reader to consider how these ideas (i.e. issues of gender inequality) are prevalent in contemporary sport and, by extension, coaching.

Focusing on the mid-nineteenth century Australia, but similar to other countries, Phillips (2000) noted that women were limited to a smaller range of activities. However, the emphasis on women's sport was not competitive success; rather, it was to prepare for motherhood. In addition, only women from wealthier backgrounds were exposed to skill acquisition and a range of competitive sports and training opportunities at school and university, with coaching predominantly undertaken by men although some girls' schools provide a few opportunities for female coaches (Phillips, 2000).

Returning to the United Kingdom, the late nineteenth century marked an increase in women's participation in sport, but many organisations still believed that sports did not contribute to the positive development of girls and women (Coakley & Pike, 2009; Park & Vertinsky, 2013). Although there were women who defied the conventions of femininity to promote competitive athletics for women (Guttmann, 2004), until the late 1960s the traditional attitudes and practices ensured that the male-dominated organisation of sports prevailed and women had few opportunities to partake. Women and girls who wanted to participate in physical activities and sports were channelled towards those that were assumed not to require strength, power and speed (i.e. characteristics associated with masculinity), such as dance, gymnastics, hockey and swimming (Hargreaves & Vertinsky, 2006). And, those who challenged these practices and chose to participate in sports that involved strength, power and speed often faced social rejection (Coakley & Pike, 2009). However, since the mid-1960s, with increased advocacy for legislation mandating equal rights, there have been dramatic increases in sport participation among girls and women (compared to previous eras) and their sporting endeavours have challenged and are continuing to contest the previously held beliefs. It is important to recognise that closely linked to the ideals of women's liberation movement are those of the civil rights movement, the gay liberation movement and rights for people with disabilities, which have had a significant impact upon participation in sport (this will be discussed later in this chapter).

In contemporary contexts, while males have moved seamlessly between working with males and females in the higher levels of sport (notable exceptions are netball and synchronised swimming in which males have experienced some resistance; Phillips, 2000), it has been assumed that men can coach women and men, but at the highest levels, women are only able to coach women (Nauright & Parrish, 2012). This has recently been challenged with the appointment of women coaches to high profile positions. Notable examples include: Becky Hammon, who, in 2014, was selected as an assistant coach of the NBA's (National Basketball Association) San Antonio Spurs. The following year, in the same league, Nancy Lieberman was named as an assistant coach for the Sacramento Kings while Jen Welter was appointed to the coaching staff of the NFL's (National Football League) Arizona Cardinals. Late in 2015, the MLB (Major League Baseball) named Justine Siegal as a guest coach for the Oakland Athletics' Instructional League club and, in August 2016, Dawn Braid was hired as skating coach for the Arizona Coyotes (National Hockey League). Outside of professional sport, in 2017, Patrizia Panico was named manager of Italy's male under-16 national team. As a performance woman athletics coach noted, 'I would very much say that there is more opportunity for second class male coaches to be at the top than second class female coaches... It's like this, the women coaches that manage to make it to the top level, are very very good.'

The underrepresentation of women in sports coaching and, by extension, sport leadership, has raised the attention of scholars in numerous countries such as Australia, Canada, Germany, the Netherlands, Norway, Sweden, the US and the UK (Acosta & Carpenter, 2014; Demers, 2009; Barker-Ruchti, Hofmann, Lindgren, Sinning & Shelton, 2013; Hovden, 2010; Knoppers & Anthonissen, 2008; LaVoi, 2014; Norman, 2008, 2010; Pfister & Radtke, 2009; Sibson, 2010; Theberge, 1993). Such work has focused on topics including: the (under)representation and marginalisation of women in coaching positions, constraints for women in coaching, media representations of women coaches, the experiences of lesbian coaches and careers of women coaches.

To make sense of the marginalisation of women coaches and the barriers or constraints they face or have faced in their practice, it is worth looking at the prevailing ideas in society (i.e. gender, race/ethnicity, social class, sexuality and disability, which were alluded to earlier in this chapter). Coaches who are not male and/or white and/

or heterosexual, for example, challenge the traditional view which has prevailed for generations and infiltrated all aspects of sport at all levels in both distinct and subtle ways. This dominance has created a challenge for women to establish credibility and achieve success in such a system (Kamphoff, 2010). As one woman athletics coach noted, 'Wherever you go, it's just assumed that you're an assistant to the man' (Purdy & Glynn, 2008). Additionally, a second athletics coach who had over fifty years of experience, reflected upon her early years as a coach:

> People's opinions [were] probably the hardest to overcome ... plenty of people would jump at the chance to point to the fact that a woman maybe shouldn't be involved in coaching male teams ... I would have had far more criticism from women ... I was letting down women or letting down what women should be doing because I was doing something different.
>
> (Purdy & Glynn, 2008)

Ideas regarding gender (and race, sexuality and disability) are deep-seated and have an immense impact upon those who do not meet the 'norm' or 'the way it has always been'. For example, in light of the traditional view of women as caregiver, often women are entrusted to coach younger age groups, less competitive levels, less prestigious sports or less visible roles (e.g. assistant to a male coach) (Messner, 2009; Reade, Rodgers & Norman, 2009). As such, a 'glass ceiling' metaphor, which refers to an unseen yet unbreachable barrier that prevents advancement in a profession, has often been employed suggesting that few to no women can reach the highest levels. This is reinforced by the lack of a career pathway for coaches, especially women, in performance sport (Barker-Ruchti et al., 2013; Barker-Ruchti, Lindgren, Hofmann, Sinning & Shelton, 2014; Christensen, 2013; Norman, 2013; Purdy & Potrac, 2014). Having limited career mobility as well as competing for a limited number of positions has impacted upon the recruitment and retention of women coaches. As a woman boxing coach reflected:

> Guys were picked for the national teams to travel to various places and I was overlooked. They used the usual excuses that it was a male team, but then when females started to be picked for internationals, it was always a male coach that went with them.
>
> (Glynn, 2008)

In an effort to make sense of the limited opportunities for women coaches, some work (e.g. Kilty, 2006; Reade et al., 2009) has argued that organisations have employed homologous reproduction (i.e. the process by which a dominant group systematically reproduces themselves in their own image) (Kanter, 1977). For example, if males occupy a majority of positions of power in sport (at all levels), it is likely that male coaches would be hired more frequently than female coaches (Kilty, 2006; Reade et al., 2009; Segas, Cunningham & Pastore, 2006).

In addition to gender ideology, heterosexist and homophobic norms that permeate sport and create climates of fear and intolerance have been identified as strong deterrents for entering/ staying in coaching (LaVoi & Dutove, 2012; Kane, 2016; Krane & Barber, 2005). Focusing on the experiences of women coaches who identified themselves as gay or lesbian, Norman (2011) noted incidents of homophobia in routine practices and interactions which left coaches feeling undervalued, trivialised, humiliated, or viewed as a sexual predator. Consequently, some coaches felt the need either to compartmentalise or deny their sexual identities.

While gender ideology and heterosexist norms have framed the positioning of women coaches in various sports, there are numerous structural issues in sport that have been identified as barriers to the recruitment and retention of women coaches. Literature identified work–life conflict, the time commitment required for the job, a lack of family friendly policies, work–family conflict and a lack of support from others (i.e. partner/spouse, peers, other coaches) as challenging in attracting and keeping women coaches. As a woman athletics coach reflected:

> It's a really big time commitment ...You've literally got to work your way up the ranks, earn respect, and for a woman, especially if you've got a family, you just can't put that amount of time in.
>
> (Glynn, 2008)

Compounding potential work–family conflicts, the organisational environment has been recognised as a barrier – namely, the scrutiny from male colleagues/parents/referees, incompatible beliefs to the organisation or having limited voice in the organisation were cited as reasons for not coaching or discontinuing coaching (Bruening, Dixon, Burton & Madsen, 2013). A woman boxing coach recalled:

> There was a [club president] who did everything in his power to stop
> me doing further training and coaching and things like that ... on one
> occasion a few years later after [athletes' success] ... he stood up ...
> and he acknowledged what I had done and he apologised ...
>
> (Glynn, 2008)

Although the coach who made this comment had ignored the efforts
of the club president, women have been deterred from coaching for
similar treatment. Being undervalued, feeling isolated or excluded
from other coaches or experiencing a lack of recognition have
been identified as reasons why women withdraw from coaching.
Other issues such as being underpaid, a lack of opportunities for
formal training and development, and difficulty getting time off
or compensation for attending courses also had an impact on the
retention of women coaches. Notwithstanding exceptions in some
sports (e.g. netball), the latter point is also of interest as formal coach
education courses, which are mostly run by men, have been viewed
as discouraging many potential female coaches from partaking in
them and, consequently, coaching (Demers, 2009). A development
rowing coach recalled:

> I looked around the room and it was the first realisation, I knew there
> weren't many women coaches out there anyways, but it was the first
> time I realised I was the only one in the room! And I suppose I felt a
> bit unsure at first going 'What am I doing here?' But it's not exactly
> rocket science so I thought I was okay. I just had to remind myself that
> I was doing okay. I guess it really just came down to having the self-
> confidence and self-belief to know I belonged there.

While the previous information provides a brief introduction to
gender ideology and its dominance in sport, it is important to
recognise that not all women coaches have the same experiences.
Rather, it is important to consider how gender, race/ethnicity, social
class, disability and sexuality interconnect to frame the experiences
of women coaches (e.g. intersectionality (Crenshaw, 1989)). It is
also of importance to consider how gender, race/ethnicity, class,
disability and sexuality interconnect to frame another experience for
women coaches. As such, a women coach who identifies as Black,

Asian, and/or minority ethnic (BAME) or a woman coach with a disability would face additional discrimination. Linking to the wider literature in sport, in the United States, sports have had a long history of ethnic exclusion which has resulted in underrepresentation at all levels (Coakley & Pike, 2009). This lack of BAME coaches has been attributed to discrimination and racism that has prevailed in sport (Cunningham, 2003; Cunningham & Sagas, 2005). Similar to ideas about gender, a dominant racial ideology has limited opportunities for coaches who are ethnic minorities. Practices such as homologous reproduction and positional segregation (e.g. frequently appointed as assistant coaches as opposed to head coaches) have been cited as limiting the prospects for BAME coaches (Cunningham, Burning & Straub, 2006; Cunningham, 2010). Additional issues such as the presence of an 'old boys' network', a lack of supports (i.e. development opportunities, networking, mentoring) and an absence of role models have impacted upon the recruitment and/or career longevity of coaches from black and minority ethnic groups (Cunningham 2003, 2010; Cunningham and colleagues 2005, 2006).

While scholars have offered numerous explanations for the underrepresentation of coaches who are women and/or from BME groups, the experiences of coaches with disabilities have not received similar attention. This is surprising given the increasing scholarship which focuses on coaches' work with athletes/players with disabilities, yet these arguments have not yet extended to how coaches with disabilities experience their work. Such work is essential as findings can help to make sports coaching inclusive to all.

The history of coaching tells us, variously, about the significance of patriarchal structures in coaching within the context of the modernisation of sport, the power of male coaches in shaping the performative and pedagogical preferences in sport cultures, and their influence in defining the bureaucratic and administrative frameworks that govern the spaces in which coaches work. In contradistinction, the herstory describes dominant ideologies, power, conflict, subordination and subjectification. However, it is important to recognise that this herstory contains many herstories, and each of these tell us something about coaching in general and the experiences of those therein.

SUMMARY

Histories and herstories of coaching are useful as they offer an understanding of how people and societies behave. And, by looking at the past, we can better appreciate the circumstances that have led to our understandings and experiences of coaching in the present day and their link to tradition, convention and history. In addition, they allow us to see counter-veiling narratives that disrupt these interpretations. By examining the history and herstory of coaching, readers can begin to understand the various continuities and discontinuities that have informed coaching practice over time. Not only do these factors have an impact on the context of the sport, but also on the daily practices of coaches. What we see is that coaching has emerged as a by-product of particular political, cultural and social forces.

The herstory of women coaches has gained attention by sport organisations that have introduced initiatives to attract and retain women coaches. Further, the introduction of women coaches into high profile leagues (e.g. NBA, NHL, MLB) strengthens conversations regarding the (under)representation of women in coaching. However, not unlike recent trends within sport history, these stories of coaching need to acknowledge a greater diversity of voice. Changes in this domain will require challenging the dominant gender, sexual and racial ideologies that prevail in sport. Rehearsing Kamphoff (2010), this will require new conversations that will challenge and advocate for institutional change within sport.

4

COACHING AS SOCIAL
CONSIDERING THE 'TAKEN FOR GRANTED' IN COACHES' WORK

Over the past two decades, researchers have increasingly recognised the social nature of coaches' work. This scholarship has been underpinned by the notion that if coaches operate as social beings within a social environment, the coaching process must be inextricably linked to the opportunities and constraints of human interaction (Cushion, Armour & Jones, 2003). With coaching positioned as a social endeavour, work has called for a greater appreciation of the 'social competencies' (i.e. the rules, structure, and organisation of the social world which inform behaviour) that are required by coaches to influence athletes/player and other stakeholders (Jones, Potrac, Cushion & Ronglan, 2011; Lemert, 1997). To do this, scholars have drawn upon the discipline of sociology, which offers a critical analysis of the social processes, social behaviour and social changes that affect coach–athlete/player relations.

Scholarly interest in the 'sociology of coaching' has resulted in an increase in empirical and theoretical work that draws upon the thinking of, for example, Erving Goffman (e.g. Jones, Armour & Potrac, 2004; Jones, 2006; Chesterfield, Potrac & Jones, 2010; Ronglan & Aggerholm, 2014), Pierre Bourdieu (Cushion & Jones, 2006, 2014) and Michel Foucault (Denison, 2010; Denison & Scott-Thomas, 2011; Denison, Mills & Jones, 2013; Denison & Mills, 2014; Denison, Mills & Konoval, 2015). These works have been useful in drawing attention to the often 'taken-for-granted', 'familiar', or 'unseen' patterns of social life inherent in sports coaching (e.g. coaches' knowledge, identity, role, interaction, power, emotions). Therefore, this chapter considers the complex social situations and interactions which are inherent in coaches' work. In particular, it provides a brief introduction to coaches' identities, interactions, power and politics.

IDENTITY

Identity is a key concept within sociology. In general, identity relates to sameness and difference, or how a person describes her/himself as unique. While our identities differentiate people from others, they share common identities with a broader group (e.g. gender identity, national identity, cultural identity) that enable them to identify with others who, we assume, are similar to ourselves (Lawler, 2008; Buckingham, 2008). This can be extended to one's social domain or occupation and/or interest, such as coaching. As such, identities are about knowing who we are as individuals and as members of collectivities. And, identity is not something a person can have (or not); identity is something a person does (Jenkins, 2008).

As opposed to being fixed or based on a person's genetic makeup or personality traits (Manza, Arum & Haney, 2013), sociologists perceive identities as being constructed through an ongoing process of engagement between the individual and the social forces that impact upon their lives (Hughson, 2012). This means that an individual may possess several identities and these identities can change.

Although literature has drawn attention to athletes'/players' identities, scholars have not afforded coaches' social identities similar consideration. This is surprising as our experiences and interactions as coaches shape our identities, which then influence our sensing of the world. As some coaches work in precarious contexts that require adaptation or reinvention, it is useful to consider how coaches' social identities can be developed, advanced, sustained and/or disrupted.

Identities provide a sense of purpose or direction (Manza et al., 2013), so how an individual defines her/himself will impact upon how s/he makes sense of her/his experiences as a coach and carry out her/his role. The subsequent quote draws attention to how a former professional basketball player began to develop his coaching identity. He reflected:

When I retired as a player, I started coaching right away. I had spent most of my life in the sport so it wasn't like I was doing something completely foreign. My playing experience was useful because I knew how the players' felt, but I found out quickly to be coach is so different to being a player. I was having to take responsibility, plan everything, and tell others what they need to do. So, I was still in the same sport, but the first couple of seasons were really hard because I really had to change my thinking from being a player and figure out what kind of coach I wanted to be, what worked, what didn't, what the players responded to, what brought success, but also, what was comfortable for me.

(professional basketball coach)

This quote is useful as it highlights that, in developing a coaching identity and making sense of how he would undertake his role, the coach drew upon several sources: his understanding of coaches gleaned from his time as a player; his initial experiences as a coach; his personal preferences; his interactions with others within the sporting context; and the meanings he associated with these experiences. This suggests that identities are fluid constructions; continuously negotiated due to time, context and interaction with others (Kondo, 1990). While identities are socially constructed and, therefore, open to change (Manza et al., 2013), the neophyte coach was not, however, free to choose whatever persona he wanted. Rather, the coach's initial identity development involved the reflection, negotiation and consideration of social influences that were interrelated with the self (i.e. his capabilities as a coach at that time). It was the success of the team and the positive feedback from the coaches around him and recruitment to a higher ranked team which led him to believe that his practices were 'working' (i.e. he was doing a good job and/or meeting expectations), thereby reinforcing his burgeoning coaching identity. Moving forward, the coach strengthened this identity through continued successful social interaction with players and other coaches. This interaction contributed to the development of social relationships (and social stability), as well as reinforced positive feelings of self-worth and social value, which are vital aspects of identity maintenance (Manza et al., 2013).

Identities are fluid creations that develop over time through the interrelationship between the self and those who comprise the social world (Manza et al., 2013). This means that identity changes may accompany career transitions (Ibarra, 1999; Kelchtermans, 2009a). For example, a coach moves from the position of Head Coach to Assistant Coach within the same season. These role changes, or career transitions, can act as catalysts for identity changes. That is:

> [a]s an assistant coach, you are close with the team and with the head coach, but as the head coach, you might have the same amount of contact, but it changes in tone ... because you are making the decisions. Sometimes the players are not as open to you because you are the head coach and there needs to be some distance between you and the players.
>
> (professional basketball coach)

While role change might impact upon how the coach views her/him self, it may also impact upon her/his ideas of what constitutes 'good' coaching practice and the resultant interaction. Similarly, a change in responsibilities with the athletes/players and/or team or a lack of progression may cause a person to question their abilities and sense of self. Such a change or 'disruption' may foster uncertainty, which makes it hard to know the social rules and how to act, consequently making it difficult to sustain a consistent self-concept or identity (Giddens, 1991). For example, following a change in position from Head Coach to Assistant, a performance athletics coach reflected:

> It's been a long time since I've had what I consider to be effective coaching from myself. Not [in this position], [I have not] done it or not consistently ... So I've got a lot of doubt about my ability at the moment ...
>
> (Purdy & Potrac, 2014, p. 789)

The quote highlights how a coach's change in role resulted in a questioning of her competence. That is, her new coaching position, which lacked consistent contact with athletes/players, challenged her understanding of the duties that a coach performs and what constitutes doing a 'good job' (Kelchtermans, 2009a, 2009b). Here, scholars have argued that when an individual is unable to perform a role in a particular way, s/he may experience strong emotional consequences, not only in terms of her/his self-esteem and job satisfaction, but also in terms of her/his continued engagement in coaching (Kelchtermans, 2009a, 2009b). Such experiences caused the coach to 'take stock … re-evaluate, revise, resee and rejudge' (Strauss, 1962, p. 65) her position as a coach. However, the decision to stop coaching was not simple to make as she had invested over two decades as a full-time coach, a position that offered little time to develop other dimensions of herself. The coach reflected:

> I often struggle to think what else I would do. Like [I'm] going to finish up [the contract] here before the end of this year and I'm really thinking hard about what my pathway is after this. And I am seriously thinking of not doing this (coaching) but I think, can I be away from it?
> (Purdy & Potrac, 2014, p. 790)

Here, questions can be raised whether the coach had over-invested in one (coaching) identity which may make it difficult for her to consider other selves or career possibilities. However, continuing in a career in which she is continuously experiencing a lack of job satisfaction and/ or lowered self-esteem may not be a workable option.

This section has briefly introduced coaches' identities as social and how they can be developed, fostered and disrupted. Of consideration is how coaches' identities provide a sense of purpose or direction as well as having implications on individuals' well-being, emotional adjustment and their overall satisfaction in their role (Stringer & Kerpelman, 2010). This section has also shown that identities are 'performed'; therefore, identities are shaped by social experiences and interactions.

INTERACTION

Social interaction is essential in the coaching process (Jones et al., 2004; Ronglan, 2011). For coaches to achieve their purpose, for example, they require interactions that are shaped by athletes/ players, other stakeholders, the environment and audience. Towards this end, academic work has focused on how coaches construct, manage and interpret their interactions (Jones et al., 2004; Ronglan, 2011). As a professional basketball coach stated:

> The interaction with players is key, and it's important to keep them on board. For example, you cannot tell a player that he is good, but leave him sitting on the bench every game. So sometimes you've got to say, 'Hey, I see your potential, but not at the moment. You can't help right now, but with a bit more practice ...' You can't say what you are really thinking, 'Your timing is bad, I can't let you play'. You cannot. You've got to give the player hope, to keep them engaged. If the player responds by pushing a bit harder, by being more aggressive in practice, I've got to reward him for that effort. And, for a couple of minutes I will let him play. If I don't, I risk losing his trust.

In considering this quote, we could focus on the coach's statement, 'You can't say what you are really thinking'. This suggests there are 'rules' regarding appropriate interaction between coach and player. These rules are one component which comprises the 'social competencies' that inform coaches' behaviour. This quote also draws attention to the coach's strategy to keep a player 'on board' (i.e. 'give the player hope') and the consequences on player's trust for the coach if the coach does not fulfil his behavioural obligations. How coaches' get players to buy into their agendas has been of particular interest to scholars who have drawn upon Erving Goffman's (1959) work *The Presentation of Self in Everyday Life* (e.g. Jones et al., 2004; Jones, 2006; Partington & Cushion, 2012; Chesterfield et al., 2010; Ronglan & Aggerholm, 2014).

Using a theatre metaphor, Goffman (1959) presented society as a stage in which social actors played roles in social situations. These roles are largely inscribed with societal expectations of behaviour, which, when performed, are intended to create, modify or maintain an impression that another person has of them. The successful execution of these roles relies upon three interconnected elements: the physical environment or setting, the appearance and manner of the social actor, and the institutionalised collective expectation (i.e. ingrained expectations of behaviour that have been constructed by the majority of a given society) (Molnar & Kelly, 2013). For example, a coach is recognisable in a sporting context as s/he engages in a set of behaviours that is understandable and meaningful to the audience of athletes/players, other coaches and stakeholders (e.g. spectators, parents). Coaches can draw upon props such as clothing (i.e. what coaches within the sport 'typically' wear), the equipment they have (i.e. stopwatch, whistle, etc.) and the language they use that help the coach to 'play the part' which is understood and appreciated by those around them. This is important because if a coach appeared at a session dressed inappropriately and did not act in accordance with the expected role in the joint interaction, the clash between the setting, manner and appearance and collective expectations would leave the 'audience' wondering how to engage in the interaction (Molnar & Kelly, 2013).

The activity that is intentionally or unwittingly employed during the performance of one's role is referred to as the 'front'. The front is 'that part of the individual's performance which regularly functions in a general and fixed fashion to define the situation for those who observe the performance' (Goffman, 1959, p. 32). Goffman referred to the region in which the 'performance' is given as the front region or front stage.

When in the front region, some aspects of the actor's activity may be accentuated. For example, Jones and colleagues (2004, 2011) drew attention to the fronts selected by coaches that were aimed at strengthening relationships and securing the 'buy in' of athletes/players. These include: exuding an aura of authority, deliberately showing a 'human side', and expressing oneself in a confident manner to convince athletes/players they know what they are talking about. While the coaches selected performances that would secure athlete/player 'buy in', that which might discredit the performance was supressed or concealed (Jones et al., 2011). Peter Stanley, a British elite athletics coach, was conscious that he needed to 'exude an aura of authority or total calm, as if it was always in the plan, even though I'm knotted in my stomach' (Jones et al., 2004, p. 139). However, not all performances are well-managed, convincing, and/ or read correctly. These have consequences as they may cast doubts among athletes/players who fail to 'buy in' to the coach's persona (Jones et al., 2004). A professional basketball player noted:

> Last season we were told we were getting this great coach which we needed because we were in a low position. But what they described and what appeared were very different. But for a coach that everyone was talking about, his practices were anything but great – nothing I had ever seen before and I've had a long career! Sure, when we'd show

up for training everything would look really good, he'd have everything ready, but when he'd set a drill, it would make no sense, and everybody would be looking at each other, even the other coaches were like, 'OK, does anyone actually understand what we need to do?' So we thought maybe he just needed some time to adjust, but it stayed the same and people started to question if he actually knew what he was doing. Practices were a joke, so we didn't have much respect for him, but because he was the coach, we couldn't show it when he was around.

This player's comment is useful in emphasising that, in addition to presenting a 'competent' front, coaches will be required to demonstrate their capacities in order to uphold it. And, as described by the basketball player, failure to do so could result in a loss of credibility in the eyes of the athletes/players (Jones et al., 2004). An elite rowing coach echoed this sentiment as he highlighted that some coaches may be more concerned about the performance and neglect to recognise that the demonstration of what they actually do is of utmost importance.

Some coaches start with a lecture where they turn up dressed nicely … first impressions and all this crap … You're their coach and the only thing that counts is what you do … They don't have to like you, they could hate your guts but they need to respect that you're a good coach and you'll help them to get better.

(Purdy, 2006)

This quote draws attention to first impressions, which may be a strategy for coaches to 'start off on the right foot' and control the course of the interaction, and the relationship, from the outset (Goffman, 1969). Such an approach would be preferable to altering a 'line of treatment being pursued once interaction is underway' (Goffman, 1969, p. 11). As the primary function of impression management is to avoid performance disruptions, the rowing coach's approach also suggests that it was important for him to present a sincere, consistent performance – one that was unlikely to be disrupted.

While the 'front region' refers to what the audience will see, that which is suppressed is left 'back stage'. The 'back stage' is a place in which the performer can relax and step out of character; it can also be a place in which impressions can be considered. For example, some coaches may privately rehearse what they are going to say or do in public (i.e. pre-match, press conference), carefully shaping their behaviour and adopting a performance which the audience would view as sincere. Coaches have highlighted that, at times, they may execute a false front – for example, adopting a 'mean' persona as a way of cajoling strong athlete/player performances (Jones et al., 2004). However, they recognise that maintaining such a rapport would be unsustainable as disruptions are likely to occur. Additionally, Goffman is careful to point out that people largely engage in performances that are not divorced from their view of themselves (Collett & Childs, 2009). The connection between the role and the self was highlighted by a coach earlier in the chapter, who stated:

> I really had to change my thinking from being a player and figure out what kind of coach I wanted to be, what worked, what didn't, what the players responded to, what brought success, but also, what was comfortable for me.

Goffman's work is useful in drawing attention to how coaches manipulate their settings, appearance and manner in order to present a specific kind of self when they encounter others. And, these performances occur and need to be understood in light of their broader social contexts. It is also worthwhile for coaches to consider how athletes/players are also engaging in impression management in an effort to be viewed positively.

Goffman's ideas have been criticised for not sufficiently addressing the role of emotional cues within human interaction. Building upon this work, Hochschild (1983) focused on the relationship between the emotions a person feels, the emotions displayed (for the benefit of others) and the social context within which the emotions are displayed (Theodosius, 2008). In her work 'The managed heart', Hochschild (1983) suggested that within social interaction, individuals frequently engage in a certain amount of acting which require that they manufacture or disguise certain emotional states (Potrac & Marshall, 2011; Potrac, Gilbert & Denison, 2013). Emotional management can include surface acting, which involves deceiving others about the emotions being experienced, but not deceive ourselves (akin to

Goffman's notion of 'back stage'), and deep acting, which involves convincing oneself in the emotions being expressed (Potrac et al., 2013). These are illustrated in the following excerpts from the diary of a development youth basketball coach:

Excerpt from diary entry #1

Yesterday I lost control and yelled at the kids. I blamed them for losing the game and could only stop myself when I saw one crying ... Later, after calming down, I apologised and told them that the 'bad coach' was leaving and the 'good coach' would take over. I'm not sure if they understood, but I cannot be that kind of coach. I WILL NOT be that kind of coach ... I've now got to convince the kids that I've changed ... I'm acting calm even though I'm anxious. I'm also hoping that by acting calm, I'll start to feel calm ... [surface acting]

Excerpt from diary entry #2

I think my strategy of acting calm started to work because all day the kids were responding to me by smiling and looking relaxed ...

Excerpt from diary entry #3

This game was really stressful, but I acted brilliantly! I was calm, supportive and controlled the situation [deep acting], and we won!

(Čyžus, 2013)

The work by Goffman and Hochschild helps us to consider how coaches develop and maintain the 'buy in' of the athletes/players. It is important to recognise this section has only offered a brief discussion of two possibilities and there are numerous 'lenses' that can be employed to consider such work. For example, another way to consider how coaches achieve the 'buy in' of their athletes/players and other stakeholders is by considering social power.

POWER

Power is considered to be 'the capacity to produce, or contribute to, outcomes by significantly affecting another or others' (Lukes, 1993, p. 504). Processes of power are pervasive, complex and often disguised in society (French & Raven, 1959). However, some argue that power exists in every interaction in ways that can be obvious and subtle, productive and repressive (McDonald & Birrell, 1999). This means that interactions are not politically neutral; rather they are influenced by the resources, objectives, assumptions, prior knowledge and expectations of the outcome that are brought by the respective parties. Therefore, a person's ability to shape interaction in the way they desire can be linked to notions of power.

Early investigations of coaches' power utilised French and Raven's bases of power (e.g. Potrac et al., 2002; Purdy, Potrac & Jones, 2008). This work suggested that for coaches to be respected, they must draw from the range of power choices (e.g. legitimate, informational, expert, reward, coercive and referent) in order to maintain an 'effective' balance. Often associated with French and Raven's (1959) bases of power is May's (1972) notion of nutrient power. In contrast to French and Raven's work, which be viewed as coach-centred, nutrient power is a more athlete-centred approach as it involves the coach sharing leadership responsibilities and decision making with the athletes.

The 'bases' of power give the impression that power is in the coach's hands. However, for this power to be exercised it needs to be given by the athlete (or person on whom the power is being wielded) (Nyberg, 1981). This suggests that the person to whom the power is wielded – in this case, the athlete – is able to resist and subvert its exercise. For example, athletes/players can resist the coach' power by not taking on the feedback, ignoring their demands, not responding to their rewards and reducing effort.

While the aforementioned work was unique in highlighting coaches' power, it received some criticism for only providing a basic understanding of power. That is, these bases don't adequately 'capture' the complexity of power and its nuances. Some scholars have drawn upon the work of Pierre Bourdieu to explore power in coaching and coach education (Cushion & Jones, 2006, 2014). Additionally, the work of Michel Foucault (a twentieth-century post-structuralist whose work has influenced the disciplines of history, sociology, psychology and philosophy) has been particularly popular in discussions of coaches' power (e.g. Barker-Ruchti & Tinning, 2010; Johns & Johns, 2000; Denison, 2007; Denison & Scott-Thomas, 2011, Denison & Mills, 2014). While Foucault has been a favourite in the field, coaching scholars have only really drawn upon particular concepts and readings of his work, namely surveillance and disciplinary technologies. These will be discussed in the following section.

A useful starting point for this discussion is the panopticon, an architectural design for a prison put forth by Jeremy Bentham in the late eighteenth century. The prison was designed so that prisoners would be contained in solitary cells arranged in a circle around a central tower. This served two purposes: to ensure that prisoners could not see those in the cells around them but were in clear view of the central guard tower. This design enabled guards to see into the cells, but the prisoners would be unable to see guards in the tower. Therefore, the assumption was that the prisoners would never know if they were being observed, but the fear of being caught breaking the rules motivated them to behave as if they were being watched all of the time (i.e. in line with the guard's/prison's expectations). Such an approach encouraged docility (i.e. to be submissive and manageable) by disciplining the prisoners to survey their own behaviours and discipline themselves to be 'obedient, conforming and non-complaining' (Denison & Scott-Thomas, 2011, p. 33). Foucault referred to this as 'disciplinary power', a form of power that is subtle and internalised.

In an attempt to understand disciplinary power, scholars have focused on the observation and assessment of athletes/players. Often at the centre of these sporting contexts is the coach who influences the customs and the rituals, identifying the approach of managing the athlete's progression, determining the skill that is required, how it will be learned, the space in which training will take place, the speed of the session, the 'ideal' effort required to undertake the session, and the amount of recovery (Denison & Mills, 2014). The coach then monitors that progress (through stopwatch/GPS, heart rates, time trials, etc.) (Denison & Mills, 2014). Here, the coaches' expertise, experience, wisdom and resources occupy an exalted position in the sporting environment which, coaches believe, gives them the right to expect athletes/players to be obedient and compliant (Johns & Johns, 2000; Cushion & Jones, 2006; Claringbould, Knoppers & Jacobs, 2015).

Denison (2007) explains that the disciplinary power coaches exert over athletes/players occurs 'subtly over time through numerous unquestioned everyday coaching practices' (p. 375). Therefore, what coaches might perceive to be a 'normal' part of the coaching process (i.e. part of the coach's role is to create and execute a predictable, manageable, progressive, controlled and strategic plan), which may be viewed to have positive results on athlete/player performances, it is worth questioning what impact this process (i.e. coaches' exercise of disciplinary power) has on athletes'/players' performances.

In considering the consequences of disciplinary power, Denison (2007) recalled his experience when coaching an athlete who underperformed in the most important race of the season. Instead of rising to the occasion, the athlete ran the race in 'an apparent daze of apathy and disinterest' (Denison, 2007, p. 381). Proceeding a discussion with the athlete about his physical and mental condition during the race, Denison concluded that the athlete had been 'psyched out'. However, following a more considered reflection which extended beyond the 'default' discourses of physiology and psychology, he recognised that many of his everyday coaching practices may have, inadvertently, worked against the athlete. That is, the traditional coaching practices which have been long established within the sport may have actually contributed to a docile runner (i.e. submissive and manageable) who was 'going through the motions' in his races, notwithstanding the contribution of a docile coach who administered training programs (Denison, 2007)!

Denison's approach to his work with the athlete highlights the importance of considering Foucauldian concepts of power, discipline and docility or the consequences (both intended and unintended) of power. While success in sport requires considerable personal discipline on the part of the athlete/player, with coaches and athletes/players deciding upon a plan, adhering to a schedule and working hard, it is worth considering how these practices have 'disciplining' effects (Denison, 2007). Towards this end, it is possible for coaches to take opportunities to reduce surveillance and monitoring (e.g. not relying upon heart rate monitors or GPS) and encourage athlete/player input in the structure, design and/or delivery of the session (Denison & Mills, 2016). However, these long-term practices are so ingrained there is the possibility that even if coaches allow athletes/players to make decisions or contribute their ideas, it is likely that the athletes/players will choose what the coaches would desire, which would still involve passivity on behalf of the athlete/player (i.e. a self-imposed docility). Therefore, it is important to recognise that actions which challenge disciplinary power need to be long-term in order to counter the long-standing practices which may also be a part, or become a part, of coaches' ongoing identity negotiation and formation.

Thus far, this section has considered the presence of social power in the coaching process, provided some ways of viewing power and the intended and unintended consequences. These discussions have evolved to consider how coaches' forge and reforge alliances in an attempt to achieve the 'buy in' of stakeholders (e.g. Potrac & Jones, 2009; Thompson, Potrac & Jones, 2015). Such practices highlight that coaching is not only power latent, but also (micro)political in nature.

MICROPOLITICS

Micropolitics is broadly understood as the use of power by individuals or groups to pursue their interests in an organisation (Blase, 1991; Hoyle, 1982). For coaches, these interests could include securing or advancing their position within a club/team, acquiring resources (e.g. equipment, time, finances), creating a positive impression, etc. Concomitantly, we could look at the interests (i.e. ideologies, motivations and goals) of stakeholders within sports contexts and how coaches attempt to navigate them in an effort to 'get the job done'. Certainly, scholars (e.g Potrac & Jones, 2009; Thompson et al., 2013) have recognised the micropolitical nature of coaches' work and suggested that it is important that coaches not only appreciate it, but are also able to read, interpret and respond to it. In the words of a professional basketball coach:

> When you join a team, you're not just working with players, you've got to think about the head coach, other assistants, management, medical staff, owners, fans and media and to survive, you've got to have a good relationship with all of them. And all these people want something from the team: the owner wants to recruit sponsors, the sponsors want to make money, the players want good statistics, coaches want to keep their jobs, the media wants something to talk about, the fans want the team to win ...

Highlighted in this quote is the recognition that although these parties work in the same organisation, it cannot be assumed that the group will be cohesive, open and collaborative (Cassidy, Jones & Potrac, 2016). Rather, there will be various ideologies and goals regarding organisational philosophy, practices and resources which may lead some to engage in strategic action in an effort to influence the setting or context (Cassidy et al., 2016). For instance, a professional basketball coach recalled a conversation he had, early in his career, with another coach which introduced him to the micropolitical nature of their work.

> I heard one coach say that the best coaches are the best liars. I asked why? Why can't the coach be honest? He said, in order for him to get things done, he's got to tell people what they want to hear.

As noted in this quote, lying offered the coach a strategy to achieve his desired ends as it enabled him to formally and informally build support amongst others to help him accomplish his goals (Blase, 1991; Kelchtermans & Vandenberghe, 1994). It must be noted that being a good liar might not be a productive long-term strategy as, over time, stakeholders might realise that the activities promised are not being carried out. However, the coach thought this to be the best course of action to maintain his position, protect his reputation (to ensure future employment) and access the resources he believed would help players perform. Towards this end, micropolitical activity involves the strategies people use to compete with each other to achieve their desired ends (or their desired working conditions). And how people, formally and informally, co-operate and build support to accomplish their goals (Blase, 1991; Kelchtermans & Vandenberghe, 1994). For the coaches featured in this section, this activity was essential for them to undertake and maintain their jobs.

SUMMARY

Coaching, by its very nature, requires role-playing, power and politics. And, awareness of these nuances can aid coaches in gaining the 'buy in' of athletes/players and other stakeholders. While discussions relating to the 'social' nature of coaching have been omitted from some coach learning initiatives, the content of this chapter serves as a starting point to consider the 'taken for granted', yet complex, nature of coaches' work. Specifically, the chapter has focused on how coaches' understandings of themselves and their positions influence the interaction with athletes/players. In doing so, it considered the strategies coaches employ to achieve their desired goals. For example, readers could reflect upon the inherent power dynamics and disciplinary nature of coaches' work and the intended and unintended consequences of their actions. As a consequence, there is potential for coaches not only to work more productively within their immediate contexts, but also to negotiate their roles and identities, employment situations and wider organisational relations beyond 'the field'.

5

CAUSES AND CONSEQUENCES

COACHES AS MOTIVATED AND AS CONSTRUCTORS OF MOTIVATIONAL CLIMATES

Coaching research was traditionally conducted by sport scientists, with psychology considered to be its parent discipline. One area that has been of interest within psychology is motivation (Franken, 2007). And, within sport, scholars have largely relied upon Self-Determination Theory (SDT) to investigate motivation and its impact upon behaviour. These investigations, however, have largely focused upon the athlete/player which is surprising given the quality of a coach's motivation can contribute significantly to her/his performance as well as impact upon the athlete's sporting experience (Gilchrist & Mallett, 2017; McLean & Mallett, 2012). Therefore, in an effort to consider why coaches do what they do and the consequences of their actions, this chapter focuses on motivation and the coach. In particular, the chapter begins by introducing SDT as a framework in which coaches' motivation and its causes and consequences can be viewed. The content evolves to consider how the environment or climate that is organised and structured by the coach can influence the goals that are adopted by athletes/players and, subsequently, impact upon their motivation. The chapter concludes with a discussion of the coach–athlete/player relationship.

MOTIVATION

> It's funny because we are always talking about athletes' motivation –
> this athlete is really motivated, but this athlete has very little motivation!
> But as coaches we don't ever talk about our motivation! We need to
> think about our motivation too. I think it makes a difference to the
> athletes to know that we want to do this as much as they do, we are
> as motivated as them.
>
> (performance swimming coach)

Motivation is generally understood as the psychological processes
that move or energise an individual to do something (Ryan & Deci,
2000). The literature has highlighted various reasons or factors
which attract people to sports coaching – for example, people might
get involved due to general interest in the sport, an enjoyment of
seeing athletes improve, as a way to support the involvement of a
family member, and as a 'natural' progression from competing in
the sport. However, coaches' motivation to carry on in the role has
received less discussion.

A popular theory of motivation that has been used in scholarly
investigations of sport is Self-Determination Theory (SDT).
Developed by Edward Deci and Richard Ryan, SDT comprises
several separate, but inter-related, theories which focus on the social
and contextual factors that facilitate or undermine self-determined
forms of motivation (Deci & Ryan, 1985, 2000, Ryan, 2002; Ryan &
Deci, 2007). To be self-determined means to act with a full sense of
volition and choice (Ryan & Deci, 2002). This means that behaviours
are fully endorsed by the individual and engaged in because they are
interesting or personally important (Bartholomew, Ntoumanis &
Thogersen-Ntoumani, 2009).

According to SDT, in order to experience effective psychological
functioning and growth, individuals are motivated to seek out
situations in which they can satisfy three psychological needs:
autonomy, competence and relatedness (Gilchrist & Mallett,
2017). The need for *autonomy* refers to the desire to control one's
actions while *competence* involves feeling efficient, effective and/or
experiencing mastery in one's behaviour. The need for *relatedness* is
concerned with feeling meaningfully connected to others or that
one belongs (to the club, team or sport). While different needs may

be more prominent than others, depending on the context and activity, all three needs need to be satisfied for optimal psychological well-being and growth.

To relate this to coaches, work focusing on women coaches' perceptions of the social environment of their sports organisations showed variation in the extent to which this environment was supportive of their psychological needs (Allen & Shaw, 2009). While the coaches had autonomy in their coaching, there was a difference in whether they felt supported or as though they *had* to operate autonomously. For example, in one organisation the coaches had independence but there were few, if any, guidelines. In contrast, in another organisations coaches' independence and initiative were encouraged within clear guidelines. Differences were also reported with regards to competence, as those within one organisation felt there was a lack of competence-development opportunities and support for them. Conversely, in another organisation, the coaches perceived there to be high quality training and preparation opportunities. There were also variations in the coaches' perceptions of the sense of relatedness with other coaches and key personnel in the organisation. For example, in one organisation coaches' perceived a lack of involvement and value from the organisation and little, if any, connection to other coaches, whereas other coaches felt a sense of connection with other coaches and the organisation. In light of these findings, it could be surmised that coaches will gain fulfilment working in contexts in which they have a sense of control over their work (i.e. training schedule, competitions to attend, athlete/player selection), an opportunity to demonstrate competence (i.e. share relevant knowledge about the sport) and feel 'part of a team' in that there is a sense of belonging or connectedness to others. Consequently, these coaches may demonstrate enhanced persistence, effort, performance, vitality, self-esteem and well-being (Deci & Ryan, 2002). Conversely, if these supportive conditions are not present, individuals have shown greater amotivation (i.e. a lack of motivation or just 'going through the motions' of the activity) which has been associated with dropout (Deci & Ryan, 2002).

Although people are motivated to fulfil their psychological needs, this motivation can vary in level and orientation (Ryan & Deci, 2000). For example, a coach could be motivated to work with a team to see how much they could achieve within the season, while another coach may be interested in gaining recognition (i.e. acclimations and a possible promotion) from the coaching community for the good work with a team. Given the difference in motivation, the quality of experience and performance would be distinct for the two coaches. Here, the coaches' motivation could be differentiated based on the reasons or goals that give rise to action (Ryan & Deci, 2000) – namely, whether a coach is motivated by *intrinsic* or *extrinsic* reasons.

Intrinsic motivation refers to doing something for its own sake. That is, the activity or experience is inherently enjoyable or interesting (i.e. a person does not require incentives to partake in it) (Ryan & Deci, 2000). For example, a boxing coach commented, 'In the early days, my priority was to train athletes to win things. I think more recently, it's become a source of satisfaction. I get a sense of satisfaction from just being involved' (Glynn, 2008). Building upon this, coaches' intrinsic rewards may also include: personal enjoyment, a sense of achievement and feelings of challenge. Such an intrinsic style of motivation has been associated with greater satisfaction, adherence and positive performances (Deci & Ryan, 1985; Vallerand, 2007).

In contrast, extrinsic motivation refers to partaking in activities to obtain an outcome (e.g. reward, recognition, approval) or to avoid a punishment (Ryan & Deci, 2000). A coach who is extrinsically motivated is engaging in the activity for external rewards (i.e. the activity is performed for reasons external to the self) (Gilchrist & Mallett, 2017). For example, coaches may be concerned with gaining status, pay, benefits, promotion, positive evaluations or better working conditions. As a boxing coach highlighted, 'Being the only woman coach I found a little bit of resistance from those around me made me more determined to prove myself and what I could do.' Here, the extrinsic reward of being recognised by her coaching peers had an impact upon the coach's motivation.

The examples above highlight the internal and external drives which influence coaches' motivation. Relating this to SDT, self-determined motivation is characterised by deriving pleasure and satisfaction (i.e. intrinsic drives) from coaching while non-self-determined motivations for coaching would relate to external (e.g. the expectations of others) and/or internal pressures (e.g. feeling of guilt). This is important as self-determined motivation has been linked to persistence and well-being, while non-self-determined motivation has been linked to burnout and exhaustion (e.g. McLean & Mallett, 2012; Lonsdale, Hodge & Rose, 2009). Although it appears that there is a stark contrast between intrinsic and extrinsic motivation, SDT proposes that extrinsic motivation can vary in the degree to which it is autonomous (i.e. having the freedom to act independently) (Deci & Ryan, 2000). Here, Deci and Ryan (1985) introduced four types of extrinsic motivation that range from self-determined to non-self-determined depending on the degree to which the behaviour has been internalised (i.e. the process of 'taking in' a value or behavioural regulation) and integrated (i.e. transforming the regulation so that it emanates from her/his sense of self) (Deci & Ryan, 2002; McLean & Mallett, 2012).To better understand this, it is useful to consider motivation as a continuum of self-determination.

A continuum of self-determination can highlight the range in motivation – from a lack of motivation or an unwillingness, to passive compliance, to active personal commitment (Deci & Ryan, 2000). At opposite ends of this continuum are amotivation (i.e. the absence of motivation and the lowest level of self-determination) and intrinsic motivation (i.e. the highest level of self-determination). The different forms of extrinsic motivation would be positioned between the two and organised in terms of the extent to which the motivation for one's behaviours emanates from one's self (Deci & Ryan, 1985). On the continuum, the first form of external motivation, *external regulation*, would be positioned closest to amotivation as it focuses on achieving an external demand such as a reward or to avoid punishment or negative feelings (e.g. coaching because it pays the bills), hence it is non-self-determined. Moving along the continuum, the second form of extrinsic motivation is *introjected regulation* – for example, a person participates out of self-imposed pressure to avoid guilt or to maintain self-esteem (e.g. coaching in order to maintain feelings of worth). Similar to external regulation, such motivation is considered to be non-self-determined because the behaviour is not fully out of choice; however, there is more autonomy than with external regulation. In contrast, *identified regulation* is a more autonomous and self-determined form of motivation which is participation initiated out of choice in order to achieve another goal; however, it is not perceived to be enjoyable (e.g. coaching enables children to engage in sport, which is of personal importance to the coach). Finally, the most autonomous and self-determined form of extrinsic motivation is *integrated regulation*. Integration occurs when there is congruence between behaviour regulation and personally endorsed values, goals and needs that are part of the self (Deci & Ryan, 2002). For example, a coach may believe that coaching is a central part of who s/he is; it defines her/him as a person. Without it, who would s/he be? It is important to note that *integrated regulation* has similar qualities to intrinsic motivation; however, as they involve achieving a goal for reasons other than inherent enjoyment, it is still considered to be extrinsic motivation (Lavallee, Kremer, Moran & Williams, 2012).

McLean and Mallett (2012), who focused on the motivation of Australian coaches in various domains, identified that coaches expressed aspects of self-determined and non-self-determined motivation. This slightly contrasts work by Vallerand and Rousseau (2001) who looked at athletes/players and found intrinsic motivation and self-determined forms of extrinsic motivation as necessary for athletes'/players' optimal functioning. However, McLean and Mallett (2012) argued that the coaches' motivational profile makes sense as, in contrast to athletes/players, coaching – particularly in the development and performance domains – requires the completion of a variety of tasks (e.g. preparing and monitoring budgets, reporting to administrators, dealing with stakeholders) that may not be driven by intrinsic means. Given that some of coaches' tasks or activities are not intrinsically interesting, it may not be realistic to attempt to eliminate non-self-determined motivation. However, a coach's levels of self-determined motivation may act as a buffer against the negative effects of non-self-determined motivation (e.g. burnout, exhaustion). Therefore, energies may be better placed on cultivating self-determined forms of motivation (Gillet, Vallerand & Rosnet, 2009; McLean & Mallett, 2012).

According to SDT, and as highlighted in this section, awareness, intrinsic goals, self-regulation and need satisfaction are fundamental for well-being (Ryan & Deci, 2000). While research has centred on the well- and ill-being of athletes/players, it has only recently begun to acknowledge the psychological needs and health of coaches (Stebbings & Taylor, 2017). Towards this end, work has primarily focused on stress and burnout. The following section offers a brief introduction to these concepts and their impact upon the sports coach.

COACHES' STRESS AND BURNOUT

> I loved coaching. I had a chance to work with great teams and great players, but over time it got too much. I got really tired of the pressure, the constant stress, the travelling. It was great for several years, but I started to feel that I was missing out on regular life.
>
> (professional basketball coach)

Research focusing on elite coaches has highlighted the high level of work pressure due to short-term contracts and expectations of athlete/team performance which is undertaken in front of an audience that is observing and scrutinising their work (e.g. Frey, 2007). In addition to the performance culture, the multifaceted and interpersonal nature of coaches' work may put sports coaches at greater risk of stress-related reactions than those in other professions which require a high degree of interpersonal interaction (Horine & Stotler, 2003; Knights & Ruddock-Hudson, 2016; McLean & Mallett, 2012).

Stress is the perceived imbalance between demands, and the resources and abilities a person has to meet these demands (Smith, 1986). Pressures such as win–loss percentage, responsibilities to athletes and managing their concerns, expectations of player development, and success at the national/international level were some of the stressors identified by coaches (Knights & Ruddock-Hudson, 2016). For coaches, stressors or the event/incident that causes stress have largely been categorised as performance-related (i.e. demands relating to the performance of the coach or the athlete), organisation-related (i.e. demands relating to the sports organisation in which they operated) and personal (i.e. the demands of home life). These stressors may be experienced in combination, with coaches left largely on their own to effectively manage.

Although research has identified that stress can contribute to heightened awareness, be energising, motivating and provide opportunities for learning, concerns have been raised regarding its contribution to anxiety, fatigue, depression, loss of confidence, and physical and emotional exhaustion which impact upon health, well-being and job effectiveness (Olusoga, Butt, Maynard & Hays, 2010). Additionally, coaches' stress can also impact upon athletes/players (Frey, 2007; Olusoga, Butt, Hays & Maynard, 2009). As a professional basketball player recalled:

> At the start of the season, the coach was approachable, we were playing well, but when we started losing, he changed. He got really controlling and paranoid. Like he kept changing his mind in practice and always wanted to know what we were talking about. We could see the assistant coaches getting nervous when he was around so we started to get nervous.

As the pressure increased through the season, the coach featured in this quote appeared to be having difficulty coping with the stressors of professional sport. A review of literature which focused on concepts, research and practice in relation to the psychological stress of sports coaches, highlighted that coaches largely employed four strategies to cope with organisational and performance stressors (Fletcher & Scott, 2010). These strategies were: emotion-focused (i.e. use of self-talk to rationalise the situation or provide positive reminders), which aimed to control emotions or mask them from athletes; problem-focused (i.e. communicate with other coaches); appraisal (i.e. reflect on the situation); and avoidance (i.e. go to the gym) (Olusoga et al., 2010; Thelwell, Weston & Greenlees, 2010). Further, UK-based performance coaches who were part of teams that had been consistent medal winners identified factors which enabled them to work in highly pressurised sporting environments (e.g. the Olympics) (Olusoga, Maynard, Hays & Butt, 2012). These were: psychological attributes (e.g. emotional control, confidence and communication), strategic preparation (e.g. contingency planning, team/athlete preparation) and skills required to cope with stress at international competitions (e.g. taking time out, team support) as essential for 'effective' Olympic coaching.

If coaches are unable to manage negative responses from stress, burnout can develop (Smith, 1986). Burnout is the product of prolonged exposure to high work-related demands (Maslach & Schaufeli, 1993). An increasing area of concern for coaches who have a high workload or are balancing multiple roles (e.g. volunteer coaching, paid work, family), burnout is a gradual process which consists of three dimensions: emotional exhaustion, cynicism and a reduced sense of accomplishment (Maslach & Leiter, 2008). With consequences including fatigue, lethargy, illness, amotivation, loss of focus, self-doubt, feelings of incompetence, anger, frustration and mood disturbances (Dubuc-Charbonneau, Durand-Bush & Forneris, 2014), burnout will impact upon coaches' abilities to do their work.

In an effort to help coaches better manage the stressors, scholars and sport psychologists have recommended psychological skills training. For example, Olusoga and colleagues (2014) introduced five collegiate UK-based university coaches to a programme of six workshops over six weeks. Each workshop consisted of several mental skills that could be used and examples of how these skills could contribute to improved performance. Throughout the intervention, coaches were encouraged to explore their experiences of coaching, stress and its influence on their thoughts and behaviours. Following the workshops, participating coaches reported positive changes in their perceptions of their ability to coach effectively under pressure and an improvement in relaxation skills particularly in competition situations (Olusoga et al., 2014). Although this project was small in scale, it provides possibilities for coach development initiatives that could be designed in light of the differing needs of coaches within various domains.

COACHES' BEHAVIOUR AND ATHLETE/PLAYER MOTIVATION

The first section of this chapter largely drew upon SDT to help make sense of coaches' motivation. Scholars have also been interested in using SDT in considering the impact of the interpersonal style of the coach on an athlete's/player's motivation and subsequent performances (e.g. Hollembeak & Amorose, 2005; Mageau & Vallerand, 2003). This work has focused on two interpersonal styles: *autonomy-supportive* and *controlling* (Deci & Ryan, 1987). Linking this to previous discussion, autonomy-supportive coaching leads to athlete/player self-determined motivation and controlling coaching leads to athlete/player non-self-determined motivation (Amoura, Berjot, Gillet, Caruana, Cohen & Finez, 2015). While the two styles are often viewed as opposites, coaches can engage in both, to varying degrees, for example, in response to contextual pressures or circumstances.

A *controlling* coaches' style is coercive, pressuring and authoritarian in an effort to impose particular ways of thinking and behaving upon athletes (Bartholomew et al., 2009). In response, athletes may feel compelled to respond in a way that satisfies the coaches' interests as opposed to their own (Mageau & Vallerand, 2003). Drawing upon wider literature, Bartholomew and colleagues (2009) identified six forms of controlling motivational strategies believed to be employed by coaches in sport contexts:

- tangible rewards or rewards which are used as leverage to control athletes'/players' behaviour;
- controlling feedback or feedback which conveys coaches' expectations about athletes'/players' behaviour;
- excessive personal control (e.g. imposing their values upon the athlete/player);
- intimidation behaviours or the use of power techniques which encourage compliance (e.g. verbal abuse, yelling, physical punishment, focusing on past mistakes, humiliation and belittling);
- promoting ego-involvement (i.e. behaviours which lead athletes to view their self-worth as contingent upon superiority over others such as fostering competition among team members and evaluating athletes in front of peers); and
- conditional regard (e.g. when a coach provides positive reinforcement for particular conduct and withdraws support/ attention when these behaviours are absent).

The problem with these behaviours is that they undermine athletes' autonomy, competence and relatedness. Instead, controlling behaviours are characterised by coercive demands, reward contingencies or a sense of obligation, all of which act as pressures for an individual to engage in the requested activity (Deci & Ryan, 2002). Consequently, concerns have been voiced by scholars regarding the use of controlling activities and the development of ill-being within athletes/players which can be manifested to further negative behaviours such as burnout, depression and eating disorders (Bartholomew, Ntoumanis & Thogersen-Ntoumani, 2011).

In contrast to controlling behaviours, *autonomy supportive* coaching can contribute to the satisfaction of a person's basic psychological needs (i.e. autonomy, competence and relatedness). When coaches support athletes' autonomy, the athletes have better performances, increased persistence, increased self-determined motivation and enhanced psychological well-being (Mageau & Vallerand, 2003). While some coaches may view themselves as autonomy-supportive, it is important to recognise that often their behaviours are influenced by the context in which they operate. For example, when coaches are under pressure or perceive athletes to be disengaged or need feedback in the middle of a match, they may draw upon a more controlling strategy. Mageau and Vallerand (2003, p. 886) identified seven autonomy-supportive behaviours employed by sports coaches. Autonomy-supportive coaches:

- provide athletes/players with as much choice as possible within specific limits and rules;
- provide athletes/players with a rationale for tasks, limits and rules;
- inquire about and acknowledge athletes'/players' feelings;
- provide opportunities for athletes/players to take initiatives and act independently;
- provide non-controlling performance feedback;
- avoid overt control, guilt-inducing criticisms, controlling statements and limit the use of tangible rewards; and
- minimise behaviours which promote ego-involvement (to be discussed in the following section).

Despite having empirical support for the use of autonomy-supportive coaching styles, and some evidence supporting the factors that predict these styles, many coaches still use strategies and techniques that do not support their athletes'/players' needs (e.g. Fraser-Thomas & Côté, 2009). Questions can be raised regarding why coaches do not adopt behaviours which have positive consequences for the athletes/players. In response, Gilchrist and Mallett (2017) argue that some coaches might not understand these behaviours, feel pressured to behave in a particular way (by others) or the way they have been coached or do not believe these behaviours will be effective in generating successful performances. Additionally, research suggests there is a link between environmental factors and coaches' likelihood of engaging in autonomy-supportive coaching behaviours. For example, increases in job pressure (e.g. Vallerand, 2007) and stress (e.g. Mageau & Vallerand, 2003) may result in controlling leadership behaviours, which have a negative effect on athletes/players.

MOTIVATIONAL CLIMATE: MASTERY AND EGO

In addition to using SDT to make sense of coaches' motivation and the impact on athletes/players, scholars have also drawn upon Achievement Goal Theory (AGT) (Nicholls, 1984) to understand the motivational climate created by the coach. Although the theory was developed in educational settings, it has been useful in sporting contexts to make sense of athlete/player motivation.

AGT is premised on the belief that individuals strive to attain competence in achievement settings. The theory proposes that variation in personal goals among individuals relates to how they interpret success and failure. It also contends that the motivational climate or how the environment is organised and structured also has an influence on the goals athlete/players adopt (Ames, 1992; Nicholls, 1984, 1989).

The motivational climate in sport is determined by how the coach operates, the organisation of the group, how their performance is evaluated and the extent to which there is social comparison (Ames, 1992). This climate promotes different treatments of the group, inducing states of ego (performance) or task (mastery) involvement (Ames, 1992). For example, if the sporting context is characterised by competition, social comparison and achievement outcomes (i.e. 'winning' and achieving outcomes, public recognition of the demonstration of ability), it is a *performance climate* in which individuals are likely to be *ego involved* (Ames & Archer, 1988). In contrast, if context is characterised by learning and the mastery of skills, it is considered to be a *mastery climate* in which individuals are likely to be *task involved* (Ames & Archer, 1988). Work focusing on motivational climates in sport has identified that ego-involving motivational climates have typically been found to be linked with decreased enjoyment (Cumming, Smoll, Smith & Grossbard, 2007; Macdonald, Côté, Eys & Deakin, 2011), while task-involving motivation climates have been related to enjoyable experiences in youth sports (e.g. McCarthy, Jones & Clark-Carter, 2008).

Looking at this more closely, for an individual who is ego-involved, improvement, understanding and learning are seen as a means to an end rather than outcomes in their own right. The individual in a more ego-involving context will try to demonstrate superiority and is concerned about how able s/he is compared to others (Nicholls, 1989). In contrast, when task-involved, an individual is trying to demonstrate mastery of the task rather than focusing on showing high ability. In this case, perceived ability is self-referenced and the person feels competent when realising learning, personal improvement and mastering a skill. This is not to say that ego-orientated athletes/players want to win while task-orientated athletes/players do not; while both want to win, the difference lies in how they interpret losses and the impact on their motivation (Duda & Whitehead, 2016). A loss for an ego-orientated athlete/player may relate to concerns over lack of ability and result in decreased motivation. In contrast, a task-orientated athlete/player may interpret a loss as the result of a lack of effort. This may increase her/his motivation as s/he focuses on increasing her/his effort (Duda & Whitehead, 2016).

To make sense of these examples, it is important to consider the underpinning theory (i.e. AGT). In a perceived task-involving sport environment, achievement is viewed in a self-referenced manner, which is considered to be more within the individual's control (Duda, 2001). In contrast, a strong ego-involving climate is assumed to lead athletes/players to focus on outcomes more outside their personal control (e.g. beating others, attaining social approval and rewards) (Duda, 2001). According to Duda and colleagues (Duda, 2001; Duda & Hall, 2001), a task-involving environmental focus should foster perceptions of competence, because the self-referenced criteria (e.g. effort) underlying judgments of competence and feelings of success are more controllable and readily achievable. This is because the emphasis in task-involving environments is on the development of competence. In contrast, in an ego-involving climate, perceptions of competence are believed to be more fragile because competence is understood in light of what others have done/are doing (Duda & Hall, 2001).

As highlighted in this section, an individual's personal goal perspective and the perceived motivational climate are significant (Pensgaard & Roberts, 2002; Roberts, 1992). As such, coaches need to consider the ego/task-involving nature of the sport and, as opposed to judging athletes/players on the outcome of the game/match, it may be of more use to consider the performance itself. Important here is that coaches are not 'locked' into one approach, rather they can foster a mastery, or performance, motivational climate based on the ways in which they define and promote success.

To help grassroots coaches foster quality motivation or create 'empowering' motivational climates, Duda and colleagues have developed Empowering Coaching™. This workshop-based programme, currently delivered in the UK and Europe, focuses on developing coaches' conceptual understanding of motivation, motivational processes and their consequences (Duda, 2013). Underpinned by AGT and SDT, the programme offers strategies for coaches in training and in competition to foster a motivational (i.e. enjoyable, engaging and supportive) climate within their teams by supporting and increasing athletes'/players' intrinsic motivation, which will lead to sustained participation in sport (see http://www.empoweringcoaching.co.uk) (Duda, 2013).

THE COACH–ATHLETE/PLAYER RELATIONSHIP

> I really think it comes down to the relationship you have with the players. I don't know how I could do my job without having the rapport that I have with the players. Without the relationship, there's no 'coaching'.
>
> (football coach)

The coach's sentiment is echoed in the literature which describes the coach–athlete/player relationship as 'not an add-on to, or by-product of, the coaching process ... it is the foundation of coaching' (Jowett, 2005, p. 412). The coach–athlete/player relationship has been a central focus in sport psychology with the relationship between the coach and athlete/player seen as one of the most important determinants of sports participation (Jowett & Poczwardowski, 2007; Sandström, Linnér & Stambulova, 2016; Serpa, 1999).

The dynamics of the coach–athlete/player relationship were first explored from a leadership approach and focused on the characteristics of the coach in terms of the communicative acts or leadership behaviours. This work was underpinned by the idea that the coaches' leadership was instrumental in enhancing the ultimate performance of the group. Consequently, investigations assessed coaches on their leadership personality, the extent to which they demonstrate leadership behaviours, and situational contingencies that affect leader behaviour. While there is still some focus on coaches and types of leadership (i.e. transformational, servant), work has expanded from a focus on coaches' behaviours to better reflect the dyadic nature of the coaching process. Consequently, there has been an increase in interest in investigating the interpersonal nature of the coach–athlete/player relationship (Yang & Jowett, 2017). Such work recognises that the coach–athlete/player relationship is influenced by the intrapersonal factors (such as the coach and athlete's/player's age, gender) and environmental factors (e.g. athletes/players in higher competitive levels of sport may have increased motivation to work more closely with coaches to achieve their goals (Jowett & Cockerill, 2003; Jowett & Meek, 2000; Sandström et al., 2016)). These investigations highlight the dynamic and unique nature of the coach–athlete/player relationship; however, researchers have identified some common dimensions of these relationships. For example, Jowett's 3Cs + I conceptual model of the coach–athlete/player relationship is premised on the belief that the quality of the coach–athlete/player relationship is formed through these four key constructs: closeness, commitment, complementarity and co-orientation.

Jowett (2005, Jowett & Pocawardowski, 2007; Yang & Jowett, 2017) view *closeness* as the emotional tone of the relationship, and reflects the degree to which the coach and the athlete are connected and the depth of their emotional attachment. This is reflected in expressions of such as 'trust', 'respect' and 'appreciation', which indicate a positive interpersonal and affective relationship (Jowett, 2005; Yang & Jowett, 2017). *Commitment* reflects coaches' and athletes'/players' intentions or desires to maintain their close athletic partnership over time (Yang & Jowett, 2017). *Complementarity* refers to the interaction between the coach and the athlete/player that is perceived as co-operative and effective. There are two sets of complementary behaviours: corresponding and reciprocal. *Corresponding behaviours* refer to the same actions that the coach and the athlete/player are expected to display in training and competition (e.g. responsiveness and openness). *Reciprocal behaviours* refer to the different actions that the coach and the athlete/player are expected to display in training and competition (e.g. when the coach directs or instructs and the athlete/player follows or executes instructions in training). These two sets of behaviours are key in determining the efficient conduct of interactions between coaches and athletes/players (Jowett & Shanmugam, 2016).

The 3Cs outline the social situation created by the coaches and athletes/players, but these constructs are interdependent. The concept of *co-orientation* (+1) is concerned with the degree to which a coach and athlete/player are able to correctly infer how the coach/athlete/player is feeling, thinking and behaving (Rhind & Jowett, 2010). As such, the positive coach–athlete/player relationship is a state reached when coaches' and athletes'/players' closeness, commitment and complementarity are mutually and causally interconnected (Yang & Jowett, 2017). While the quality of the relationship between a coach and an athlete/player is formed through these four key constructs, the resultant positive outcomes, such as satisfaction, fulfil the three basic psychological needs of autonomy, competence and relatedness (Jowett & Shanmugam, 2016).

Empirical work in this area has identified that the better the quality of the coach–athlete/player relationship, the more satisfied athletes/players and coaches are with performance, training and coach treatment, and the higher the levels of team cohesion (Jowett, 2009; Jowett & Chaundy, 2004; Jowett, Shanmugam & Caccoulis, 2012). Relationship quality has also been found to link to positive perceptions of self-concept and passion for the sport (Jowett, 2008; Lafrenière, Jowett, Vallerand, Donahue & Lorimer, 2008). Because they have the opportunity to develop relationships with their coaches that are close, committed and complementary, athletes/players in individual sports are likely to be more satisfied than athletes/players who participate in team sports (Rhind, Jowett & Yang, 2012).

The 3Cs +1 model can be used to stimulate conversations between coach and athlete/player regarding their working relationship. This can assist in addressing or preventing counterproductive atmospheres which are often created when a coach is not acting in a way perceived by the athletes/players as what they should and vice versa. As such, the 3Cs + 1 conceptual framework can draw attention to the importance of communication between coach and athlete/player.

SUMMARY

The purpose of this chapter has been to focus on motivation and the coach. The initial chapter content utilised SDT to better understand coaches' motivation, its causes and consequences. It has been established that coaches will gain fulfilment working in contexts in which they can satisfy three needs: autonomy, competence and relatedness. Therefore, it would be useful for readers to consider how these needs are addressed (or not) in their own practice. While the initial discussions in this chapter focused on the coach, these extended to consider the impact of coaches' autonomy-supportive or controlling behaviours on athletes/players. Autonomy-supportive coaches acknowledge athletes' feelings and perspectives and involve them in the decision-making process (Reeve, 2009). In contrast, those adopting a controlling style would employ a highly directive style of interaction which requires that athletes/players behave in a particular way (Bartholomew, et al., 2009; Deci & Ryan, 1985). Felton and Jowett (2013) highlight that contexts in which coaches employ behaviours that are controlling and generally negative will have consequences on athletes'/players' abilities to satisfy their need for competence (necessary for psychological functioning and growth). Additionally, such behaviours may make athletes/players feel afraid, upset, nervous and hostile (Bartholomew et al., 2011; Felton & Jowett, 2015).

Following a discussion of SDT in considering coaches' motivation and their behaviour on athlete/players, the chapter progressed with a discussion of AGT to make sense of the motivational climate coaches can create and its influence on athletes'/players' goal perspectives (i.e. ego or task). These are significant in motivation and, ultimately, have an influence on athletes'/players' enjoyment in the sport. The chapter culminated with a discussion of the coach–athlete relationship (Jowett & Cockerill, 2003). This relationship is considered by some to be the heart of coaching, and coaches who fail to acknowledge the importance of it risk not developing their athletes/player to their full potential (Jowett, 2005; Lyle, 1999).

6

COACHES' METHODS AND ATHLETE/PLAYER LEARNING

> I was working on one athlete and saying 'Move your hands away, move your hands away', thinking of the technique I was trying to get and then I realised, okay, this is Ana. Why isn't Ana moving her hands properly? Maybe she doesn't understand what I'm saying or I'm saying it the wrong way, so I changed something or did it another way or whatever, but it immediately brought my focus onto the person and now I was dealing with Ana and Simona and Maria, rather than just a group of athletes to whom I was teaching a technique. And it just kind of struck me then 'Ah, this is the way you go about it. This makes it much more interesting!'

The above quote from Chapter 1 presents the thinking of a neophyte rowing coach who had started to consider how her approach could better influence the learning (and performances) of her young athletes. In doing so, she begins to hint at the messiness of how an athlete/player learns, how a coach teaches, what is being taught and the context in which learning occurs. To better understand the process of knowledge production that occurs in the interactions between the coach, the athlete/player, and the sporting content and context, scholars have drawn upon the sub-discipline of pedagogy. The term 'pedagogy' usually refers to children as learners, however, within the literature the term is also used in the context of adults, although the more appropriate term is 'androgogy' (Armour, 2011).

Learning has been, and continues to be, a topical area within sports coaching. Certainly, coaches are influential in shaping the learning and development of athletes/players. In work focusing on sport coaches and athlete/player learning, three theories are often discussed: behaviourism, cognitivism and constructivism. While these theories are in agreement that learning involves 'acquiring and modifying knowledge, skills, strategies, beliefs, attitudes and behaviours' (Schunk, 2014, p. 2), they differ in how it occurs. Therefore, this chapter begins with a discussion of these three theories, highlighting their differences. The second half of the chapter focuses on the connection between athlete/player learning and popular methods that coaches use: directive/command, task, reciprocal, guided discovery and problem solving.

BEHAVIOURISM

Behaviourism has its roots in late nineteenth/early twentieth century psychology with John Watson generally considered to be the founder. However, Ivan Pavlov, Edward Thorndike and B.F. Skinner were involved in key developments within this area (Rachlin, 1991). Behaviourism has significantly influenced the content and delivery of education in the western world. The hallmark of behaviourist theories is that they focus on behaviour, explaining learning in terms of environmental events (Schunk, 2014) – that is, we learn through a process of stimulus-response and selective reinforcement. This means that all behaviour can be explained without consideration of what is happening within the learner's brain during learning (Chambers, 2011).

John Watson (1878–1958) was an American psychologist, who, with his graduate student Rosalie Rayner, developed an experiment entitled, 'Albert B'. The purpose of the experiment was to identify if classical conditioning (famously used by Pavlov with dogs) could be used to condition an emotional response in humans. Watson and Rayner exposed nine-month-old boy, Albert, to a series of neutral stimulus (i.e. a rat, rabbit, monkey, masks and burning newspapers), to which Albert had no reaction. Because the stimulus was neutral (resulted in no reaction), the researchers could use one of the items to test if they could condition a response. For example, when they introduced a hite rat to Albert they made a loud noise caused by hitting a hammer against a metal pipe. Albert was disturbed by this loud noise (unconditioned response), and upon hearing it began to cry. Each time the rat was introduced to Albert, the noise occurred. After repeatedly pairing the rat (conditioned stimulus) and the noise (unconditioned stimulus), Albert associated the rat with fear (conditioned response) (Huber, 2013).

In relating this example to coaching, consider an athlete who decides to try a new sport. Before conditioning, the lack of experience and knowledge of the new sport meant that the sport itself did not elicit a response (neutral stimulus). However, during the first week of training, the athlete witnesses the coach shouting at the other athletes and punishing them for making mistakes. The new athlete finds the coach's behaviours (negative unconditioned stimuli) upsetting. Consequently, she develops a hatred for the new sport (negative conditioned response) and does not want to continue participating.

Watson's work in classical conditioning led to the belief that the learner is a passive recipient of knowledge. However, Thorndike and Skinner did not agree with this view of learning and positioned the learner as more active. As discussed in the subsequent paragraph, in contrast to classical conditioning, operant conditioning suggests that behaviour is shaped or maintained by its consequences.

Edward Thorndike (1874–1949) was a prominent American psychologist who proposed that learning involves forming associations or connections between sensory experiences (perceptions of stimuli/events) and neutral impulses or responses that are demonstrated behaviourally (Schunk, 2014). Such an approach to learning is based upon trial and error (i.e. selecting and connecting). For example, one of Thorndike's most known works was the puzzle box experiment in which a cat was placed into a cage, with food placed outside of it. The cat would randomly try different ways to escape the box to get the food and, eventually, after moving around the box, would stumble upon the lever that opened the hatch. Over several trials, the cat made fewer errors to find the lever and was faster at escaping from the box. This suggested the cat had learned that there were favourable consequences to pressing the lever; thereby it adopted the behaviour. Focusing on the relationship between the cat's behaviour and its consequences, Thorndike proposed the law of effect. This is explained in the following way:

If a stimulus that follows a response makes that response become more likely, we say that the response was reinforced. If the stimulus makes the response become less likely, we say that it is punished.

(Carlson & Buskist, 1997, p. 145)

In addition to the law of effect, Thorndike also identified the law of exercise. This referred to the *law of use*, in which a response to a stimulus strengthens the connection and the *law of disuse*, in which a response is not made to a stimulus. Consequently, the connection is weakened or forgotten (Schunk, 2014). Further work by Thorndike identified that rewards strengthened the connections, but punishment did not weaken them (Thorndike, 1932). Rather, connections were weakened when alternative connections were strengthened. This is interesting because the work identified that punishment may suppress a response, but it only provides feedback on what not to do (i.e. it does not offer information on the correct behaviour). Therefore, when athletes are told that they are doing something incorrectly, they understand what *not to do*. However, if an athlete does something incorrectly, but is also given corrective feedback and an opportunity to practise solving problems correctly, they learn the appropriate method (although they do not forget the incorrect method) (Huber, 2013).

B.F. Skinner (1904–1990) was an American psychologist who built upon Thorndike's work. Skinner was interested in how positive reinforcement worked. To do this, Skinner placed a hungry rat in a 'Skinner box'. The box contained a lever on one side and, as the rat moved about the box, it would accidentally knock the lever. In doing so, a food pellet would be released into a container. After a few trials, when the rat was put into the box, it would go directly to the lever. Skinner explained that the positive consequence of receiving food ensured the rat would repeat the action each time it was put into the box. While Skinner demonstrated how rewards can increase behaviour, he also showed the impact of negative reinforcement. Similar to the initial experiment, Skinner placed a rat in the Skinner box and, instead of providing a reward, he subjected it to an unpleasant electric current. As the rat moved about the box, it would knock the lever that switched off the electric current. The rat quickly 'learned' to go straight to the lever to shut off the unpleasant stimulus after a few times of being put in the box (i.e. escape learning). In contrast to the first experiment (i.e. the food pellet), the consequence of escaping the electric current (i.e. the removal of an unpleasant reinforcement) ensured they would repeat the action (Schunk, 2014). Skinner then developed this work by teaching the rats to avoid the electric current. To do this, he turned on a light just before the electric current was switched on. The rats soon 'learned' to press the lever when the light came on because they knew that this would stop the pending electric current (i.e. avoidance learning) (Schunk, 2014). From this work, Skinner believed that learning occurs through trial and error.

As Skinner identified, reinforcement can increase the chances that a behaviour will recur (Schunk, 2014). This suggests that in sport, skills could be taught or shaped through reinforcement. While positive reinforcement refers to receiving something that can increase the likelihood of a response (e.g. positive feedback), negative reinforcement refers to removing something unpleasant that would increase behaviour (e.g. criticism). In contrast, punishment can be used to decrease the frequency of an action (but it does not offer information relating to the correct behaviour). This could include asking an athlete/player to pay a fine or remove something pleasant to decrease the undesired behaviour (e.g. benching the athlete/player during a training session). Also, coaches could ignore the negative behaviour of an athlete/player, hoping that by removing her/his attention, the athlete/player will cease the negative activity, this is referred to as extinction. It is important to note that a reinforcer will only strengthen a behaviour if it is 'situationally specific' and if the athlete/player desires it (Schunk, 2014). That is, what may be a reinforcer for one person, may be considered to be a punisher to another (Morgan, 2008). Therefore, a coach would need to know how an athlete would view a potential reinforcer to know its possible effect.

Behavioural theories contend that learning involves the formation of associations between stimuli and responses. For example, learning is viewed as a change in the rate, frequency of occurrence, or form of behaviour or response which occurs largely as a function of environmental factors (Schunk, 2014). Coaches who adopt a behaviourist approach to learning would place athletes in controlled environments (stimuli) and direct them toward specific behaviour changes (or learning) based upon pre-determined achievement objectives set by the coach. Sessions would be characterised by rote learning, repetition, reinforcement, drill-based activities, and trial and error towards a fixed outcome (Chambers, 2011). Skills are commonly taught through a 'one-size-fits-all', 'all-at-the-same-time' approach with the focus on 'what' to coach and less on the complexities associated with the skills in game play (Light, Harvey & Mouchet, 2014).

COGNITIVISM

In the late 1950s, psychologists found behaviourists' explanations of learning too simple and too dependent upon observational behaviour. Consequently, understandings of learning shifted to the learner's mental processes (Merriam & Bierema, 2014). Those interested in cognitive theories of learning aimed to address the issues of how information is received, organised, stored and retrieved by the mind. Therefore, cognitive theories are underpinned by the assumption that learners actively seek and process information (Schunk, 2004). As such, learning is not concerned so much with what learners *do*; rather, it is *what* they know and *how* they come to acquire it (Jonassen, 1991).

Although there are different strands of cognitivism, they are underpinned by the belief that learning builds upon previous experience (Gould, 2009). In this way, individual information has limited meaning in itself and accumulating more knowledge does not necessarily constitute learning (Schunk, 2014). Learning can only occur when one can relate to the information and see how it 'fits' within the 'bigger picture' (Gould, 2009). For cognitivists, learning is considered to be 'a change in cognitive structures; the way in which we perceive events and organise experiences to arrive at understanding' (Gould, 2009).

Jean Piaget (1896–1980), a Swiss cognitive psychologist, viewed learning to be a developmental cognitive process. Believing that children thought differently from adults, Piaget developed a four-stage model of how the mind processes information. The first two stages focus on how people move from the infancy stage (birth to age 2) of sensorimotor responses to stimuli, to the preoperational stage (ages 2 to 4) in which they are able to represent objects in symbols and words (Merriam & Bierema, 2014). Following this, a child moves to the concrete operational stage (ages 7 to 11) in which they can understand concepts and relationships to the operational stage (age 11+) in which they can reason hypothetically and think abstractly (Merriam & Bierema, 2014). In Piaget's stage model, children's intellectual development is not simply based on increased information; rather, as children progress through the stages, there are changes in how they think. Piaget used the term *schema* to describe a unit of cognitive structure (Huber, 2013). Schemas include, for example, representations of events, stories and skilled actions. Schemas then, are adjusted or changed through assimilation and accommodation. *Assimilation* occurs as new information is incorporated into existing schema, while *accommodation* is the process in which existing schemas are altered or new schema formed as a person learns new information (Huber, 2013). Given its concern with the progressive adaptation of an individual's cognitive schemes, Piaget's work is evidenced in sporting practices which have been designed to be 'developmentally appropriate'.

SOCIAL COGNITIVE LEARNING THEORY

Cognitive learning theory provides an explanation of how the brain processes information; however, some working within this area believed that learning occurs in a social environment. Social cognitive learning theory, a subset of cognitivism, acknowledges that people acquire knowledge, rules, skills, strategies, beliefs and attitudes by observing others (Schunk, 2014).

Albert Bandura (1925–1976), a Canadian psychologist, found that people could learn new actions by observing others performing them (Merriam & Bierema, 2014). Contrasting behaviourists, Bandura identified that reinforcement was not necessary for learning to occur (Schunk, 2014). Rather, he was interested in how people could learn actions by observing others performing them (Schunk, 2014). He identified that learning through observation was dependent upon the learner's attention, retention, production and motivation. *Attention* refers the learner's focus on the relevant event so that it is perceived in a meaningful way (Schunk, 2014). For example, an athlete's attention can be directed by accentuating features of the task, subdividing complex activities into parts, demonstrating the usefulness of the modelled behaviour. *Retention* refers to how well the learner will remember the behaviour and can recall what was observed (Huber, 2013). This is increased through repetition (live or video) and relating the material to information previously learned (Schunk, 2014). Assuming the learner has the ability to execute the skill or task being modelled, the learner then reproduces the behaviour in light of the mental representation they retained (i.e. production). In a sports context, this can be assisted by the coach or peers who can provide feedback (Huber, 2013). However, important to this process is the learner's motivation. *Motivation* influences learning because people are more likely to engage in the previous three processes (i.e. attention, retention, production) for activities they feel are important, performing actions which will result in rewarding outcomes and avoiding those which will be received negatively (Schunk, 2014).

Cognitive theories pay attention to the acquisition of knowledge and skills, the formation of mental structures and the processing of information and beliefs (Schunk, 2014). Towards this end, learning is an internal mental phenomenon inferred from what people say and do. Therefore, in contrast to behaviourism, cognitivists view learning as largely detached from the environment and asocial in nature. However, similar to constructivism (to be discussed in the following section), cognitive theories view learners as 'active seekers and processors of information' (Schunk, 2008, p. 132). Coaches who accept a cognitivist approach to learning would break down tasks into steps, which begin with the most basic and build towards the more complex (depending on the athlete's/player's schema or prior knowledge). The coach prepares and transmits the information, but also empowers the mental processes of the athlete/player (Chambers, 2011).

CONSTRUCTIVISM

In contrast to behaviourism and some cognitive approaches, constructivists believe that humans create meaning as opposed to acquiring it. That is, learning is a social process in which learners construct new knowledge. Consequently, learning is seen as a process of continual adaptation and responsiveness to a constantly changing environment (Light, 2008). This recognises athletes'/players' previous knowledge (what they bring to the learning environment/

sporting context) and focuses on the construction of new knowledge or the modification of knowledge based on their learning experiences within the session. Thus, learners build personal interpretations of the world based on individual experiences and interactions, and knowledge emerges in contexts within which it is relevant (Schunk, 2014). Such a perspective positions the coach as a facilitator who asks in-depth and challenging questions to guide the learner with learner enquiry, discovery, autonomy and self-motivation viewed as critical to the success of the learning process (Leonard, 2002).

A popular constructivist theory featured in coaching scholarship is Len Vygotsky's Social Development Theory. Len Vygotsky, a Russian scientist (1896–1934), viewed learning as occurring in a cultural context and involving social interaction. He believed that an individual acquires new mental functions and patterns of thought from the assistance of tools (i.e. cultural objects, language and social institutions – churches, schools) and scaffolding (i.e. support from others) when it is offered within the zone of proximal development (ZPD) (Schunk, 2014).

ZPD is the zone in which learning occurs. This 'zone' is just beyond their range of experience with the assistance of a coach or more capable peer who can help bridge the distance from what the learner can do independently and what they can do with assistance (Schunk, 2014). Here the ZPD is not formed just within the learner, it is the interaction between the learner, the more 'capable' other and the cultural tools that are shared within a culturally mediated interaction (Cobb, 1994; Wells, 1999). Therefore, learning occurs as the athlete/player, bringing their own understanding to the interaction, constructs meaning by integrating these understandings with their experience in the context (Schunk, 2014). The influence of the cultural-historical setting is key to Vygotsky's theory as it not only provides the context in which scaffolding (i.e. assistance from others) takes place, but also enables the learner to develop an improved awareness of themselves, their language and their role in the world (Schunk, 2014). Such participation in the cultural world transforms mental functioning, enabling new forms of awareness to occur.

In contrast to behavioursim and cognitivism, constructivism comprises a range of theories which suggest that learning is most effective when it is active, interactive and authentic (Newmann, 1994). In adopting a constructivist approach to learning, coaches would actively encourage athletes/players to draw upon prior learning and experience to construct new meanings and understandings (Chambers, 2011). However, this would require that coaches understand the athlete's/player's prior learning in order to build upon it (i.e. construct) new learning. To do this, coaches would need to provide 'task-orientated, hands-on, self-directed activities which are orientated towards design and discovery' (Chambers, 2011, p. 47). At a practical level, this would include creating opportunities for active engagement, participation in groups, frequent interaction and feedback and connections to 'real-world' contexts (Chambers, 2011).

Learning is complex. As illustrated in the first part of this chapter, understanding ways athletes/players may receive and make sense of information is important to coaches who wish to create optimal learning experiences for athletes/players. Coaches' sessions are often structured in ways that reflect their assumptions and beliefs about what learning is and how people learn. However, many coaches may not have considered connections between athlete/player learning and methods or, by extension, there may be disconnect between the learning that they seek and the methods they use within their sessions. Therefore, identifying the underpinning theory of the methods coaches' use is useful as it draws attention to the intended and unintended consequences on athlete/player learning.

COACHES' METHODS

The term 'method' is commonly used when referring to the strategies that coaches use in structuring and designing their sessions. This is often confused or used synonymously with 'style'; however, methods should be viewed as principles in action whereas style is a manner of self-expression (Cassidy et al., 2009; Tinning, Kirk & Evans, 1993). To clarify, 'techniques and methods are available to all [coaches], the way in which they are used determines the [coaches] style' (Willee, 1978, p. 20). Therefore, coaches may draw upon similar methods, but they may use very different styles.

A popular approach to viewing coaches' methods is Mosston's spectrum of teaching styles (Mosston, 1966). Given that methods are principles in action and style is a manner of self-expression, in this chapter Mosston's work will be referred to a spectrum of methods. The spectrum includes eleven methods that are presented on a continuum from viewing athletes/players as passive or active learners. Here, the passive approaches (or coach-centred methods) are those that promote a robotic approach to sporting performance whilst the active learning approach (or athlete/player-centred methods) would positively impact upon decision making and problem-solving abilities of the athlete/player. In 1996, Mosston's spectrum was adapted by Kirk and colleagues who reduced it to five methods which ranged from coach-centred to athlete/player-centred (i.e. directive/command, task, reciprocal, guided discovery and problem solving). This approach was used by Cassidy et al. (2004, 2009) and will also be adopted in this chapter.

Coaches may draw upon more than one method in their session as, often, the choice of method is influenced by the nature of the subject matter and the context in which the learning will occur (i.e. indoor/outdoor) (Kirk, Naught, Harahan, Macdonald, & Jobbing, 1996). Additionally, coaches' choice of methods would reflect their views of learning, in particular, the relationship between the coach, learner, subject matter and the learning environment (Armour, 2011; Cassidy et al., 2009).

Table 6.1 provides a brief description of the five methods that will be discussed in light of behavioursim and constructivism. Notably absent here is a discussion of cognitivism; however, there is some overlap between cognitivist theories and constructivism. Additionally, cognitivism might be evident in how coaches decide which skills are relevant to the age group they are coaching and in how they demonstrate skills and/or provide instruction.

BEHAVIOURISM AND COACHES' METHODS

As mentioned previously, behaviourism is a theory that focuses on the modification of behaviour through stimulus-response and selective reinforcement. Successful learning, then, is determined through changes in behaviour (Chambers, 2011). In relation to coaches' methods, behaviourism underpins the direct or command method which is popular among coaches. As highlighted in Table 6.1, a directive or command method positions the coach as the knowledgeable one who provides the information and direction to the athletes/players. The coach privileges demonstration and feedback

Table 6.1 Coaches' methods (based on information from Mosston & Ashworth, 2008 and Cassidy et al., 2009)

Method	Characteristics
Directive/ command	• The coach makes the decisions about how athletes/players are organised, the subject matter, how the tasks should be executed (privileges demonstration), when tasks start/stop and/or change. The coach supervises and corrects athlete/ player errors. • The athlete/player performs accordingly (i.e. replicating the subject matter).
Task-based	• The session comprises several different tasks (e.g. circuit) which can be undertaken simultaneously. • The coach makes decisions regarding the task, what will be accomplished and how (e.g. the order of the task, equipment information, intervals), but provides time for each athlete/ player to work individually. This enables the coach to provide individual feedback. • The athlete/player can work independently from the coach and has the opportunity to make some decisions (e.g. the order of the task, starting time, pace and rhythm, stopping time, interval, location, attire/appearance and to ask questions for clarification).
Reciprocal instruction	• Requires athletes/players to work with one another in partnerships. • The coach designs the session to suit the abilities and needs to the athletes/players. The coach matches the athletes/players so that one is more skilled/knowledgeable than the other. The coach introduces the task, provides the performance criteria, asks for clarification, observes the partnerships, listens to the interaction and provides feedback to the group. • In partnerships, one athlete/player takes the role of a 'doer' who performs the task, while an 'observer' offers immediate and ongoing feedback (the roles reverse following achievement of the behaviour).
Guided discovery	• Incorporates activities/tasks that encourages athlete/player independence. • Through a logical and sequential design of questions, the coach attempts to gradually lead the athlete/player to discover the end result (i.e. a concept, movement, etc. which is unknown to the athlete/player). • By responding to the coach's questions, the athlete/player engages in the discovery of concepts.
Problem solving	• The coach establishes a problem (e.g. a situation the athlete/ team has experienced) or question/situation/issue and sets the parameters (e.g. equipment, time, location). • Athlete/players engage in the task by discovering and producing solutions (e.g. combination of movements, strategy).

(i.e. the information that the coach would like to see replicated) and provides reinforcement. An example is a fitness coach who leads the warm up or the warm down. The fitness coach decides which activities to include, the order of activities and the time allocated for each activity without differentiating for each athlete/player. Some would argue that this approach maximises learning as it organises information into logical progressions. However, others argue that it takes little account of learner's needs and interests which limits its effectiveness (Cassidy et al., 2009; Kirk et al., 1996).

Another example of behaviourism is the task-based method. This method comprises several different tasks, which are arranged in stations (e.g. a circuit). Such an approach enables athletes/players to work more independently from the coach as it places slightly more responsibility on the learner than the directive or command method. There is space for the coach to recognise the diversity of the athletes/players by creating or adapting tasks which will meet their needs (Cassidy et al., 2009). Additionally, a task-based method could have social benefits. However, similar to the direct or command method, the coach still controls the flow of information (they decide what tasks to include), which encourages athletes/players to reproduce the coach's knowledge. As this method (and the direct or command method) encourages athletes/players to memorise rather than understand, there is limited opportunity for athletes/players to understand the nuances of the game/activity.

CONSTRUCTIVISM AND COACHES' METHODS

Recent work in coaching has endorsed methods which are underpinned by constructivism. These methods appeal to coaches who believe that athletes/players should be primarily responsible for their own learning. That is, in contrast to being a passive sponge soaking up knowledge, the athlete/player is viewed as 'a thinking, feeling and physical being that interprets and makes sense of learning experiences shaped by the knowledge and inclinations that [s/he] brings to the learning experience' (Light & Evans, 2010, p. 104). Three methods that are underpinned by constructivism are reciprocal, guided discovery and problem solving.

RECIPROCAL INSTRUCTION METHOD

Similar to directive/command and task-based methods, reciprocal instruction still involves the coach selecting and sequencing the subject matter. However, it moves beyond behaviourism in that learning becomes social as athletes/players work together to discuss or develop the material to suit their needs (Kirk et al., 1996). Such an approach enables athletes/players to undertake these roles (although the coach may have initial involvement in teaching them how to perform them) (Kirk et al., 1996). It also enables coaches to organise athletes/players according to ability and experience or knowledge of the sport. For example, putting the less experienced athletes/players with those who are more experienced (i.e. a more capable peer). This would allow athletes/players to appreciate the skills and perspectives of others as well as encourage the development of feedback and an improved understanding of skill execution, enabling athletes/players to improve their analytical, physical and communication skills (Cassidy et al., 2009). Additionally, pairs could be joined together to form small groups, encouraging co-operative learning (Kirk et al., 1996). However, it may be naïve for a coach to think that all athletes/players want to help one another. Rather, a more experienced athlete/player may view sharing their knowledge and helping another player as threatening to her/his position on the team.

GUIDED DISCOVERY AND PROBLEM SOLVING

Guided discovery, as a method, requires helping athletes move through a series of tasks in response to a number of questions. These questions are carefully aimed at helping the athletes discover a concept or a solution. For example, rugby coach Wayne Smith – former coach of the New Zealand men's rugby team, the All Blacks – provided an example of how he used questioning with his players. He described a scenario used in a training session in which he puts three attackers against two defenders (Kidman, 2005). 'The obvious thing would be for the second attacker to draw the last defender and pass to the outside guy because he is the one in space' (Kidman, 2005, p. 197). Based on the players' responses to the scenario, the coach can ask questions regarding their understanding (i.e. if the player does or does not understand what needs to be done, but cannot execute the skill). For example, Smith (in Kidman, 2005, p. 197) talked through a conversation he might have with one of the attacking players:

Coach:	What did you do?
Player:	I held onto the ball.
Coach:	Where was the space?
Player:	Outside.
Coach:	Why did you hold onto the ball?
Player:	I couldn't get the pass away.
Coach:	Why couldn't you get the pass away?
Player:	He was on me too quick.
Coach:	How could you give yourself a bit more time?
Player:	I could slow down?
Coach:	What would you need to do to slow down?
Player:	Take shorter steps.

As illustrated in this example, the athlete requires cognitive processing to work through the questions posed by the coach. However, the outcome has been determined by the coach, so her/his expertise is still paramount to the approach (Kirk et al., 1996). This differs to the problem-solving method which allows for a more varied outcome. Continuing with an example from rugby, a coach might use the following scenario: 'There's 15 minutes remaining, you're leading by 2 points and playing into the wind. The opposition has one front row forward suspended for 10 minutes and it's a lineout on the halfway line.' The coach gives the players 10 minutes to discuss options. After that time, the coach calls the group together and asks them about the scenario, their options (e.g. their priorities with respect to applying pressure, pitch position, penalty or possession of the ball) and, as a group, discusses how this information could be useful in future matches.

Problem solving places less emphasis on the coach, as the athletes/players take responsibility for solving the problems. Solving problems requires the athlete/player to draw upon her/his previous knowledge, preferred pace at which to work and develops skills in taking responsibility for her/his learning (Kirk et al., 1996). This method would suit tasks that require more complex cognitive processes, such as adapting game play.

TEACHING GAMES FOR UNDERSTANDING (TGFU)

One of the most well-known constructivist approaches is Teaching Games for Understanding (TGfU). TGfU was developed in the early 1980s in response to educators' concerns that children (and adults) were good performers of skills, but were poor 'players' who did not understand the games they were playing (Almond, 2010). Therefore, at its core, TGfU places emphasis on players developing an understanding of the game and the learning of skills within contexts that resemble the full game to give them meaning and authenticity. In contrast to telling players what to do, this approach challenges them to find out. Here, games are useful to present problems to participants regardless of their age, ability and experience. In addition to improving understanding of the game, athlete/player motivation may also be influenced.

TGfU is useful as it allows for a range of learning strategies. For example, offence and defence strategies can be developed through guided and progressive practice conditions that more appropriately simulate the game environment (Hubball, Lambert & Hayes, 2007). Some coaches believe that TGfU does not provide opportunities to learn skills; however, it has been argued that skill acquisition is best developed in circumstances that most resemble the situations in which it will be used (as opposed to teaching it in isolation) (Almond, 2010). Therefore, a games-based approach enables athletes/players to improve the cognitive dimensions of their play without detracting from skill development (Light, 2006).

In Australia, TGfU developed into Game Sense in the mid-1990s. Similar to TGfU, Game Sense is a player-centred, games-based approach which aims to promote game appreciation, tactical awareness and decision making, and is premised on the belief that skills learnt within the context of games or game-like situations are more easily transferred to competitive matches (Light, 2006). Furthermore, athletes/players who understand the dynamics of the sport and are disposed towards independent problem solving are likely to learn more effectively (Light & Wallian, 2008).

While TGfU and Game Sense are appealing in that they could contribute toward, for example, an improved understanding of the game, better game play and increased athlete/player motivation (Light & Wallian, 2008), the success of these approaches hinges upon the coach's ability to ask meaningful and probing questions. These questions need to extend the athlete's/player's knowledge and encourage the athletes/players to respond (Kidman, 2005). In order to achieve these aims, coaches need to consider the types of questions they use. For example, lower order questions (i.e. those that focus on 'what' and 'where') require little cognitive involvement, so would not be of use in extending athlete's/player's knowledge. In contrast, questions that encourage athletes/players to analyse and integrate previous knowledge or encourage decision making and/or problem solving (i.e. those that focus on 'why' and 'how') require more cognitive involvement. Therefore, coaches need to ensure they are using relevant and meaningful questions that engage and challenge as opposed to asking questions for the sake of it. Wayne Smith, rugby coach, cautioned that some coaches may feel the need to over-question athletes/players (Kidman, 2001). Additionally, there is a danger that the coach could set irrelevant problems or accept any solution (Cassidy et al., 2009). This may be due to an uncertainty of how to create meaningful problems, a lack of clarity of the types of questions to use, when to ask questions, or feel the need to advise rather than let the athletes work through the scenario/situation (Kidman, 2001). Here, coaches need to read the situation as it unfolds.

TGfU and Game Sense have been adopted by coaches working with athletes/players of all levels and domains. As mentioned earlier, Wayne Smith utilised the Game Sense approach with the Canterbury Crusaders and the All Blacks. While some coaches, clubs and/or sports organisations have embraced TGfU and Game Sense, not all have been as accepting. Some have argued that coaches may be hesitant to engage with these methods as they challenge 'traditional' coaching practices (Reid & Harvey, 2014). That is, TGfU and Game Sense require that the coach acts as a facilitator of learning rather than a director of it (Light & Evans, 2010). This may make coaches uncomfortable as it challenges their understanding of 'what coaches do' (i.e. the coach is the 'expert') and their beliefs and assumptions about what comprises 'good' coaching (Harvey & Jarrett, 2014; Reid & Harvey, 2014). Also, TGfU and Game Sense require that coaches have a deep understanding of the game, but many coaches feel they do not know the games well enough to deliver sessions in this way.

Finally, coaches also need to consider the expectations of the athletes/players (as mentioned in Chapter 4). If coaches are willing to challenge the time-honoured methods which have prevailed in their sport and engage in Game Sense or TGfU, it would be useful to explain to the athletes/players what they are doing and why; allowing the athletes/players to become used to the different approach (Cassidy et al., 2009).

SUMMARY

The methods coaches use often link to their ideas of how athletes/players learn, the culture of the sport (i.e. what coaching 'looks like', what a 'normal' training session looks like), their experiences of coaches who used similar methods and athletes'/players'/parents' expectations. However, these ideas appear to be based on assumptions that the familiar or observed behaviours are not problematic. Additionally, coaches might know that something works, but do not know why. In an effort to provide a 'foundation' for coaches' decisions regarding the methods they use, this chapter has drawn attention to behavioural, cognitivist and constructivist learning theories. This was followed by a discussion of five methods used by coaches (i.e. direct/command, task, reciprocal, guided discovery and problem solving) which require various levels of coach involvement, but have differing implications on athlete/player learning. For example, a rote-drill practice, which is characteristic of coaches who use the directive/command approach, would not be productive if the coach's aim is to develop athlete's/player's decision making and problem solving. This aim would be better met by constructivist approaches such as Teaching Games for Understanding (TGfU) and Game Sense which provide problem-based learning, encouraging athletes to find relevance in existing knowledge and experience, and make connections to the outside world (Gore, Griffiths & Ladwig, 2004). Additionally, while scholars are increasingly arguing that the most effective way to learn is via constructivism, readers can consider the practices relating to behaviourism and cognitivism (e.g. feedback, evaluation) which still serve a useful purpose in training sessions. The take home message here is that coaches need to consider how the methods they adopt influence athlete/player learning.

7

LEARNING THE LABOUR

CONSIDERING COACHES' LEARNING INITIATIVES

The preparation and development of coaches have been popular areas of discussion among policy makers, coach educators and researchers. Their interests lie in better understanding how to 'best' support and facilitate coaches' learning. However, in light of the contested and complex nature of coaching, and with coaches ranging from volunteer to full-time and working in increasingly diverse contexts, it is difficult to create an education programme which addresses the needs and interests of *all* coaches. Consequently, coach education or coach learning initiatives – also referred to as coach development, coach certification or continuing professional development (CPD) – differ across and within nations as well as vary according to sport.

Formalised coach learning initiatives (e.g. coach certification) have been recognised as a gatekeeper to get involved in coaching. However, questions have been raised whether traditional forms of CPD are valuable in enhancing learning (Armour, 2011; Cushion et al., 2003; De Martin-Silva, Fonseca, Jones, Morgan & Mesquita, 2015; Wright, Trudel & Culver, 2007). There are numerous criticisms relating to coaches' CPD which have highlighted that it is too narrow in scope, ineffective for practice, disconnected to prior learning and from the context in which learning will be applied, and is unable to meet the demands of coaches (Armour, 2011; Jones et al., 2004; Jones & Turner, 2006). Further, questions have been raised whether such opportunities encourage coaches to move beyond what they already know (Armour, 2011; Jones &

Turner, 2006). Notwithstanding that these initiatives are usually mandatory for coaches, and given the time demands and cost of these initiatives, particularly for those who are volunteers and coaching in their leisure time, it is important to ensure that time devoted to professional learning is time well spent for coaches (Armour, 2011).

Before discussing some of the learning initiatives available to coaches, it is important to clarify the terminology used in this chapter. The term 'coach education' may be restrictive because it represents notions of formality typically captured in the structures of formal education. Additionally, coach education may imply there is an 'end' point; however, to keep informed with current knowledge, coaches would need to engage in a 'lifelong' process of CPD. The term 'coach learning', in contrast, is more appropriate and will be used in this chapter because it embraces continuous knowledge construction from inside and outside of educational settings.

The chapter comprises a brief outline of coach learning initiatives which are prevalent in a variety of sports and nations. Consistent with much of the literature which focuses on coaches' learning, the following content is organised according to Coombs and Ahmed's (1974) conceptual model of learning. This model distinguishes between formal, informal and non-formal learning initiatives which interconnect to characterise coaches' learning experiences. These initiatives are reflected in the subsequent chapter content.

FORMAL

When coaches are asked about their learning, they often refer to the formal opportunities in which they engage. According to Coombs and Ahmed, formal learning is 'something that takes place in an institutionalised, chronologically graded and hierarchically structured education system' (1994, p. 8). Such learning initiatives comprise compulsory attendance, standardised curricula which focuses on coaching theory, sport-specific techniques and tactics, and coaching practice and results in the achievement of a degree, certificate or 'badge' (Trudel & Gilbert, 2006). These include standardised coach education programmes delivered by governing bodies or sports federations and university degrees. Examples of the former are: Canada's National Coaching Certification Programme

(NCCP), Australia's National Coaching Accreditation Scheme (NCAS) and the UK Coaching Certificate (UKCC). These large-scale coach education programmes were developed in response to moral and legal issues relating to coaches' practice and to increase the competency of coaches (Trudel & Gilbert, 2006). Therefore, to be deemed 'ready' to coach, those who participate in these programmes must be able to demonstrate a *minimum level* of competency.

With content largely focusing on coaching theory, sport-specific techniques/tactics and coaching practice, the programmes were originally designed on the assumption that coaches' careers existed on a continuum from novice to expert with coaches expected to accumulate what was deemed to be 'appropriate' knowledge and key concepts as they progressed along the continuum (see discussions in Chapter 6 relating to behaviourism and cognitivism) (Trudel & Gilbert, 2006). Such a view positions learning as a series of stage-like progressions, assuming that coaches' expertise increases as they progress through the continuum. These programmes are often tasked with addressing the various needs and interests of coaches (volunteer to full-time professional) and often large numbers that exist across significant geographical landscapes. That said, there has been an increase in alternative delivery methods such as MOOCs (i.e. massive open online courses) and other distance learning initiatives.

Many of these formal initiatives have been criticised for failing to meet the needs of those for whom development opportunities are aimed (Armour, 2010). Here, the literature suggests that coaches are not satisfied with these opportunities, suggesting that the courses are too narrow in scope, are lacking in 'relevant' content or reinforce what coaches 'already know' (Jones et al., 2004; Jones, Morgan & Harris, 2012). Furthermore, content is often considered either too basic (as in simple drills) or too abstract (as in bio-scientific content) to be used in practice (Jones et al., 2004) with coaches struggling to see the relevance of the course material to reality of their everyday practice (Vargas-Tonsing, 2007). Consequently, these courses have had relatively low impact on coach learning (Cushion et al., 2010; Mallet, Trudel, Lyle & Rynne, 2009).

Additionally, as programme developers prescribe the design of the curriculum, content, method of delivery, assessment tasks, feedback and technical/tactical approaches, some courses have been likened to indoctrination (Chesterfield et al., 2010; Mallett et al., 2009) as they may expose the coach to a single set of values and attitudes of which the coach is expected to adopt (Cushion et al., 2010). Consequently, coaches learn, internalise and construct these values and behaviours, which results in the development of coaches who are homogenous, disciplined and versed in certain forms of knowledge but not in others (Lang, 2010; Lang, 2015). However, coaches are unlikely to challenge the status quo for fear of failing the course. This may encourage some coaches to adhere to the values, attitudes and behaviours of the coach educators who facilitated the course following its completion; other coaches may 'adopt' the approach promoted on the course as a way of achieving the qualification, but upon completing the course, return to their original approach or practice. As a tennis coach stated:

> At the end of the day you are there to pass and if you want to pass you take [the information] in and you relay it back to them in a way that seems as though you've agreed. Whether you do or not is another matter.
>
> (Griffiths, 2015)

In spite of the shortcomings of formal learning opportunities, there are positives. Some coaches have reported that these courses have provided an initial interest and enthusiasm for coaching, a useful opportunity to engage with other coaches, and are appreciative of the practical components. Additionally, coaches who do not have an extensive knowledge of the sport or coaching experience have found the courses to be useful and, consequently, have gained greater awareness and understanding. Finally, it is important to highlight that developers of some of these formal programmes have recognised the shortcomings of their provision and created various programme strands which group coaches with similar needs (and interests) to create more meaningful learning experiences.

Coach education programmes have largely been the domain of governing bodies or sports federations. However, in some countries, higher education institutions (i.e. universities) serve as the main educator of coaches. Degree programmes address the limitations of many of the large-scale certification provision by offering more breadth and depth; however, some programmes have been criticised for lacking real-world relevancy as they privilege scientific elements of coaching and neglect to pay similar attention to the socio-pedagogical (De Martin-Silva et al., 2015). Additionally, in some nations, these degrees do not act as 'stand alone' qualifications for coaches; rather, coaches must also undertake the National Governing Bodies' certificate programme in order to be deemed 'competent' to coach.

As this section has identified, there are numerous limitations of formal education programmes. However, these programmes often are viewed as a 'starting point' or 'minimum' in terms of coaches' learning. Consequently, there have been increasing calls for consideration of other forms of coach learning initiatives, which would more adequately prepare coaches for their work; these include non-formal and informal coach learning.

NON-FORMAL

Often used in conjunction with formal coaching (or instead of), non-formal learning refers to 'organised, systematic, educational activity carried on outside of the formal system to provide select types of learning' (Coombs & Ahmed, 1974, p. 8). These include: coaching conferences, seminars, workshops and clinics (i.e. short courses which focus on a specific area) which are provided by 'knowledgeable others' (Mallett et al., 2009). Non-formal initiatives differ from formal learning as they present an alternative source of learning to the structured approach (e.g. a short course targeting a particular topic) which can be aimed at a subgroup of a population (e.g. volunteer participation coaches, performance coaches) (Cushion et al., 2010). These opportunities can compensate for some of the shortcomings of formal education identified earlier. Also, non-formal educational opportunities have the potential to be highly varied, extensive and ongoing. However, some programmes have been criticised for being short-term, voluntary and lacking prerequisites. Also, in relation to some sport-specific conferences, questions have been raised about the credibility of the information shared. As one coach highlighted:

> I've been to a few conferences for [performance] coaches. But at the
> last one I asked a couple of questions after one of the speakers and
> one of the guys at the conference said to me, 'If you expect them to

come here and tell you everything, and to be honest, you're fooling yourself.' So why do they get up and speak if they're not? One of the coaches did a presentation and in it she said she had nothing to do with her athletes through the whole winter. Nothing at all she said. Well that's just a load of bunk because everyone has seen her at the winter training camps with her athletes! So she told us a load of rubbish! From that experience, I have the mentality that if I can pick up one thing at a conference, I'm probably doing all right.

(Purdy, 2006)

While non-formal coach learning initiatives have been useful to disseminate information to coaches, learning from experience and from other coaches (informal learning) is still cited as the primary source of knowledge for coaches (Gilbert & Trudel, 2001; Mallett, Rossi, Rynne & Tinning, 2016; Mesquita, Isidro & Rosado, 2010). Informal learning and the related coach learning initiatives will be discussed in the following section.

INFORMAL

Given the relatively small amount of time a coach might spend in a formalised learning environment in comparison to the number of hours s/he spends in the sporting venue, coaching and interacting with athletes/players and/or other coaches, it is unsurprising that coaches place more value on informal learning (Gilbert, Côté & Mallett, 2006). Informal learning has been described as 'the lifelong process by which every person acquires and accumulates knowledge, skills, attitudes and insights from daily experiences and exposure to the environment' (Coombs & Ahmed, 1974, p. 8). These learning opportunities are usually unorganised, unsystematic and could be unintentional, however, they account for a majority of a person's learning over the life course (Coombs & Ahmed, 1974). Examples of informal learning include: previous experience as an athlete, informal mentoring, practical coaching experiences, and interaction with peer coaches and athletes.

Experience as an athlete/player has been extensively reported in the literature as an important source of coaches' knowledge (e.g. Bloom, Durand-Bush, Schinke & Salmela, 1998, Cushion et al.,

2003; Mallett, 2010). Playing experience contributes to development of the rules and procedures of the sport, the field-specific (technical and tactical) coaching content and an understanding of the culture of the sport (Mallett et al., 2009; Mallett, 2010). Additionally, this experience is useful in helping the coaches understand how performance feels for the athletes/players which helps them better relate to the athletes/players (Schempp, Manross, Tan & Fincher, 1998). However, the value of these past experiences differ according to coach, with some coaches stating they are relatively unimportant in comparison to other sources of learning (Schempp et al., 1998).

While the value of experience as an athlete/player in contributing to coaches' learning is contested, athletes'/players' observations of their coaches are influential in the career development of coaches (Cushion, 2006). For athletes/players, observation of coaches throughout their sporting careers contributes to knowledge construction (i.e. initial conceptions of what and how to coach) (Cushion et al., 2003; Mallett et al., 2009, 2010). These experiences can also be viewed as channels through which methods and the culture of coaching become integrated into the behaviour, style or understandings of the aspiring coach (Cushion et al., 2003). For example, a grassroots coach noted, 'The coach that I had was very good; he was very technical so I'd say that I am very technical.' If observations of others are useful in coaches' development, questions can be raised regarding the focus of coaches' attention and the consequences for their subsequent learning. There are numerous examples of questionable practices within sporting contexts which are continuously being denounced, yet are still evident in coaches' practice. Therefore, coaches need to carefully consider why they are adopting certain behaviours and their intended (and unintended) consequences.

Notwithstanding the value of experience in sport and observations of other coaches, learning from practical coaching experience and discussions with others have been identified as the primary sources of coaching knowledge (e.g. Cushion et al., 2003; Mallett, 2010; Mallett et al., 2009). For example, a professional basketball coach noted that in the early stages of his career he tried to get as much experience as possible. Given the choice to work with a team which had twenty-six games per season versus a team with fifty-two games, the coach selected the latter as 'it would give me more time to work on my coaching'. However, work experience alone is insufficient to develop coaching knowledge and refine coaching practices (Mallett et al., 2009). Scholars have highlighted the importance of self-reflection in making these experiences meaningful and to develop and refine coaching knowledge and practices (e.g. Mallett, 2010; Trudel & Gilbert, 2006).

Recognising the benefits of informal learning, coach educators have attempted to 'formalise the informal' by incorporating reflection, communities of practice and mentoring into their coach learning initiatives. As these initiatives have been formalised, some might not consider them to be 'informal' coach learning initiatives; however, in this chapter, they will be included in this section due to their 'informal' origins.

REFLECTIVE PRACTICE

Most of coaches' learning takes place through experience in the practice environment (Gilbourne, Marshall & Knowles, 2013). Yet, for learning to occur, we need to examine, analyse and consider these experiences in order for it to become knowledge (Aitchison & Graham, 1989). Towards this end, reflection offers a way to look at practice, make sense of it and 'learn' (Gilbert & Trudel, 2001). Reflection and reflective practice have been increasingly discussed in relation to coach learning as reflective practice offers coaches the opportunity to access, make sense of, and learn from the relevant knowledge-in-action that enables them to learn how to coach (Knowles, Gilbourne, Borrie & Neville, 2001). To help the practitioner 'know' what it means to reflect and to aid coaches in framing their knowledge and learning from practical experiences, scholars have introduced conceptual tools such as landscape maps, (Ghaye, 2001; Ghaye & Lilllyman, 2000) or models of reflection (Gibbs, 1988; Johns, 2000; Atkins & Murphy, 1994; Schön, 1983; Smyth, 1991) (Knowles et al., 2001). Here, coaches have commented that engaging in reflective practice led to an improved self-awareness which was accompanied by heightened confidence; a better understanding of the context in which they were operating and a heightened appreciation of the needs of the athletes/players

(Cropley, Miles & Peel, 2012). Also, reflection aided coaches in initiating change in their practice (Cropley et al., 2012).

Although researchers have worked with coaches to promote reflective practice, coaches have highlighted several barriers to reflection: finding time to reflect in a structured manner, struggling to be motivated to reflect as there was no 'immediate effect', and feelings of vulnerability and discomfort when reflecting upon emotions (Cropley et al., 2012).

Given the possibilities for reflective practice to aid coaches' learning, scholars have questioned the amount of attention given to the development of reflective skills within coach learning initiatives (Knowles, Borrie & Telfer, 2005). However, it is important to note that a lack of clear structures to support coaches in the development of reflective skills and limited attention to the area on these courses could only result in a superficial understanding and practice of reflection (Knowles et al., 2005).

COMMUNITIES OF PRACTICE

> I'm always in contact with other coaches, we're always sharing ideas, I'm always looking for new things from them, I'm always giving them stuff.
> (performance field hockey coach)

As mentioned previously, the most prevalent form of coaches' learning, is through interaction with other coaches. That is, when human beings interact with each other (and the world) and in the pursuit of enterprises, they learn (Wenger, 1998). Such learning underpins coach learning initatives such as communities of practice (CoP). A community of practice is 'a group of people who share a common concern, set of problems or a passion about a topic and who deepen their knowledge and expertise in this area by interacting on an ongoing basis' (Wenger, McDermott & Snyder, 2002, p. 4). For example, following the bi-weekly training session, consider a pair/ group of coaches meeting for a coffee/drink to 'catch up'.

To develop a community of practice, coach educators could consider creating opportunities which involve mutual engagement, joint enterprises and a shared repertoire (Wenger, 1998). *Mutual engagement* refers to discussions in which coaches negotiate their practice, for example, meetings in which coaches consider season preparation, the content of training sessions and competition preparation (Culver & Trudel, 2006). This mutual engagement is negotiated among the members ensuring that it is a *joint enterprise* which is 'never fully determined by an outside mandate, by prescription, or by an individual participant' (Wenger, 1998, p. 80). A *shared repertoire* then enables the community members to negotiate meaning, reflecting the community's history of mutual engagement but also enabling it to be indefinite (Culver & Trudel, 2006). Towards this end, learning occurs as a member of a CoP develops her/his knowledge and (strengthens) her/his identity by engaging in a joint activity which enables her/him to develop an understanding of practice and become accountable to other members of the 'community' (Culver, Trudel & Werthner, 2009).

While communities of practice appear to be a more 'natural' way of learning for coaches, Culver and Trudel (2006) caution that all interactions between coaches do not constitute a CoP. For example, there are examples of coach education initiatives which have incorporated 'communities of practice'; however, these initiatives do not fulfil Wenger's (1998) criteria (i.e. mutual engagement, joint enterprise, shared repertoire). Rather than being viewed as communities of practice, these initiatives may be more akin to non-formal coach learning provisions, informal knowledge networks (IKN) and networks of practice (NoP).

IKNs involve the informal exchange of information; however, there is no commonality that binds these discussions (e.g. the development of shared practice). Such an approach is consistent with inviting a coaching colleague, a technical specialist or sport psychologist to help 'solve' a coaching problem (Culver & Trudel, 2006). For example, a performance coach commented:

> Often I find myself needing [information] for [an athlete] … I have to go and read about it and then talk to the physio and those things are a constant learning curve, but that [learning process starts] from an athlete!
>
> (Bertz & Purdy, 2011, p. 37)

Differing from communities of practice and IKN are NoP. These involve members who do not meet face to face, yet they regularly provide advice or help (Culver & Trudel, 2006). Easily facilitated through web-based mediums, NoPs have a wide reach (Culver & Trudel, 2006). Given that IKN and NoP are largely coach-driven modes of interaction and learning, coach educators need to consider how these learning opportunities could be maximised; in particular, how could they support or facilitate opportunities for coaches to exchange ideas and practices in less formal environments? It is important to recognise, however, that some coaches may be unwilling to engage in a CoP because the competitive nature of some levels of sport may preclude coaches from sharing their knowledge (Culver et al., 2009; Lemyre, Trudel & Durand-Bush, 2007; Wright et al., 2007). Therefore, coach educators need to think carefully about when and for whom communities of practice may be beneficial.

MENTORING

Throughout this chapter, it has been established that much of coaches' learning is from interacting with other coaches. Another way to do this is through mentoring programmes. Mentoring has been accepted as a way of developing high-quality practitioners in a variety of fields, including sport. A highly effective way for new coaches to learn their role (Bloom et al., 1998), mentoring refers to a 'relationship in which a person of greater rank, experience or expertise teaches, guides and develops a novice in a profession' (Alleman, Cochran, Doverspike & Newman, 1984, p. 329). In contrast to formal and non-formal coach learning opportunities, in mentoring, the relationship between the mentor and mentee is unique; driven by issues, concerns or areas which are considered to be relevant to them (not by an outside party). Consequently, it has the potential to be viewed to be more valuable by the learner. Towards this end, coaches may find mentoring appealing because such relationships offer access to sport-specific knowledge and nurture collegiality in a domain criticised for being competitive (Griffiths, 2015). Additionally, mentoring may be more compatible with the coaches' beliefs about learning in general (to be discussed later in this chapter). It also has a role in supporting accelerated learning and career growth, the potential to increase confidence and self-esteem, encourage professional growth, and improve self-reflection and problem solving (Hobson, Ashby, Malderez & Tomlinson, 2009; Parker, Douglas & Kram, 2008).

There are two main approaches to mentoring: natural/informal; and formal. Natural or informal mentoring occurs when a coach seeks a mentor from within the sporting community. Unplanned, based on mutual chemistry and trust, the mentee coach controls the agenda and interactions (Colley, Hodkinson & Malcolm, 2003). While informal mentoring is prevalent in coaching, for some coaches, the process of finding a mentor was often the case of 'being at the right place at the right time' (Bloom et al., 1998, p. 274) and difficult to replicate. In contrast, formal mentoring programmes have been established which involve a more structured approach with mentors assigned to coaches. However, given the unique and serendipitous nature of informal mentoring relationships, concern has been raised regarding making mentoring relationships too formal as it could hinder the creation of a rapport and impact upon the development of trust and openness. This has an effect on the quality of the relationship and the learning that is likely to occur. Consequently, Trudel and Gilbert (2006) ask if it is possible for a formalised and structured mentoring programme to be as effective as the informal version.

Only recently have investigations centred on mentoring in coaching. For example, Griffiths (2010) focused on a formalised mentoring programme for novice coaches in the UK. This work involved seven mentors and eighteen mentee volunteer coaches from a range of sports. The mentee coaches found the interaction between mentor and mentee helpful, as it enabled sharing of practice, problem setting and solving, opportunities to observe, to be observed and to receive feedback. However, for a majority of mentors and mentees the formalised relationship ended prematurely due to beliefs that they were unfulfilling or as a result of inactivity.

In considering the premature end of the formal mentoring programme. Griffiths (2010) identified that it was characterised by irregular contact, a lack of familiarity between mentor and mentee, a lack of acceptance by coaches, and a mentoring process which was perceived to be a general information resource. Additionally, the programme was comprised of a lack of mentoring competence, confused role expectations (i.e. some mentors viewed themselves as information-givers; to be available to 'give out' information or promptly return correspondence), and poor interpersonal relationships (the pairings were assigned by a third party so there was an absence of a mutual chemistry) (Griffiths, 2010). Some coaches commented that they had poor access to the mentor (who was not always linked to the coach's sports club), and weak mentor-mentee relationships (i.e. some coaches already had informal mentoring in place and these relationships were stronger than the formal mentoring relationship) (Griffiths, 2010).

For coach educators or programme developers, Griffiths' work (2010, 2011) has identified that it is important to introduce participants into the complexities of mentoring as a learning. In particular, those involved in the mentoring programme need to have opportunities to critically reflect (in a meaningful way) on their personal learning experiences and their understandings of learning and mentoring (Griffiths, 2011). Also, for mentoring to be productive, expectations of both parties need to be managed. For example, there needs to be clarity regarding the competencies, skills and motivations of mentors in the initial stages of programme development (Griffiths & Armour, 2012). Additionally, it is important that there is compatibility between mentor and coach. Consequently, not all coaches should be mentors nor would all mentee coaches work well with all mentors. And, the developmental needs of coaches at various points in their careers would call for different mentoring relationships (Griffiths, 2011). Finally, if designing such programmes for coaches, one should be cautious if adopting a mentoring model which has been developed for other contexts (e.g. business) as they may not be transferable (Griffiths, 2011).

WHAT DO 'GOOD' COACH LEARNING INITIATIVES LOOK LIKE?

In considering productive coach learning, it is worth emphasising that adults and children learn differently. As coaches are predominantly adults, it would be useful to consider how they learn. In a review of models of adult learning, Tusting and Barton (2003b, pp. 1–2) identified several key points which would have implications on the design of meaningful coach learning initiatives.

- Adult learners have their own motivations for learning. This means that learners build upon their existing knowledge and experience and 'fit' learning to their own purposes. These purposes relate to their 'real' lives, practices and roles. Applying this to coach learning initiatives then, this suggests that if the coach learning initiative is linked to the needs and interests of the learners, they might be more motivated. As a starting point then, it would be of use for coach educators or programme facilitators to highlight the value of such learning in improving coaches' performances. Additionally, consideration of the needs and interests of learners also provides a rationale for the involvement of more coaches in the construction of sport and/ or context specific resources that better speak to their needs.

- Adult learners have a drive towards self-direction and becoming autonomous (i.e. independent) learners. This would imply that learning is initiated by the learner. Therefore, if learners find themselves in situations in which others are imposing their ideas upon them, they may experience resentment and resistance (Knowles, 1984).

- Adult learners have the ability to learn about their own learning processes and benefit from discussions about it. This would mean that it would be useful to create opportunities for learners to discuss their experiences of learning. Towards this end, coach educators or facilitators could also draw coaches' attention to different theories or approaches to learning to help learners contextualise the process.

- Adults can learn by engaging in practice. Learning is generated when people encounter problems and issues in their real lives and think about ways to resolve them. Therefore, it would be useful to draw upon the coach's experiences and then assist the learner to connect these experiences with new ideas, concepts, theories and experiences (Merriam & Bierema, 2014). Here, a problem-centred learning may be useful as it is engaging and lends itself to immediate application (Merriam & Bierema, 2014).

- Adults reflect and build upon their experience. As reflective learning arises out of the complexities of their own experiences, learning is unique to each person. Consequently, much of learning happens in incidental ways. Reflective learning enables learners to 'see' situations in new ways which can be potentially transformative, personally, socially and professionally. However, it is important to recognise while there are ways to encourage reflective learning, there is no guarantee that it will happen.

It is interesting that CPD opportunities are often developed in ways that ignore what is widely known about learning. A useful starting point then, would be to consider if the CPD is grounded in a detailed understanding of learning theory and practice (Armour, 2011). In addition, coaches' professional learning needs to recognise the complexity of coaching practice, the diverse contexts in which coaches work and individuals with whom the coaches interact. Such consideration may begin to address criticisms of many formal coach learning initiatives which have been deemed being 'fine in theory but divorced from the gritty realities of practice' (Jones et al., 2012, p. 313). Towards this end, coach educators have the opportunity to create programmes that will enable coaches to 'move beyond existing practice, to innovate, to experiment, to adapt, to reflect, and to build underpinning knowledge and skills for the requirements of 'higher levels' of coaching' (Lyle, 2002, p. 280).

SUMMARY

Coaches bring vast amounts of experience to each learning episode (Armour, 2011). Therefore, when considering productive coach learning initiatives, it would be essential to consider the coaches' past experiences. Here, there will be differences between how a group of individuals will react when participating in the same learning opportunity. These differences can be partly explained by looking at their personal learning biographies (Trudel, Gilbert & Werthner, 2010). A learning biography involves the negotiation of learner identities over time and in the context of particular learning environments. This would have influence on what the coach/learner chooses to pay attention to and what s/he chooses to learn in different situations (Werthner & Trudel, 2006). It also helps to highlight the discomfort in the event these previous learning experiences (i.e. knowledge, skills, attitudes, values, emotions, beliefs and senses) are challenged (Trudel et al., 2010). As such, coach educators need to be sensitive and considerate of this process.

The purpose of this chapter has been to consider coaches' learning initiatives. In doing so, it has raised questions whether coaches' learning is 'best' facilitated through the acquisition of knowledge (e.g. formal and non-formal learning) or the process of social participation in specific situations (e.g. non-formal learning) (Griffiths, 2011). While formal learning initiatives are prevalent in many nations, questions have been raised whether they have had a significant impact on actual coaching practice. As a performance athletics coach highlighted, formal learning opportunities are

> like passing your driving test. It doesn't make you a good driver ... just because you've got the certificate doesn't mean you're a good coach. It's the building blocks ... There's a lot more driving to do ...
>
> (Bertz & Purdy, 2011, p. 34).

8

CROSSING LINES

CONSIDERING PROBLEMATIC COACHING BEHAVIOUR(S)

Many coaches may believe they are working in the best interests of the athlete/player; however, research is increasingly drawing attention to coaches' poor practice. This literature has predominantly focused on the emotional, physical and sexual abuse of young athletes/players. Nevertheless, dubious coaching practices extend beyond child and youth sport – that is, there are numerous examples of problematic coaches' behaviours within adult sporting contexts which are also of concern. For example, Rutgers University fired basketball coach Mike Rice after a videotape aired showing him shoving, grabbing and throwing basketballs at players in practice and using homophobic slurs (Pearson & Brady, 2013). More recently, the University of Illinois released head football coach Tim Beckman after allegations of physical abuse, bullying over injuries and verbal threats (Ganim, 2015). Although these examples focus on two coaches working within the collegiate sport system in the USA, it is likely that these are not isolated incidents. Furthermore, these two examples show that some organisations are taking a stand against such behaviours by releasing the coaches from their contracts, however sports organisations (local, nationally and internationally) demonstrate varied approaches towards athlete/player welfare. These global differences may be in part due to respective political, economic, historical and cultural differences that have influenced the evolution of sports cultures and the priorities in coach development.

Coaches' awareness of the problematic nature of these behaviours and their prevention is key in the development of safer sporting spaces at all levels. Even though some coaches are aware that elements of their practice are abusive (and carry on anyway), others may be unintentionally engaging in some of these behaviours. As such, this chapter raises awareness of poor practice which 'crosses lines' in terms of what may be deemed morally and/or legally acceptable within sport. In particular, the chapter focuses on abuse and exploitation in the coach–athlete relationship, drawing attention to physical, emotional and sexual abuse. This terminology usually refers to exploitative behaviours towards children and adolescents, however in this chapter, it will also be used to discuss the maltreatment of adult athletes/players (as opposed to the terms: assault, harassment, bullying and physical or sexual violence). Following the discussions of the types of abuse, the content changes focus slightly to discuss how fears of false accusations are also impacting upon some coaches' practice. Although this chapter focuses on problematic behaviours of coaches, it is important to recognise that there are numerous perpetrators of maltreatment in sport, including parents, peers, medical and support staff (Kavanagh, Knowles, Brady, Rhind, Gervis, Miles & Davison, 2016; Stirling, 2009).

ABUSE IN SPORT

Given the growing focus on athlete/player welfare in sport, abuse in sport is receiving increasing attention in academic literature. Work published in the past two decades has provided several explanations as to why coaches might abuse or exploit athletes/players. Two of the more prevalent arguments presented relate to the power-ridden nature of the coach–athlete relationship (discussed in Chapter 4) and a performance-focused culture of sport.

The sporting context has been, and continues to be examined in relation to power, and this power is manifested in numerous ways. For example, coaches may view themselves as experts who are in the position to enhance, restrict or terminate the progression of athletes/players. Athletes/players, aware of the coaches' power over their sporting future, may respond through subordination and/or dependence and accept their coach's questionable behaviour in order to remain in the sport. This may be more pronounced with youth, particularly those at the 'stage of imminent achievement' (i.e. on the cusp of the elite level) when the high stakes of nearing the top level may result in a more compliant athlete/player and, consequently, be more susceptible to harm (Brackenridge & Kirby, 1997; Farstad, 2007; McPherson, Long, Nicholson, Cameron, Atkins & Morris, 2017). Notwithstanding the power inherent between coach and athlete/player, the coach's influence can also extend to other coaches or stakeholders in sporting contexts. This was highlighted by Jacobs, Smits and Knoppers (2016) whose work with gymnastics coaches found that coaches feared retribution (e.g. being ousted or ostracised), which led them to neglect to engage in peer control or report abusive behaviour.

In addition to consideration of power relations, scholars have identified the culture of sport, particularly that of performance sport, and the emphasis on winning as ways coaches justify dubious coaching behaviours or methods (Cushion & Jones, 2006; Owusu-Sekyere & Gervis, 2014). Adopting a 'win at all costs' approach situates the athlete/player as an instrument to be used in the pursuit of sporting success, and, consequently, places the athlete in a position of vulnerability. Towards this end, coaches have been accused of challenging the fine line between harm and reasonable action when pushing the human body to physical and emotional limits (Telfer, 2010). As a consequence of this environment, it is argued that athletes/players are vulnerable to exploitation. And, this might be more intense and more relevant to coaches whose careers and income depend greatly on their athletes'/players' performances. For example, following the 2012 Olympics, Japan's National Women's Judo coach, Ryuji Sonoda, resigned over allegations that he harassed and physically abused his players. Sonoda defended his actions stating that he was under pressure to produce a gold medal (Miller & Nakazawa, 2015).

This section has briefly set the scene regarding sport as a site for problematic coaching behaviour. The following sections will build upon it by focusing on coaches' practice in relation to physical, emotional and sexual abuse, and harassment.

EMOTIONAL ABUSE

> Many coaches have a split personality ... They would never yell or
> scream at their own kids but the moment they put on their coaching

clothes, yelling and screaming become acceptable behaviour. They know it is not right; otherwise they would not keep the curtains and doors closed.

(Jacobs et al., 2016, p. 7)

This statement was made by a director working in elite youth gymnastics who was contributing to a project which was investigating the institutional context of emotional abuse in youth sport (Jacobs et al., 2016). Although this work focused on elite gymnastics in the Netherlands, it is important to note that coaches who engage in emotionally abusive behaviour can be found across sports, levels and cultures (these acts may also be referred to as bullying). The above quote is useful as it draws attention to the abusive practices of some coaches, which, although considered to be inappropriate ('otherwise they would not keep the curtains and doors closed'), are often unchallenged by stakeholders (i.e. athletes/players, directors, parents). Towards this end, concerns have been raised that some may view this conduct as 'normal' within sporting contexts; therefore, it is useful to draw attention to the types of emotional abuse with sport settings. It is hoped, then, that in doing so coaches reflect on their interactions with athletes/players, the appropriateness of such behaviours and, if necessary, consider alternatives.

Emotional or psychological abuse involves patterns of deliberate non-contact behaviour within a critical relationship between an individual and caregiver that has the potential to be harmful (Stirling & Kerr, 2013). In sport, three types of emotionally abusive coach behaviours have been identified: physical, verbal and the denial of attention/support (Stirling & Kerr, 2008). Physical abusive behaviours include incidents in which coaches have thrown objects either at, or in the presence of, an athlete, and punching walls and/ or breaking training equipment when frustrated with an athlete's performance (Stirling & Kerr, 2008). For example, one athlete interviewed as part of a project on emotional abuse in organised sport recalled, 'When we got to the end of the game [the coach had] thrown a chalkboard at me' (McPherson et al. 2017, p. 50).

In contrast to physical forms of emotional abuse, verbal forms of emotional abuse relate to behaviours such as: yelling, shouting, belittling, threats, name-calling, humiliation and degrading comments, including inappropriate comments about weight and physical appearance (Gervis & Dunn, 2004; Stirling & Kerr, 2008; Stirling & Kerr, 2013). For example, in Stafford, Alexander and Fry's (2015) work on the sport experiences of young adults (age 18–22) in Australia, athletes/players reported that the higher the level of sport they achieved, the more the coaches shouted or swore at them. These findings are consistent with earlier work by Gervis and Dunn (2004) who interviewed British athletes/players in the sports of diving, football, gymnastics, hockey, netball, and track and field athletics. These athletes/players also noted that these actions increased once athletes/players reached the elite level (Gervis & Dunn, 2004).

The third type of emotional abuse employed by coaches is the denial of attention and support. This involves, for example, ignoring athletes/players or excluding them from training sessions (Stirling & Kerr, 2008). Interestingly, data from interviews with fourteen retired elite swimmers revealed that of the three types of abuse, the coach's denial of attention/support had the strongest negative affect on athletes/players (Stirling & Kerr, 2008). One explanation for the differences in athletes'/players' views of the severity of the three types of emotional abuse could relate to the extent to which each of the behaviours threatens the athlete's self-esteem and their relationship with the coach. As Stirling and Kerr (2008) explain, the denial of attention/support as a form of punishment suggests to the athlete that they are not 'worthy of attention' (p. 179). While such actions have a negative impact on the relationship between coach and athlete, they also impact upon the athlete's sense of self-worth which, in turn, has implications on their ability to cope with other forms of emotional abuse (i.e. physical and verbal) (Stirling & Kerr, 2008).

Emotional abuse may occur as the result of a coach's attempt to push an athlete to a higher level of functioning and/or out of anger and loss of emotional control (Stirling, 2013). As mentioned previously in this chapter, these behaviours might be the result of the context that promotes winning and, consequently, has normalised such behaviour (Stirling, 2013). Rehearsing the work of Jacobs et al. (2016), these coaching behaviours were accepted to the extent that the directors of elite gymnastics clubs did not realise that they were witnessing emotionally abusive behaviour. This is also supported by Stirling and Kerr (2008) who highlighted that the former athletes/

players they interviewed rarely identified their coaches' behaviours as 'emotional abuse'. Former athletes/players recalled feeling stupid, worthless, upset, angry, guilty, depressed, humiliated, fearful, hurt, inferior and lacking in self-confidence as a result of the behaviour of their coaches (Gervis & Dunn, 2004). These feelings led to a 'destructive cycle' in which their deteriorating performance led to an intensification of emotionally abusive coaching behaviour. And, for some athletes/players who participated in this project, the emotional abuse from the coach resulted in residual emotional and psychological problems (Gervis & Dunn, 2004).

Athletes'/players' acceptance or lack of awareness that such behaviours constitute emotional abuse could be the result of their socialisation in the sport. That is, as they begin at the novice stage they observe more advanced athletes/players being yelled at, belittled or humiliated so adopt the belief that emotionally abusive actions of the coach are required in order to succeed (Stirling & Kerr, 2008). A similar rationale can be applied to novice coaches who witness the behaviours of performance coaches and believe these to be appropriate; consequently, emotionally abusive coaching continues. It is interesting to note that if these behaviours were adopted by those working in instructional settings (e.g. schools) in some Western nations, there would be serious consequences (Stirling & Kerr, 2008). However, emotional abusive coaching behaviours have not received similar treatment.

PHYSICAL ABUSE

In the introduction to this chapter the cases of two coaches – Mike Rice and Tim Beckman – were highlighted regarding allegations of physically abusive coaching behaviours (e.g. shoving, grabbing and throwing basketballs at players, physically abusing football players). Looking outside of the United States, interviews with former female artistic gymnasts in Portugal revealed that coaches employed numerous physical punishments (e.g. coaches physically pushed, kicked or slapped athletes/players) (Pinheiro, Pimenta, Resende & Malcolm, 2014). Furthermore, in exploring athletes'/players' experiences of physical abuse in organised sport in Australia, McPherson and colleagues (2017) interviewed an athlete who recalled, 'he'd physically grab us, push us like into position ... he was

... manhandling us really ... and sometimes he'd give you a slap ... across the back of the head if you didn't do things correctly' (p. 50). These examples suggest that physically abusive coaching behaviours are indicative of accepted coaching practice in many sports and across cultures. Indeed, the coaches highlighted may consider their approaches to be 'appropriate training' or 'reasonable physical discipline' as opposed to physically abusive. This is significant as it reinforces earlier concerns (i.e. emotional abuse) regarding the dangers of coaches' ingrained cultural practices, and the potentially damaging consequences (ethical, personal, legal or otherwise) their actions may have on athletes/players in their care.

Although physically abusive coaching behaviours are not limited to child and youth sport, the literature examining athlete/player welfare has predominantly focused on physical issues around children's safety, protection, security and well-being. This work recognises child physical abuse in sport as acts of physical assault inflicted on the child athletes/players; forced overtraining leading to risk of injury; and training forced or encouraged while the child athletes/players is injured or exhausted (Alexander, Stafford & Lewis, 2011). More specifically, in child and youth sport, these include: exposing athletes/players to inappropriate training regimes, competing in too many games/tournaments that are close together with limited recovery time, encouraging training and competing of athletes/players while they are pain or injured, overtraining, physical punishments and the use of inappropriate training practices (Fasting & Brackenridge, 2009; Oliver & Lloyd, 2015; Pinheiro et al., 2014).

In sport (child, youth and adult), there is a very thin line that divides intensive training from abusive and exploitive practices (David, 2005; Oliver & Lloyd, 2015). This 'line' is evident, for instance, when coaches introduce exercise that could cause potential harm (i.e. forcing an athlete/player to train when exhausted or injured); exercise in which there is no actual or perceived benefit; and when physical activity is used as a form of punishment (e.g. running laps, running sprints, push-up, sit-ups, etc.) (Alexander et al., 2011; Kerr, 2010). While the use of exercise as punishment is no longer considered to be an accepted method of discipline in many countries, it appears still to be pervasive among coaches (Burak, Rosenthal & Richardson, 2013) and is likely to continue unless it is actively challenged. Recently, a clear message was sent by the Québec-based disciplinary committee of Hockey Lac St-Louis who forced an ice hockey coach to sit out a season after ordering 11 and 12 year-old peewee AAA players (i.e. the highest level for the under 13 age category) to do push-ups following a 7-2 loss (The Canadian Press, 2016).

There is no sport that is immune to the physically abusive practices of coaches: research has drawn attention to women's artistic gymnastics (WAG) in particular as a site of physical and emotionally abusive behaviours by coaches in a variety of countries (e.g. Jacobs et al., 2016; Pike & Scott, 2015; Pinheiro et al., 2014; Stirling & Kerr, 2008). Women's artistic gymnastics is a sport that is aesthetically driven and relies upon early specialisation (Barker-Ruchti & Tinning, 2010). Within this sport, children are subjected to intensive training programmes from a young age and are encouraged to practice up to eight hours a day, six days a week (David, 2005; Barker-Ruchti & Tinning, 2010). Such intensive physical (and psychological) demands on young athletes/players, whose developing bodies are susceptible to injuries, have raised concerns relating to overtraining or dangerous training, ultimately suggesting that the training itself could be viewed as a form of physical abuse (Matos, Winsley & Williams, 2011; Oliver & Lloyd, 2015). Such thinking may surprise coaches who have been immersed in sporting contexts in which these practices may be common. While they may argue that success in the sport demands such commitment from the athlete/player, it is worth considering how these practices could be safer for the participants. Recognition of early signs of overtraining, ensuring training loads are appropriate, employing injury-prevention strategies, making sure athletes/players can rest and recover (Oliver & Lloyd, 2015), and recognising the importance of developing non-sport related identities are starting points to help coaches challenge physically abusive training programmes.

Although the aforementioned literature has highlighted various physically abusive behaviours, the failure to appropriately condition and physically prepare and protect athletes/players could also be considered to be a neglect of coaches' duties. Neglect refers to 'a failure to care for the [athlete's/player's] physical and/or psychological needs which could result in the serious impairment of the child's health or development' (CPSU, 2017). In sport, this could refer to, for example, a coach's lack of care for the athlete's/player's health, exposing athletes/players to undue cold or heat without ensuring adequate clothing or hydration, encouraging athletes/players to play through injury, failure to adhere to sport safety rules or to provide appropriate equipment, and denial of access to appropriate medical care (Partington, 2016). Such practice echoes early criticisms in the literature (e.g. Donnelly, 1997) which question 'traditional' coaches whose interests focus on athletes'/players' performances as opposed to viewing athletes/players as human beings (Pinheiro et al., 2014).

SEXUAL HARASSMENT AND ABUSE (ALSO KNOWN AS SEXUAL VIOLENCE)

Several high-profile convictions and scandals, including the recent disclosures of historical sexual abuse involving football coaches and youth players in the United Kingdom, have highlighted that sport is not immune from sexual abuse. However, while the media has drawn attention to sexual abuse, they have not given similar attention to sexual harassment. Sexual harassment is generally agreed to involve 'unwanted sexual attention' (Fasting, Chroni & Knorre, 2014) and can be classified into three distinct, yet related, areas: gender harassment, unwanted sexual attention and sexual coercion (Fitzgerald, Gelfand & Drasgow, 1995).

Gender harassment is the most prevalent type of sexual harassment (Leskinen, Cortina & Kabat, 2011). It refers to a range of verbal and non-verbal behaviours which convey insulting, hostile and degrading attitudes about the victim's gender (Fitzgerald et al., 1995) – for example, sexist jokes, anecdotes and comments, or insulting or derogatory conduct towards a person because of their gender. In sport, such comments may be unrecognised as harassment, rather they are often accepted as 'banter' among teammates or with coaches. A second form of sexual harassment is unwanted sexual attention. This refers to verbal and non-verbal behaviours that are unsolicited, offensive and unreciprocated (Fitzgerald et al., 1995) – for example, staring, gestures, showing pictures or objects with sexual allusions (Chroni et al., 2012), sexual name calling, attention which causes fear, alarm or distress, and being touched without permission.

Although sexual harassment is an issue that does not discriminate based on gender, studies in sport have largely focused on male harassment of females, particularly in relation to some male coaches' interactions with female athletes/players as well as female–female harassment (Fasting, Chroni, Hervik & Knorre, 2011). Work in this area is developing; however, what is concerning (based on information from the existent work) is that athletes/players and coaches may experience gender harassment, unwanted sexual attention and sexual coercion, but not consider these experiences to be sexual harassment (Welsh, Carr, MacQuarrie & Huntley, 2006). Consequently, unacceptable behaviours have been tolerated and no disciplinary action taken against the offending coaches or athletes/players. Additionally, while coach education initiatives have drawn attention to good practice and safeguarding children, discussions of sexual harassment are often missing (Fasting et al., 2011). Nonetheless, an improved understanding of sexual harassment may help coaches consider their communication styles, postures, gestures and group management techniques which may be linked to problematic practice (Fasting & Brackenridge, 2009) and create a safer (i.e. physically and emotionally) environment for other coaches and athletes/players. Towards this end, the coach's repertoire could be redeveloped to provide a more appropriate range of possibilities (Fasting & Brackenridge, 2009). Fasting et al. (2000, 2011, 2014) used the following points to help athletes/players and coaches better understand their 'everyday' interactions in sporting contexts which are forms of sexual harassment:

> a) Unwanted physical contact, body contact (for example, pinching, hugging, fondling, etc.).
> b) Repeated unwanted sexually suggestive glances, comments, teasing and jokes, about the recipient's body, clothes, private life, etc.
> c) Ridiculing of sport performance of the athlete/player because of gender or sexuality (for example, 'Football is not suitable for girls').
>
> (modified from Fasting et al., 2014, p. 122)

Whereas the preceding information relates to sexual harassment, this chapter also highlights the prevalence of sexual abuse in sport, focusing on non-consensual sexual relationships and sexual abuse/ assault prevalent within sporting contexts. Sexual abuse refers to behaviours relating to grooming or entrapment, in which a child unwittingly complies with sexual behaviour, or is coerced to comply through force (Fasting & Brackenridge, 2009).

As already mentioned, grooming often plays a central role in sexual abuse (CPSU, 2015). Grooming can generally be understood as any strategy a perpetrator uses to coerce a person to engage in sexual interactions with them (CPSU, 2015). In other words, grooming is a *conscious* process by the abuser which is aimed at developing 'co-operation' from the athlete/player, making it appear that the abuse is consensual (Brackenridge, 2001). Relating this to sport, Brackenridge noted:

> Sexually abusive coaches spend a long time ... grooming their athletes. This process is a crucial precursor to sexual approaches and involves building trust, gradually pushing back the boundaries of acceptable behaviour and slowly violating more and more personal space through verbal familiarity, emotional blackmailing and physical touching.
>
> (Brackenridge, 1997, p. 122)

Given the seemingly innocent interactions in the initial stages of grooming, these behaviours may be perceived by the athletes/players as acceptable and without any sexual connotations (Vanden Auweele et al., 2008). This adult–child touch or contact is subtly increased through the use of touching 'games' or 'accidental' touch that progressively becomes more sexual to blur the boundaries of 'normal' behaviour and evaluate whether a child has been groomed sufficiently for abuse to begin (McAlinden, 2006). For coaches (and other stakeholders), it is important that they are aware of these processes so that they can recognise the 'danger signs' (and report these concerns), which can aid in the protection of athletes/players and ultimately create safer sporting spaces.

Although there are more males than females participating in sport, the 'male abuser–female victim' has been the prevailing narrative in the literature. Work has highlighted that male athletes/players have suffered sexual abuse in the context of their sport and this abuse often goes unreported (Hartill, 2009). This low rate of disclosure of sexual abuse among boys is concerning as it has been largely attributed to a lack of understanding of abuse. In other words, many boys did not recognise or downplayed the abusive nature of the treatment inflicted on them (Alaggia & Millington, 2008; Fondacaro, Holt & Powell, 1999; Hartill, 2009). These behaviours may go unreported as many victims often feel that reporting them will not accomplish anything and they are concerned about retaliation or future victimisation (Cense & Brackenridge, 2001). Further, many athletes/players are often deterred from reporting incidents of sexual abuse due to the myths, fears and taboos relating to the topic (Parent & Bannon, 2012).

The examples provided in this section draw attention to various abusive behaviours (i.e. emotional, physical and sexual), however, there continues to be a 'code of silence' within sport. Coaches, athletes/players and other stakeholders may be desensitised and not recognise these behaviours as dubious; alternatively, they may be afraid of the consequences of reporting these behaviours so they often go unreported. Increasing education regarding emotional, physical and sexual abuse, and harassment as well as providing safe processes for reporting, may, in some part, contribute to safer sporting spaces.

FEAR OF ACCUSATIONS

While the media has played a part in drawing attention to coach–athlete/player sexual abuse, it could also be somewhat responsible for creating a hypersensitivity among coaches regarding what is appropriate practice. This sensitivity has extended to a fear that any physical contact with athletes/players may be misinterpreted as grooming (Lang, 2015). As such, it has been suggested that a fear of accusations of child abuse has become a dominant mechanism in shaping the work of many sports coaches (Johnson, 2015). The following vignette highlights the growing concerns of many coaches in some Western nations regarding the use of physical contact or 'touch' in coach–player interactions.

Swimming coach David has strict rules: he is never alone with a swimmer. In training sessions, team meetings or travelling to tournaments, he makes sure another adult is present at all times. All instructions are provided verbally or via demonstration, and Coach David ensures that during a session, he never physically touches a swimmer. In celebrating performances, he is happy with a high-five, but hugs are not permitted. Before training, the swimmers leave their phones (which have photographic or video recording capabilities) at the building's main reception and Coach David does

> the same. Although his daughter is a swimmer in the squad and he's known most of the children and their parents for years, Coach David still feels he needs to protect the swimmers and himself. 'People might think I'm over the top, but you can never be too careful. One false allegation and my career is over. I want to ensure that I'm *never* in a position to be falsely accused of abuse.'

Recent work suggests that coaches, especially males, are becoming more cautious in their practice out of concern of being accused of (sexual) abuse (Marshall & Mellon, 2011; Piper, Taylor & Garratt, 2012). As such, Coach David's actions, unproblematically positioned as self-protective, may resonate with coaches who have modified their practice due to concerns of false accusations of child abuse. As Lang (2015) argues, such protective strategies are understandable, given one of the manifestations of these concerns is coaches' anxiety about adult–child physical contact.

This brief vignette provides a useful starting point in drawing attention to the 'moral panic' – i.e. an exaggeration or fabrication of risk and projection of societal anxiety onto a group (Goode & Ben-Yehuda, 1994) – that is growing in many Western societies in relation to the risk of child abuse, especially child sexual abuse (Brackenridge, 2001). Some argue that this moral panic has been created by child protection regulations within sport, which have shifted too far towards prescription and over regulation (Hardman, Bailey & Lord, 2014; Piper, Duggan & Rogers, 2013). Such a view has generated anxiety and confusion among some coaches around what actions are permitted as well as an uncertainty about what is considered to be acceptable coach–athlete/player engagement (Piper et al., 2012). This has contributed to the creation of an environment in which safety from abuse defines every act of adult–child touch as suspicious (Lang, 2009). In response, sporting clubs and coaches have adopted prescriptive and proscriptive environments in which coaches exercise caution by avoiding any behaviour which could be construed as suspect (Piper et al., 2013).

In sport, coaches often use physical contact which is aimed at instruction or to demonstrate effective technique to athletes/players (i.e. 'instructional touch') or which is crucial to the development of positive social and personal relationships (i.e. 'caring touch') (Field, 2003; Lang, 2015) – for example, physical contact as an effective pedagogic tool when teaching or developing sport-specific skills and can be used for pastoral care purposes (i.e. congratulate or console a child who has performed well/badly) (Lang, 2015; Öhman & Grundberg-Sandell, 2015). However, as Coach David's story suggests, increasing concerns in some societies about adults' potential to harm children may have influenced ideas about physical conduct from being considered to be an acceptable way of demonstrating warmth and instruction to athletes/players to a signal of dangerous intent. Consequently 'no touch' is becoming, either intentionally or unintentionally, the most practical way of minimising risk, regardless of whether is it pedagogically appropriate or desirable (McWilliam & Sachs, 2004). For example, Lang's (2015) work with UK youth swimming coaches identified, in an effort to manage the risk of being accused of abuse, that coaches did not differentiate between positive and negative touch; rather, they limited their use of all forms of adult–child touch. This was echoed by Piper and colleagues (2012), who found that for some coaches this 'no touch' policy was so strong they were even reluctant to provide physical contact to assist a child whose life was in danger.

While limiting the use of all forms of adult–child touch may be a more extreme form of 'defensive' coaching strategies adopted by coaches, others have made smaller modifications to their practice. As Lang's (2015) data highlighted, if 'no touch' was not possible, coaches limited their touch to areas of the body considered less 'risky'. Additionally, coaches reported that they increased their visibility in the sporting context or sought verbal consent from athletes/players before employing instructional touch in their work (Gleaves & Lang, 2017; Lang, 2010, 2015). The latter reaction is interesting as obtaining athlete/player consent is not an unproblematic process. For example, a child may consent to a behaviour, but not feel comfortable with it. Additionally, seeking consent assumes that the child is able to differentiate between acceptable and unacceptable behaviours, which might not be the case.

While the moral panic has influenced some coaches to modify their practice to various degrees, evidence suggests that unfounded allegations of child sexual abuse are extremely rare both in and beyond sport (Brackenridge, Bringer & Bishopp, 2005; Lang, 2015; Gleaves & Lang, 2017). The low rate of false accusations suggests that the moral panic within the coaching community is largely based on abstract, discursive experiences as opposed to personal experience (Brackenridge et al., 2005). Therefore, it is important for coaches to be aware of the counter narrative. For example, Gleaves and Lang (2017), who focused on UK parents' perspectives of youth swim coaches' uses of physical contact, identified that parents were critical of coaches who avoided or restricted their use of physical contact in order to protect themselves at the expense of the impact on the children with whom they worked. Although aware of coaches' concerns regarding the moral panic in relation to the use of physical contact, these parents considered such an approach to be a disregard of coaches' professional and moral duties. Parents identified circumstances when adult–child physical contact was appropriate in sport: to prevent, minimise or treat physical harm to a child (particularly when performing dangerous moves, e.g. diving); to teach a child a sport-specific technique or skill; and for moral support (i.e. to congratulate or support following their performance) (Gleaves & Lang, 2017). It is important to recognise that this work was based upon a small sample of parents' views of physical contact in child and youth sport, but it serves as a useful starting point in challenging the dominance of the 'moral panic'. Towards this end, Lang (2015) advocates that coaches and coach educators need to consider challenging the moral panic and focus on encouraging the development of positive touch.

While the chapter content to this point has focused on questionable coaching behaviour in relation to physical, emotional and sexual abuse, it is likely that related discussions will not cease until there is widespread institutional change within sport. The issue here is that such a process would require challenging ideologies of what constitutes acceptable coaching practice. Although such an approach sounds difficult, there are examples of coaches who transformed their coach-centred practices (i.e. a person who view athletes/players as a means to an end) to a more athlete/player-centred approach (see Denison, Mills & Konoval, 2015; Jacobs, Claringbould & Knoppers, 2014); so change is possible.

SUMMARY

As highlighted in this chapter, abuse and harassment in sport is an international issue with sport increasingly recognised as a site which does not always place the welfare of the athletes/players (child and adult) at its core. The United Nations International Children's Emergency Fund (UNICEF) has highlighted that all people have the right to participate in sport in a safe and enjoyable environment. Unfortunately, this does not appear to be the 'reality' in many contexts.

Some researchers have attributed coaches' dubious behaviours to asymmetrical power relations between coaches and athletes/players. These relationships are not only believed to have led to the victimisation of athletes/players, but also contributed to a 'code of silence' with athletes/players (and/or other stakeholders) feeling intimidated by the coach or unable to report incidents of abuse out of concern for their selection and maintenance of their athletic career. Another explanation has positioned coaches' questionable conduct as the result of prioritising sporting success over the welfare of the athlete/player, especially within the higher levels. However, as the increasing scholarship focusing on the (mis)treatment of athletes/players suggests, these coaching behaviours do not enhance athlete/player performance!

Moving forward, it is important that coaches develop a critical reflection of themselves and their practices (and their duties of care) *foremost*, before considering the performative demands of their sports and their athletes/players. And, coaches (and organisations) need to be better prepared to adapt, change and negotiate their current practices in ways that better ensure athletes/players are protected. Readers may consider ways to facilitate such changes, however, part of this strategy will entail several improvements – first, coaches' and organisations' understanding of what is and is not acceptable for athletes/players; second, accepting their roles in 'bad practice'; third, recognising their individual and collective capacities to act; and last, ensuring appropriate practical, organisational and/or cultural shifts are genuine and sustainable. This is not to say that performative agendas are of secondary concern to coaches (indeed, in many contexts coaches may consider this their raison d'être). Rather, what matters is that developing and maintaining a culture in which all individuals' well-being and safety is assured as a cornerstone priority for both coaches and organisations.

9

TWELVE HOUR DAYS, SIX DAYS A WEEK, FIFTY WEEKS A YEAR

CONSIDERING THE CAREERS OF PERFORMANCE COACHES

Media portrayals of performance (i.e. elite and professional) coaches have often positioned their work and careers as seamless and unproblematic. Additionally, the focus of academic literature on coaches' progress from novice to expert (e.g. Côté & Gilbert, 2009; Erickson, Bruner, MacDonald & Côté, 2008; Nash & Sproule, 2009), may have contributed to the assumption that coaches' careers can be presented as a 'one size fits all' series of linear stages and milestones. Coaches may hold the view, for example, that their progression will consist of movement from assistant to head coach where they will remain throughout their career or, following the achievement of the highest level of coaching certification, feel entitled to work with elite athletes/players. However, these ideas have been challenged by academic literature that has highlighted such portrayals of coaches' careers as failing to adequately reflect the career 'realities' experienced by coaches (Barker-Ruchti, Lindgren, Hofmann, Sinning & Shelton, 2014; Christensen, 2013; Purdy & Potrac, 2014; Purdy, Kohe & Paulauskas, 2017). These linear or 'one size fits all' models have also been criticised for a lack of consideration of the cultural and institutional contexts of sport (Christensen, 2013), as well as the changing nature of careers in contemporary society. Such unproblematic portrayals of careers may contribute to coaches' feelings of frustration, confusion and dissatisfaction as their expectations (i.e. linear trajectory) may not match the 'reality' of their experiences in professional and elite contexts. For example, Maeve, a coach working in elite-level athletics who had seen her career progress from working with junior, under 23 and senior athletes highlighted,

> I got really close [to the Olympics] ... and I was completely pissed off at not getting an Olympic squad or [the role of] assistant coach. I think by rights I should have been an assistant coach but I was given the non-priority athletes [and not invited into the Olympic village] and [an apprentice coach who had been identified and developed by the sport] was given the top group. I was so pissed off ... God it annoyed me. Sure, he had been an international athlete but [in his career] he had only coached one junior athlete – that was it. And I was really, really unhappy about that.
>
> (Purdy & Potrac, 2014, p. 788)

One way of making sense of Maeve's frustration at being overlooked for the Olympic position could be related to her view of coaching as a 'traditional' career and profession. This understanding was reinforced as Maeve's experiences within the sport had been predominantly linear or progressive, involving more responsibility and increased access to rewards as her career lengthened. Consequently, Maeve believed her career would continue to proceed in such a way. However, with an 'apprentice' coach securing the position instead of the more experienced Maeve, her career expectations were challenged. It is unsurprising that the situation led Maeve to feel angry and frustrated. However, the situation left Maeve questioning: 'For me the ladder stopped. But why did [the apprentice coach] have more chance of moving on?' (Purdy & Potrac, 2014, p. 788).

Maeve's story may resonate with other coaches who have similar experiences or also perceive their careers to be linear and progressive (i.e. increasing in responsibility as the career progresses), but have fallen short of the top positions. Additionally, scholars know relatively little about how coaches in performance contexts experience working in environments in which their interactions and relationships are frequently 'bound up in the production and consumption of [sporting] performances' (Roderick, 2006, p. 246). Therefore, the purpose of this chapter is to draw attention to the careers of performance coaches.

In contrast to previous chapters, which utilise data to support the discussion, this chapter is designed around the analysis of interview data from four elite coaches in athletics and rowing as well as six professional basketball coaches (referred to as Professional Basketball Coaches A, B, C, D, E and F). The content of this chapter highlights the characteristics of 'traditional' and 'contemporary' careers and the various turning points experienced by elite and professional coaches in the processes of becoming a coach, being a coach and leaving coaching.

To recognise the unique assumptions and expectations which frame coaches' practice, in this chapter, the terms elite and professional are used to distinguish between differing contexts within the performance domain. This differentiation is important as the contexts will impact upon how coaches organise and undertake their work. In this chapter, the term 'professional coach' is used to describe coaches who are concerned with weekly performances of a team within a league, while 'elite coaches' are focused on longer-term goals such as world championships or the Olympics. While a professional coach can also be an elite coach, at the time of interview, these coaches were working within professional clubs.

MAKING SENSE OF COACHES' CAREERS

Irrespective of performance context, investigations of the careers of elite female coaches have highlighted a certain amount of 'chance' in their employment histories noting that the coaches did not necessarily strategically develop their careers; rather, they 'fell' into positions that became available and moved 'up and down' between positions (Barker-Ruchti et al., 2014). In addition to this type of mobility being consistent with Maeve's experience (mentioned at the outset of this chapter), these movements challenge the notion that coaches' careers fit neatly within a series of chronologically ordered milestones. Therefore, we could question the dominant view of the 'one size fits all' model of coaching careers as it fails to adequately reflect these differences as well as the serendipitous nature of individual's coaching careers (Christensen, 2013).

As opposed to viewing careers as linear, an alternative view of careers which reflects the reality of coaches' career experiences is needed. A more contemporary understanding would appreciate that careers are increasingly characterised by frequent job changes, shifts in employers and work status, and more fluid and individual career choices (Sennett, 1998). Towards this end, a career would be viewed as an 'evolving sequence of a person's work experiences over time' (Gunz & Peiperl, 2007, p. 4). The promotion of such a view would be helpful for coaches as it more adequately 'captures' the realities of their career experiences, which will help developing coaches better manage their expectations.

BECOMING A PERFORMANCE COACH

For many, the decision to pursue a career as an elite or professional coach extended from their playing careers, as the athlete/player neared retirement from competing in their chosen sports (Barker-Ruchti et al., 2014; Christensen, 2013). Additionally, several coaches commented that their decision to move into coaching was the result of their inability to achieve their athletic goals. For example, although the athlete's ultimate aim was to compete at the Olympics, they knew their athletic skills would not enable them to realise this dream. As an elite athletics coach reflected: 'I couldn't make it as an elite athlete, but I could get to the Olympics as a coach.'

In considering pursuing coaching as a career, some coaches commented that their love of the sport was critical in their decision in selecting coaching. As Professional Basketball Coach A reflected, 'I didn't want to leave it!' Such a sentiment has been recognised by scholars (e.g. McGillivray, Fearn & McIntosh, 2005) who highlighted that athletes/players may move into coaching as the resources they have invested in sport may make them feel it is the only thing they believe they know how to do. Towards this end, staying within sport enables coaches to maintain their strong sport-related identities and existing social support systems (i.e. relationships with friends/colleagues in the sport) (McLean & Mallett, 2012).

Although coaches may have experienced a range of points of entry into coaching, the coaches' initial understandings of their work were similar. Both elite and professional coaches noted that their primary or first engagement in the field required them to be heavily dependent upon their experiences of participating in performance sport programmes and their observations of other coaches. For these coaches, the transition from 'thinking like an athlete' to 'thinking like a coach' occurred when they more seriously considered pursuing it as a career. At this juncture, the athletes/players recalled making a conscious effort to 'gather' as much information about coaching. For example, when recalling his transition from competing to considering a future within the sport, a professional basketball player who had moved into coaching (Professional Basketball Coach B) recalled: 'I started to prepare myself for coaching ... I start to watch coaches, the things they did, what they were doing in practice, what I liked, what I didn't like ...' In another case, Professional Basketball Coach C commented on discussions with other players which helped him think about how coaches in the professional sporting context understood and approached their work.

> When I was playing in Europe, I had contacts in other teams so talking to them was always interesting. I knew that I wanted to be a coach so these discussions helped prepare me. So, I talked to other players: How does your team do this? Why does this coach have success? Why don't the players stay for a long time in that team? Is it about the money, or are there other conditions that make them want to stay? And for me, these were the questions that were useful when thinking about what I could do as a coach.

Although Coaches B and C recalled their initial learning which focused on observing various coaches' practice or gathering information regarding how other coaches undertook their work, the valuable experience they acquired as players should not be understated. In interviews with fifteen development and elite sport coaches, Trudel and Gilbert (2006) noted that over 90 per cent were competitive athletes/players in the sport they coached. This background in the sport was viewed positively as it provided insight into the culture of the sport and the technical and tactical areas. Additionally, scholars have suggested that the match or competition experience gleaned as an athlete/player aids in the development of analytical skills while observation of their coaches throughout their sporting careers contributes to knowledge construction (i.e. initial conceptions of what and how to coach) (Cushion et al., 2003; Rynne, Mallett & Tinning, 2006, 2010). People continue to debate whether successful playing careers are useful in predicting the 'successful' careers of coaches, with investigations in this area indicating that success in the highest levels of sport is not essential, rather it is the individual's knowledge of the sport that is important (Mallet et al., 2009; Rynne, 2008). Although a successful athletic career may provide more access to coaching positions and allow a coach to get a 'foot in the door', the coaches' record becomes more pertinent for future employment (Mallett et al., 2009).

While experience and observation play a role in the development of prospective coaches' knowledge, the importance of formal education varies according to context. Tertiary education, for example, plays an important role in the development of coaches in North America, Europe, Asia, South Africa and Australia (Trudel & Gilbert, 2006; Lynch & Mallett, 2006). In contrast, other regions and countries may rely more upon coaching certification provided by national sports federations or sports confederations. However, unlike 'traditional' education which follows a linear pathway, Christensen's (2013) work with ten Danish elite coaches drew attention to unique pathways of learning and education which were adopted by coaches. The coaches, who worked within badminton, rowing, football/soccer, handball and swimming had varying engagements in coach education at different points in their elite careers. Some had completed elite (i.e. high performance) coach education prior to their appointment as coaches in elite sport contexts; others completed formal education alongside their first position as an elite sports coach (several years after their appointment), and some had not engaged in formal coach education at all. These trends were echoed by the coaches interviewed in this chapter which identified that those working in elite sport had engaged in coach certification programmes run by national sports federations at various points in their careers. And, the professional coaches were required to have a university degree and to engage in annual CPD (i.e. continuous professional development) provided by their national federations.

BEING A PERFORMANCE COACH

The disposable and replaceable nature of professionals (i.e. athletes/ players and coaches) in sporting contexts has been criticised in the literature for several decades (Ingham, Blissmer & Davidson, 1999; Roderick, 2012; Stewart, 1989); however, it is still an accepted 'reality' of coaches' work. Coach turnover in elite and professional domains has been attributed to a performance-based or an outcome-based culture, which has resulted in an environment in which job loss, short-term contracts and employer change are regular features (Andrews & Silk, 2012; Roderick, 2006). Notwithstanding the emotional toll that accompanies the precarity of coaches' positions, the highly public nature of the work of many of these coaches and the associated scrutiny from audiences who have a strong knowledge of the field (or perceive themselves to possess a high knowledge of the field) can heighten feelings of uncertainty and vulnerability (Roderick, 2006). Professional Basketball Coach D noted: 'You always need to be worrying, you know, working in that job. Always … Coaches have a rule, when you sign the contract you start to look for the next one!' As evidenced in this quote, coaches are aware of the external forces which may disrupt their careers, particularly in professional sport, thus they are not unexpected (though the timing may be!). However, the more experienced coaches know that these potential end points exist and work accordingly (to be discussed later in this chapter).

In performance sport, there are logical annual (end of season) or quadrennial (end of an Olympiad) times for leadership change (Wagstaff, 2017). Although there may be some situations in which elite sport has replaced coaches outside of these times, this appears to be more frequent in some professional sports. As a professional player noted, 'If the team is losing, it means the first finger points to the coach, and then maybe a player.' 'Pointing the finger' at the coach, then, assumes that a change in the coach leads to an improved team performance (van Ours & van Tuijl, 2016). However, scholars have identified if deciding to replace a coach does not result in an improvement in results, the decision is still viewed more positively than deciding not to act and not have an improvement in results (Besters, van Ours & van Tuijl, 2016).

In addition to poor performances, a lack of respect from athletes/players is frequently cited as a contributing factor to a head coach's contract termination (Fee, Hadlock & Pierce, 2006). For example, a professional basketball player recalled:

> The [General Manager] asked me and a couple of the other guys, including the captain, to talk. He asked us what was going on with the team and we told him, the coach had destroyed the chemistry, everyone was playing for themselves ... He asked us if they changed the coach would things improve? We told him 'It could not be worse' and he said ... 'Ok, it's done.'

The athlete's comment draws attention to the importance of obtaining and maintaining an athlete's respect. As demonstrated in this quote, the respect from athletes/players cannot be underestimated, as, without it, coaches cannot function (Jones et al., 2004). In contrast to being fired for poor results, which is not always within the coaches' control, coaches can actively develop respect from those with whom they work. For example, coaches have commented on the various strategies they employ to maintain the respect of athletes/players, including presenting an expert persona perceived by the athletes/players as a person who knows what they are doing, is in control of events and is consistent in their behaviour, while also appearing to have the athletes'/players' best interests at heart (Jones et al., 2004). While poor results and a loss of respect can contribute to the termination of coaches' contracts, coaches may be dismissed in response to the dissatisfaction of stakeholders (i.e. owners, shareholders, sponsors, media, fans). As a professional player recalled:

> We kept losing and kept losing. It got to the point when, the fans – we have some of the best fans in Europe – it got to the point when ... we would lose ... and at the end of the game, all fans are booing and shouting at us, 'Shame, shame, shame!'

In this case, the media and fans exerted pressure on the club to take action. For the club, doing something seemed better than doing nothing at all, so the coach was released (van Ours & van Tuijl, 2016).

Despite the frequency in which coaches are replaced (i.e. some clubs have been known to change coaches up to four times per season), the professional coaches noted that it was not something they thought about, believing that focusing on their vulnerability would undermine or distract them from doing their job. Therefore, coaches accepted their working conditions (uncertainty and all) and focused on doing the best job they could. As Professional Basketball Coach C commented:

> You just don't think about it, you know, you don't think that something can happen ... because if you're always thinking 'Wow, they can fire me', you will be worrying. So what will happen will happen, and you need to concentrate what you need to do – to prepare the players and prepare for the next game.

As identified in this quote, in professional sport, coaches' reputations largely rest on the results of their athletes/teams (Bachan, Reilly & Witt, 2008; de Tios Tena & Forrest, 2007). Therefore, the short-term and easily dissolvable nature of these contracts which characterise coaches' careers require that the coaches ensure they remain marketable. The coaches interviewed also discussed the importance of protecting their 'name' (i.e. reputations), which was their currency for further employment. As one coach noted, 'Especially now with phone cameras and everything, you have to be aware. You can't do anything that is not good for your name or for your career.' One way of interpreting the coach's concerns about surveillance and protecting his reputation is by considering the 'synopticon'. In contrast to the panopticon in which 'the few' watch 'the many' (discussed in Chapter 4), the synopticon refers to 'the many' watching 'the few' (Doyle, 2011). For example, athletes'/ players' and fans' observations of the coach which, as Mathiesen (1997) explains, can act as a disciplinary mechanism which can direct and control the individual.

In addition to monitoring their behaviour, the coaches highlighted that they attempted to retain their credibility and their professional reputation by resigning from positions in which they felt they had limited security. For example, 'It was only time before [the owner] would cut me ... I [didn't] want to kill my name so it was better for me to leave ...' (Purdy et al., 2017). Consequently, the coach moved back onto 'the market', looking for another position either as a head coach or assistant, within the same level or possibly within a lower league. Such movements challenge the traditional view of coaches' careers as linear and progressive.

CAREERS OF HORIZONTAL AND VERTICAL MOVEMENTS

In contrast to 'traditional' careers which are progressive, involving more responsibility and increased access to rewards as the career lengthens (Christensen, 2013; Stambulova, 2010), coaches' careers appear to be characterised by both vertical and horizontal movements (Barker-Ruchti et al., 2014). For example, depending on the available opportunities coaches may move up and down leagues or in and out of different systems. Head coaches might find employment as assistant coaches and assistant coaches might be promoted to the position of head coach.

> When you are the head coach, you're taking responsibility, and you're planning everything, and you're telling assistant coaches what to do. To be a player, that's the easiest thing, because all you need to do is attend practice; ok, you might need to arrive fifteen minutes early, but the coaches take care of everything else.
>
> (Professional Basketball Coach D)

A majority of the literature focuses on head coaches with assistant coaches largely left unrecognised. Yet, assistant coaches are often responsible for position specific areas or roles such as scouting and conditioning which require different interactions and skills to that of the head coach (Wiman, Salmoni & Hall, 2010). For example, differing from the head coach, the assistant coaches usually work more closely with the athletes/players and, at times, their responsibilities can extend to off-field activities. For example, 'When I was an assistant, sometimes I would go out in the evenings with the players, especially around important games, just to make sure they didn't do stupid things' (Professional Basketball Coach A).

In considering whether to accept a position as an assistant coach, the coaches considered whether they were willing to accept the requirements that accompanied the position as well as if they could work with the other members of the coaching team. For example, 'If you agree to take the position, then you're supposed to follow your role as a helper, or supporter for the head coach' (Professional Basketball Coach F). However, there were times during the season when the head coach's contract was terminated and the assistant coach was given the opportunity to move into the position as head coach either temporarily in lieu of the arrival of a new appointment or in a more permanent position. The decision to accept this promotion was not always easy. Here coaches highlighted that if they had a strong relationship with the former head coach, moving into the position may be viewed as betrayal (and could negatively impact upon future career opportunities), so would not accept the position without discussing it with the former head coach. In addition, the assistant coaches considered whether they could make a positive impact on the team. As Professional Basketball Coach D reflected upon the decision to move from assistant coach to head coach.

> It was difficult to decide whether I should take the head coach position and take over the team. I only had two months before the season ended and the team was down – in the league and emotionally. I knew that I would have no time to do anything with them because the playoffs were starting ... But I accepted the position and it was huge pressure, huge pressure ... In this level, it only matters if you win, but I was also pushing myself, to use the opportunity to finish the season well, to help the club finish well because when you are losing throughout the season; it's bad, but if you win the league, you are saving something or at least you're saving part of the season. And it was a hard decision to make, but it was the right decision. I knew that when I started to see that the team was following me ... after the first, second, third practice I saw that it would not be difficult to lead them.

While the previous information draws attention to the spells of unemployment which may characterise coaches' careers, ranging from a few days to several months in duration, the coaches did not consider that these would be permanent. Rather, when unemployed, they continued to engage in the sport. As Professional Basketball Coach F reflected:

> In the beginning, it was very good to stay at home with my family, to wake up in the morning to eat breakfast with them, but two weeks, one month later, I wanted to do something. I wanted to work. I was going to the games, watching the top league, and what happened was there were changes [with another team] and [the coach called me] 'What do you think? Maybe you want to be an assistant', and I said, 'Yes, why not?'

As evidenced in this quote, the coaching profession is a relatively insular, highly interconnected network (Ronglan & Havang, 2011). While coaches are largely left on their own to manage their careers within an invariably disorderly and unpredictable context, their networks (i.e. other coaches, administrators) become increasingly important in obtaining positions (Borges, Rosado, Oliveira & Freitas, 2015; Orlowski, Wicker & Breuer, 2016). Consequently, coaches who are well connected are more likely to find jobs after being fired. The concept of the boundaryless or protean careers (Hall, 1996) may be of use here as it suggests that careers are built on experience and networks. Akin to coaches' experiences within sport, these boundaryless or new forms of careers are recognised as precarious as it is not always easy to develop networks and career capital (McRobbie, 2002).

CAREER MOBILITY

Given the short-term and limited job market, geographical mobility can be crucial for an individual's career, particularly in performance sport. The literature has suggested that coaches' decisions to migrate are affected by a combination of 'push' and 'pull' factors (Elliott, 2012, 2014). These factors could be organised into three areas: job-related, social and competitive (Orlowski et al., 2016). Push factors refer to the forces that influence coaches to leave their home country or country of residence (e.g. a perceived lack of opportunities in the home country, no incentive to stay, low salaries, politics within the sport governing body, low social recognition) (Bale & Maguire, 1994). Pull factors refer to the forces that attract coaches to positions outside of their home country or country of residence. For example, better working conditions, financial incentives, the opportunity to work in a better league/programme or as a stepping stone towards a higher league/programme. These also include the technology available, the competitiveness of the training environment and geographical proximity. Decisions to move are also influenced by socio-cultural similarities, family support, children's education, and the seeking of new experiences (e.g. new culture, language and the challenging nature of the position) (Elliott, 2012, 2014; Orlowski et al., 2016).

To return to the focus of this section, the culmination of these issues and forces here were coaches recognising the 'push' and 'pull' factors that influenced their career decisions.

HOME LIFE

Coaching is a time-consuming profession as coaches' work frequently entails practices in the afternoons/evenings, non-balanced work schedules, moderate to heavy travel, and weekend and holiday obligations (Dixon & Sagas, 2007; Cunningham & Sagas, 2005). While research has focused on work–life issues which impact upon the recruitment and retention of women coaches (see Chapter 3), most accounts of coaches' experiences focus on their achievements in the sport, with little attention given to their home lives. Exceptions are Gmelch and San Antonio (2001) and Ortiz (2004) who focused on the female partners of male professional athletes/players (major league baseball and a mixture of major league baseball, professional (American) football, professional basketball and professional ice hockey players respectively). Their work identified that the partners experienced social isolation, feelings of alienation due to seasonal or mid-season relocation due to the sportsperson being traded, released from their contract or injured. Looking at this more carefully, frequent relocation also makes it difficult to maintain close friendships or develop new friendships and sustain family relationships (Ortiz, 2004). Consequently, some partners prefer not to relocate, opting to stay in their home country where they can be supported by friends and family, meaning that leaving visits to/from the sportsperson were limited to holidays. These findings correspond to the data generated by the professional coaches. Given there was no guarantee they would maintain their position through the season, the coaches often worked in cities/countries away from their families. The rationale for doing so was to not 'disrupt' family life, particularly if children were in school. This restricted family visits to breaks during the season and summer holidays. As Professional Basketball Coach B reflected:

> When there are school holidays, my family visits me because it is very difficult to get back home. So I see them at Christmas and Easter ... But that was our decision; we decided as a family ... At the beginning it was tough, and for the family too, but that was the decision we made.

Although the coaches' might not see their families frequently, they noted that various technologies enabled them to stay in contact or 'parent by phone'. As Professional Basketball Coach A noted:

> Some issues [my wife and I] were deciding over the phone, Skype or whatever. But we were lucky that there wasn't a time when we had problems with our kids. I always told my wife, 'As soon you have problems or if it is too difficult for you by yourself, I'll leave everything and I'll come back.'

It is important to recognise that the literature in this area (e.g. Gmelch & San Antonio (2001); Ortiz (2004)) and the data provided in this chapter highlight prevailing traditional gender ideologies among professional coaches (i.e. male coach with a female partner who is largely responsible for managing the family). While there has been attention on the work–family interface of women coaches, the 'voices' of partners have been largely unheard. However, considering coaches' wider lives (i.e. outside of the sport) can not only help us to understand what it is like to be an elite or professional coach, but may also be of use for sports organisations and/or clubs to consider the support provided to coaches and their families.

LEAVING PERFORMANCE COACHING

While coaching can be rewarding, research exploring elite coaching has underlined the struggles of dealing with high work pressure and highly-perceived expectations (e.g. Olusoga et al., 2009). When experiencing a large workload and high pressure at work, coaches are at risk of serious negative health outcomes such as professional burnout (Bentzen, Lemyre & Kenttä, 2015; Lundkvist, Gustafsson, Hjälm & Hassmén, 2012). It is unsurprising then that some coaches would find alternative employment. As Professional Basketball Coach E reflected:

> I was missing my family and my country so much. I really got tired because you always have this pressure, this constant tension ... I spent so much time and wasted so much time with other people ... so much time in competition, time with the team. And I wasted so much energy, especially mental energy. I lost my patience, and I wanted to get back to a normal life. I felt crazy. I had so much – I had a lot of

> money, but I didn't have a normal life. Normally after work people go home and spend time with family, spend time together, but I was working. I had even forgotten what weekends meant. I had forgotten about vacations. I had forgotten how to properly communicate with my family; I was always involved in my job.

As reflected in this coach's comment, for many coaches work is all-consuming. This has been highlighted in the literature, with coaching described as a

> multi-faceted, high paced work setting full of practices, recruiting, off-season workouts, administrative duties, and teaching responsibilities that have created an environment where only those willing to work twelve hour days, six days a week, for fifty weeks a year can thrive.
>
> (Dixon & Bruening, 2007)

It is unsurprising then that sports coaching has been identified as an inherently stressful occupation (Gould, Greenleaf, Guinan & Chung, 2002). While some coaches noted they thrived on their work and involvement in sport (see Chapter 2), for others, the persistently high demands and pressurised environment began to have a negative impact on their lives. As Professional Basketball Coach E reflected:

> I became nervous and this was starting to impact upon all areas of my life. Once, after practice, I went home for dinner with my family ... I hadn't even start to eat dinner before I started to talk about my job. One of my children did something and I started to yell at them and they started to cry ... it was awful. But it was a wake-up call, and I started to think, 'There's something wrong with me'... After that, I realised that I could not talk about my job when I was at home.

The literature relating to transitioning out of sport has largely focused on elite athletes/players (see Knights, Sherry & Ruddock-Hudson, 2016). However, retiring from coaching has not received similar attention. The work addressing coaches has largely been conducted from a psychological perspective. For example, Lavallee (2006) focused on fifty-six UK coaches who had retired from full-time positions at the national level and were in the process of transitioning into another career outside of sports coaching. Findings indicated that these coaches had relatively low levels of career awareness and had done little post-sport career planning during their coaching careers. This work echoed the results of a similar earlier investigation of Australian coaches, which suggested, despite aware of the insecure nature of their jobs, coaches were reluctant to consider careers outside of coaching (Lavallee, 2006).

According to Lavallee (2006), numerous skills from coaching can transfer into other areas (e.g. leadership, communication and performing under pressure); the time intensive and demanding nature of the sport often leaves coaches with little time to consider pre-retirement planning. However, the involvement of coaching associations and sports organisation in supporting career transitions of coaches is interesting as, given the insecure nature of elite sport, it is questionable whether coaches would reach out to such organisations for career advice. Coaches may consider this to be too risky if others (particularly their current employer) become aware of their intentions to change careers. As such, to preserve their 'name' and their positions, seeking support outside of sport or not at all may be viewed as the only workable option. Furthermore, with professional and elite coaching positioned as contemporary careers, there is no agreed career end point. There are numerous examples of coaches who continue working past seventy years of age. For example, Sir Alex Ferguson (Manchester United 1986–2013) and Giovanni Trapattoni (Republic of Ireland 2008–2013), retired in their mid-seventies. At the time of writing this chapter, there are numerous examples of coaches working past this age – for example, Malcolm Arnold (born 1940) is an athletics coach for Great Britain and rowing coach Mike Spracklen (born 1937) is working with the Russian rowing team.

SUMMARY

The purpose of this chapter was to draw attention to the careers of performance coaches. In doing so, it has highlighted characteristics of the occupational sector in which elite and professional coaches operate. The coaches featured in this chapter operated in contexts in which they were only as good as their last game/team. Consequently they focused on creating and preserving reputations which would enable them to remain marketable. Here, the coaches, as 'self entrepreneurs' (Rose, 1989), focused on building and self-managing their careers. However, instead of linear trajectories which depict 'traditional' careers, the coaches' careers were characterised by a series of horizontal and vertical movements either at 'home' or abroad as they strategically accepted and resigned from positions which would enable them to maintain their reputations (key in seeking further employment). Relying upon networks within sport to search for and obtain new opportunities, the coaches accepted or rejected assistant coaching posts if they were unable to support the views of the head coach, were unable to work within a different sporting domain, or were unsure that they could make a positive impact.

While the coaches in professional sporting contexts had experienced short spells of unemployment, they continued to 'fall' into other positions. For these coaches, flexibility, adaptability, patience and access to a wide network of other coaches brought success. Although some of the coaches viewed the insecure nature of their work as a challenge, for some, the continuous stress and sacrifices which encroached on other areas of their lives contributed to their decisions to retire. Even though this work has highlighted the experiences of some coaches in elite and professional sporting contexts, it is not attempting to suggest that these are similar for all coaches in these contexts. Rather, it serves as a starting point for readers to consider how coaches' athletic careers, gender, ethnicity, sexuality, wider cultural beliefs and expectations, and the socio-political milieu of particular sporting organisations are strongly related to their career 'development' (Christensen, 2013).

REFERENCES AND FURTHER READING

Note: All uncredited extracts/quotes throughout the book refer to personal conversations with the author.

Abraham, A., Collins, D., & Martindale, R. (2006). The coaching schematic: validation through expert coach consensus. *Journal of Sports Sciences, 24*(6), 549–564.

Acosta, R.V., & Carpenter, L.J. (2014). *Women in intercollegiate sport: a longitudinal, national study thirty-seven year update*. Brooklyn, NY: Brooklyn College.

Adams-Curtis, L., & Forbes, G. (2004). College women's experiences of sexual coercion: a review of cultural, perpetrator, victim, and situational variables. *Trauma Violence Abuse, 5*, 91–122.

Aitchison, J., & Graham, P. (1989). Potato crisp pedagogy. In C. Criticos (ed.), *Experiential learning in formal and non-formal education* (pp. 15–21). Durban: University of Natal.

Alaggia, R., & Millington, G. (2008). Male child sexual abuse: a phenomenology of betrayal. *Clinical Social Work Journal, 36*(3), 265–275.

Alexander, K., Stafford, A., & Lewis, R. (2011). *The experiences of children participating in organised sport in the UK*. London: NSPCC.

Alleman, E., Cochran, J., Doverspike, J., & Newman, I. (1984). Enriching mentoring relationships. *Personnel and Guidance Journal, 62*, 329–332.

Allen, J.B., & Shaw, S. (2009). Women coaches' perceptions of their sport organizations' social environment: Supporting coaches' psychological needs? *The Sport Psychologist, 23*, 346–366.

Almond, L. (2010). Revisiting the TGfU brand. In J.I. Butler & L.L. Griffin (eds), *More teaching games for understanding: moving globally* (pp. vii–x). Champaign, IL: Human Kinetics.

Ames, C. (1992). Classrooms: goals, structures, and student motivation. *Journal of Educational Psychology, 84*(3), 261–271.

Ames, C., & Archer, J. (1988). Achievement goals in the classroom: students' learning strategies and motivation processes. *Journal of Educational Psychology, 80*, 260–267.

Amoura, C., Berjot, S., Gillet, N., Caruana, S., Cohen, J., & Finez, L. (2015). Autonomy-supportive and controlling styles of teaching: opposite or distinct teaching styles. *Swiss Journal of Psychology, 74*(3), 141–158.

Andrews, D.L., & Silk, M.L. (eds) (2012). *Sport and neoliberalism: politics, consumption and culture*. Philadelphia, PA: Temple University Press.

Armour, K. (2010). The learning coach … the learning approach: professional development for sports coach professionals. In J. Lyle & C. Cushion (eds), *Sports coaching: professionalisation and practice* (pp. 153–164). London: Churchill Livingstone Elsevier.

Armour, K. (2011). *Sport pedagogy: an introduction for teaching and coaching*. London: Prentice Hall/Pearson.

Arthur, M.B. (2008). Examining contemporary careers: a call for interdisciplinary inquiry. *Human Relations, 61*(2), 163–186.

Arthur, M.B., Hall, D.T., & Lawrence, B.S. (1989). *Handbook of career theory*. New York: Cambridge University Press.

Atkins, S., & Murphy, K. (1994). Reflective practice. *Nursing Standard, 8*(39), 49–56.

Bachan, R., Reilly, B., & Witt, R. (2008). The hazard of being an English football league manager: empirical estimates for three recent league seasons. *Journal of the Operational Research Society, 59*(7), 884–891.

Baier, A. (1987). Hume: The woman's moral theorist? In E.F. Kittay & D. Meyers (eds), *Women and moral theory* (pp. 37–55). Totowa, NJ: Rowman & Littlefield.

Baier, K. (1958). *The moral point of view: a rational basis of ethics*. Ithaca, NY: Cornell University Press.

Baldock, A. (2011, 18 October). Wales coach Warren Gatland reveals he considered cheating. *The Independent*. Retrieved from www.independent.co.uk/sport/rugby/rugby-union/international/wales-coach-warren-gatland-reveals-he-considered-cheating-2372262.html.

Bale, J., & Maguire, J. (1994). *The global sports arena: athletic talent migration in an interdependent world*. London: Frank Cass Publishers.

Bale, J., & Sang, J. (1996). *Kenyan running: movement culture, geography and global change*. London: Frank Cass Publishers.

Barker-Ruchti, N. (2008). 'They must be working hard': an (auto) ethnographic account of women's artistic gymnastics. *Cultural Studies ↔ Critical Methodologies, 8*(3), 372–380.

Barker-Ruchti, N., & Tinning, R. (2010). Foucault in leotards: corporeal discipline in women's artistic gymnastics. *Sociology of Sport Journal, 27*, 229–250.

Barker-Ruchti, N., Hofmann, A., Lindgren, E.C., Sinning, S., & Shelton, C. (2013). *Top-level women football coaches: tracing exceptional career pathways. Report for the International Centre for Sports Studies* (CIES). Retrieved from http://iki.gu.se/digitalAssets/1492/1492523_barker-ruchti-et-al_final-report-2014.pdf.

Barker-Ruchti, N., Lindgren, E., Hofmann, A., Sinning, S., & Shelton, C. (2014). Tracing the career paths of top-level women football coaches: turning points to understand and develop sport coaching careers. *Sports Coaching Review, 3*(2), 117–131.

Bartholomew, K., Ntoumanis, N., & Thogersen-Ntoumani, C. (2009). A review of controlling motivational strategies from a self-determination theory perspective: implications for sports coaches. *International Review of Sport and Exercise Psychology, 2*, 215–233.

Bartholomew, K., Ntoumanis, N., & Thogersen-Ntoumani, C. (2011). Self-determination theory and the darker side of athletic experience: the role of interpersonal control and need thwarting. *Sport and Exercise Psychology Review, 7*, 23–27.

Becker, A.J., & Wrisberg, C.A. (2008). Effective coaching in action: observations of legendary collegiate basketball coach Pat Summitt. *The Sport Psychologist, 22*(2), 197–211.

Bentzen, M., Lemyre, P.N., & Kenttä, G. (2015). The process of burnout among professional sport coaches explored through the lens of Self-Determination Theory: a qualitative approach. *Sports Coaching Review, 3*(2), 1–16.

Bertz, S., & Purdy, L. (2011). Coach education in Ireland: observations and considerations. *Journal of Coaching Education, 4*(3), 29–43.

Besters, L.M., van Ours, J., & van Tuijl, M.A. (2016). Effectiveness of in-season manager change in English Premier League football. *De Economist, 164*(3), 335–356.

Blase, J. (1991). *The politics of life in schools*. Newbury Park, CA: Sage.

Bloom, G.A., Durand-Bush, N., Schinke, R., & Salmela, J.H. (1998). The importance of mentoring in the development of coaches and athletes. *International Journal of Sport Psychology, 29*, 267–281.

Booth, D. (2005). *The field: truth and fiction in sport history*. Abingdon: Routledge.

Borges, M., Rosado, A., Oliveira, R., & Freitas, F. (2015). Coaches' migration: a qualitative analysis of recruitment, motivations and experiences. *Leisure Studies, 34*(5), 588–602.

Bowes, I., & Jones, R.L. (2006). Working at the edge of chaos: understanding coaching as a complex, interpersonal system. *The Sport Psychologist, 20*, 235–245.

Brackenridge, C.H. (1997). 'He owned me basically …' Women's experience of sexual abuse in sport. *International Review for the Sociology of Sport, 32*, 115–130.

Brackenridge, C.H. (2001). *Spoilsports: understanding and preventing sexual exploitation in sport*. Abingdon: Routledge.

Brackenridge, C., & Kirby, S. (1997). Playing safe: assessing the risk of sexual abuse to elite young athletes. *International Review for the Sociology of Sport, 32*(4), 407–418.

Brackenridge, C.H., Bishop, D., Moussalli, S., & Tapp, J. (2008). The characteristics of sexual abuse in sport: a multidimensional scaling analysis of events described in media reports. *International Journal of Sport and Exercise Psychology, 6*(4), 385–406.

Brackenridge, C., Bringer, J.D., & Bishopp, D. (2005). Managing cases of abuse in sport. *Child Abuse Review, 14*(4), 259–274.

Bringer, J., Brackenridge, C.H., & Johnston, L. (2001). The name of the game: a review of sexual exploitation off males in sport. *Current Women's Health Reports, 1*, 225–231.

Brown, J.D. (1998). *The self.* London: Routledge.

Brown, G., & Potrac, P. (2009). 'You've not made the grade, son': de-selection and identity disruption in elite level youth football. *Soccer & Society, 10*, 143–159.

Bruening, J., Dixon, M., Burton, L., & Madsen, R. (2013). Women in coaching: the work-life interface. In P. Potrac, W. Gilbert & J. Denison (eds), *Routledge handbook of sports coaching* (pp. 411–423). Abingdon: Routledge.

Buckingham, D. (2008). Introducing identity. In D. Buckingham (ed.), *The John D. and Catherine T. MacArthur Foundation series on digital media and learning* (pp. 1–24). Cambridge, MA: The MIT Press.

Burak, L.J., Rosenthal, M., & Richardson, K. (2013). Examining attitudes, beliefs, and intentions regarding the use of exercise as punishment in physical education and sport: an application of the theory of reasoned action. *Journal of Applied Social Psychology, 43*, 1436–1445.

Busen, N.H., & Engebretson, J. (1999). Mentoring in advanced practice nursing: the use of metaphor in concept exploration. *The Internet Journal of Advanced Nursing Practice, 2*(2), 10.

Bush, A.J., Silk, M.L., Andrews, D.L., & Lauder, H. (2013). *Sports coaching research: context, consequences and consciousness.* Abingdon: Routledge.

Busser, J.A., & Carruthers, C.P. (2010) Youth sport volunteer coach motivation. *Managing Leisure, 15*, 1–2, 128–139.

Carlson, N.R., & Buskist, W. (1997). *Psychology: the science of behaviour.* Boston, MA: Allyn and Bacon.

Carter, N. (2010). Coaching cultures. *Sport in History, 30*(1), 1–7.

Cassidy, T., Jones, R.L., & Potrac, P. (2004). *Understanding sports coaching: the social, cultural and pedagogical foundations of coaching practice.* Abingdon: Routledge.

Cassidy, T., Jones, R.L., & Potrac, P. (2009). *Understanding sports coaching: the social, cultural and pedagogical foundations of coaching practice* (2nd edn). Abingdon: Routledge.

Cassidy, T., Jones, R.L., & Potrac, P. (2016). *Understanding sports coaching: the pedagogical, social and cultural foundations of coaching practice* (3rd edn). London: Routledge.

Castles, D. (2010, August 1). Jose: his new life as Hollywood director. *The Sunday Times*. Retrieved from www.thesundaytimes.co.uk/sto/sport/football/European_football/article359320.ece.

Cense, M., & Brackenridge, C.H. (2001). Temporal and developmental risk factors for sexual harassment and abuse in sport. *European Physical Education Review, 7*(1), 61–79.

Chambers, F. (2011). Learning theory for effective learning in practice. In K. Armour (ed.), *Sport pedagogy: an introduction for teaching and coaching* (pp. 39–52). London: Prentice Hall/Pearson.

Chesterfield, G., Potrac, P., & Jones, R.L. (2010). 'Studentship' and 'impression management': coaches' experiences of an advanced soccer coach education award. *Sport, Education and Society, 15*(3), 299–314.

Child Protection in Sport Unit (CPSU) (2015). *CPSU briefings: understanding the grooming process*. Retrieved from understanding-the-grooming-process-jan-2015.pdf.

Child Protection in Sport Unit (CPSU) (2017). Child abuse in a sports setting. Retrieved from https://thecpsu.org.uk/help-advice/introduction-to-safeguarding/child-abuse-in-a-sports-setting/

Christensen, M. (2013). Outlining a typology of sports coaching careers: paradigmatic trajectories and ideal career types among high-performance sports coaches. *Sports Coaching Review, 2*(2), 98–113.

Chroni, S., Vertommen, T., Bettina, R., Rhind, D., Papaefstathiou, M., Maria, M., Knorre, N., Hartill, M., Fasting, K., & Zurc, J. (2012). *Prevention of sexual and gender harassment and abuse in sport: initiatives in Europe and beyond*. Frankfurt: Deutsche Sortjugend im Deutschen Olympischen Sportbound.

Claringbould, I., Knoppers, A., & Jacobs, F. (2015). Young athletes and their coaches: disciplinary processes and habitus development. *Leisure Studies, 34*(3), 319–334.

Clark, J., & Nash, C. (2015). Technology in sports coaching. In C. Nash (ed.), *Practical sports coaching* (pp. 259–276). Abingdon: Routledge.

Coakley, J. (2009). *Sport in society: issues and controversies* (10th edn). New York: McGraw-Hill.

Coakley, J., & Pike, E. (2009). *Sport in society: issues and controversies.* United Kingdom edition. New York: McGraw-Hill.

Cobb, P. (1994). Where is the mind? Constructivist and sociocultural perspectives on mathematical development. *Educational Researcher, 23*(7), 12–20.

Collett, J.L., & Childs, E. (2009). Meaningful performances: considering the contributions of the dramaturgical approach to studying family. *Sociology Compass, 3*, 689–706.

Colley, H., Hodkinson, P., & Malcolm, J. (2003). *Informality and formality in learning: a report for the learning skills research centre*. London: Learning and Skills Research Centre.

Collins, L., & Collins, D. (2015). The adventure sports coach in adventure sports coaching. In M. Berry, J. Lomax & C. Hodgson (eds), *Adventure sports coaching* (pp. 5–23). Abingdon: Routledge.

Coombs, P.H., & Ahmed, M. (1974). *Attacking rural poverty: how non-formal education can help*. Baltimore, MD: John Hopkins University Press.

Corfield, P.J. (2008). *All people are living histories – which is why history matters*. Retrieved from www.history.ac.uk/makinghistory/resources/articles/why_history_matters.html.

Côté, J., & Gilbert, W. (2009). An integrative definition of coaching effectiveness and expertise. *International Journal of Sport Science & Coaching, 4*, 307–323.

Côté, J., Salmela, J., & Trudel, P. (1995). The coaching model: a grounded assessment of expert gymnastic coaches' knowledge. *Journal of Sport & Exercise Psychology, 17*(1), 1–17.

Crenshaw, K. (1989). Demarginalizing the intersection of race and sex: a black feminist critique of antidiscrimination doctrine, feminist theory, and antiracist politics. *University of Chicago Legal Forum, 140*, 139–167.

Cropley, B., Miles, A., & Peel, J. (2012). *Reflective practice: value, issues, and developments within sports coaching*. Sports Coach UK original research. Leeds, UK: SCUK.

Cross, N. (1995). Coaching effectiveness in hockey: a Scottish perspective. *Scottish Journal of Physical Education, 23*(1), 27–39.

Crotty, M. (1998). *Foundations of social research: meaning and perspective in the research process*. London: SAGE.

Culver, D., & Trudel, P. (2006). Cultivating coaches' communities of practice. In R.L. Jones (ed.), *The sports coach as educator: reconceptualising sports coaching* (pp. 113–127). London: Routledge.

Culver, D., Trudel, P., & Werthner, P. (2009). A sport leader's attempt to foster a coaches' community of practice. *International Journal of Sports Science & Coaching, 4*, 365–383.

Cumming, S.P., Smoll, F.L., Smith, R.E., & Grossbard, J.R. (2007). Is winning everything? The relative contribution of motivational climate and won-loss percentage in youth sport. *Journal of Applied Sport Psychology, 19*, 322–336.

Cunningham, G.B. (2003). Already aware of the glass ceiling: Race-related effects of perceived opportunity on the career choices of college athletes. *Journal of African American Studies, 7*(1), 57–71.

Cunningham, G.B. (2010). Understanding the under-representation of African American coaches: a multilevel perspective. *Sport Management Review, 13*(4), 395–406.

Cunningham, G., & Sagas, M. (2005). Gender and diversity in sport organizations: introduction to a special issue. *Sex Roles, 58*(1/2), 3–9.

Cunningham, G.B, Burning, J.E., & Straub, T. (2006). The under-representation of African Americans in NCAA Division I-A head coaching positions. *Journal of Sport Management, 20*(4), 387–413.

Cushion, C. (2006). Mentoring: harnessing the power of experience. In R.L. Jones (ed.), *The sports coach as educator: reconceptualising sports coaching* (pp. 128–144). London: Routledge.

Cushion, C.J., & Jones, R.L. (2006). Power, discourse and symbolic violence in professional youth soccer: the case of Albion F.C. *Sociology of Sport Journal, 23*(2), 142–161.

Cushion, C., & Jones, R.L. (2014). A Bourdieusian analysis of cultural reproduction: socialisation and the hidden curriculum in professional football. *Sport, Education and Society, 19*(3), 276–298.

Cushion, C.J., Armour, K.M., & Jones, R.L. (2003). Coach education and continuing professional development: experience and learning to coach. *Quest, 55*, 215–230.

Cushion, C.J., Armour, K.M., & Jones, R.L. (2006). Locating the coaching process in practice: models 'for' and 'of' coaching. *Physical Education and Sport Pedagogy, 11*(1), 83–99.

Cushion, C., Nelson, L., Armour, K., Lyle, J., Jones, R., Sandford, R., & O'Callaghan, C. (2010). *Coach learning and development: a review of literature.* Leeds, sports coach UK.

Čyžus, K. (2013). *Coaching emotions* (unpublished MSc thesis). University of Worcester, UK.

Csikszentmihalyi, M. (2002). *Flow: the psychology of happiness.* London: Ebury Publishing.

Csikszentmihalyi, M., Whalen, S., Wong, M., & Rathunde, K. (1993). *Talented teenagers: the roots of success and failure.* New York: Cambridge University Press.

d'Arripe-Longueville, R., Fournier, J.F., & Dubois, A. (1998). The perceived effectiveness of interactions between expert French judo coaches and elite female athletes. *The Sport Psychologist, 12*, 317–332.

David, P. (2005). *Human rights in youth sport: a critical review of children's rights in competitive sports.* Abingdon: Routledge.

Day, D. (2012). *Professionals, amateurs and performance: sports coaching in England, 1789–1914.* Oxford: Peter Lang.

Day, D. (2013). Historical perspectives on coaching. In P. Potrac, W. Gilbert & J. Denison (eds), *Routledge handbook of sports coaching* (pp. 5–15). Abingdon: Routledge.

Day, D., & Carpenter, T. (2015). *A history of sports coaching in Britain: overcoming amateurism.* Abingdon: Routledge.

Deci, E.L., & Ryan, R.M. (1985). *Intrinsic motivation and self-determination in human behavior.* New York: Plenum Publishing Co.

Deci, E.L., & Ryan, R.M. (1987). The support of autonomy and the control of behavior. *Journal of Personality and Social Psychology, 53*, 1024–1037.

Deci, E.L., & Ryan, R.M. (2000). The 'what' and 'why' of goal pursuits: human needs and the self-determination of behaviour. *Psychological Inquiry, 11*, 227–268.

Deci, E.L., & Ryan, R.M. (2002). *Handbook of self-determination research*. Rochester, NY: University of Rochester Press.

De Dios Tena, J. & Forrest, D. (2007). Within-season dismissal of football coaches: Statistical analysis of causes and consequences. *European Journal of Operational Research, 181*(1), 362–373.

De Martin-Silva, L., Fonseca, J., Jones, R., Morgan, K., & Mesquita, I. (2015). Understanding undergraduate sports coaching students' development and learning: the necessity of uncertainty. *Teaching in Higher Education, 20*(7), 669–683.

Demers, G. (2004). Why female athletes decide to become coaches – or not. *Canadian Journal for Women in Coaching, 4*(5). [online] Retrieved from www.coach.ca/women/e/journal/july2004/index.htm.

Demers, G. (2009). 'We are coaches': program tackles the under-representation of female coaches. *Canadian Journal of Women in Coaching, 9*(2), 1–9. Retrieved from www.coach.ca/files/WiC_Journal_April_2009_Vol_9_No_2.pdf.

Denison, J. (2007). Social theory for coaches: a Foucauldian reading of one athlete's poor performance. *International Journal of Sports Science and Coaching, 2*, 369–383.

Denison, J. (2010). Planning, practice and performance: the discursive construction of coaches' knowledge. *Sport, Education and Society, 15*(4), 461–478.

Denison, J., & Mills, J.P. (2014). Planning for distance running: coaching with Foucault. *Sports Coaching Review, 3*, 1–16.

Denison, J., & Mills, J. (2016, 27 June). *Beginning to coach with power in mind*. Retrieved from www.mcmillanspeed.com.

Denison, J., & Scott-Thomas, D. (2011). Michel Foucault: Power and discourse: the 'loaded' language of coaching. In R.L. Jones, P. Potrac, C. Cushion & L.T. Ronglan (eds), *The sociology of sports coaching* (pp. 27–39). Abingdon: Routledge.

Denison, J., Mills, J.P., & Jones, L. (2013). Effective coaching as a modernist formation: a Foucauldian critique. In P. Potrac, W. Gilbert & J. Denison (eds), *The Routledge handbook of sports coaching* (pp. 388–398). London: Routledge.

Denison, J., & Mills, J.P., & Konoval, T. (2015). Sports' disciplinary legacy and the challenge of 'coaching differently'. *Sport, Education and Society, 22*(6), 772–783.

Dixon, M., & Bruening, J. (2005). Perspectives on work–family conflict: a review and integrative approach. *Sport Management Review, 8*, 227–254.

Dixon, M., & Bruening, J.E. (2007). Work-family conflict in coaching I: a top-down perspective. *Journal of Sport Management, 21*, 377–406.

Dixon, M.A., & Segas, M. (2007). The relationship between organizational support, work-family conflict, and the job-life satisfaction of university coaches. *Research Quarterly for Exercise and Sport, 78*(3), 236–247.

Donnelly, P. (1997). Child labour, sport labour. *International Review for the Sociology of Sport, 32*, 389–406.

Doyle, A. (2011). Revisiting the synopticon: reconsidering Mathiesen's 'The Viewer Society' in the age of Web 2.0. *Theoretical Criminology, 15*(3), 283–99.

Doyle, W. (1992). Curriculum and pedagogy. In P. Jackson (ed.), *Handbook of research on curriculum* (pp. 486–516). New York: Macmillan.

Dubuc-Charbonneau, N., Durand-Bush, N., & Forneris, T. (2014). Exploring levels of student-athlete burnout at two Canadian Universities. *Canadian Journal of Higher Education, 44*(2), 135–151.

Duda, J.L. (2001). Achievement goal research in sport: pushing the boundaries and clarifying some misunderstandings. In G.C. Roberts (ed.), *Advances in motivation in sport and exercise* (pp. 129–182). Champaign, IL: Human Kinetics.

Duda, J.L. (2013). The conceptual and empirical foundations of Empowering Coaching™: setting the stage for the PAPA project. *International Journal of Sport and Exercise Psychology, 11*(4), 311–318.

Duda, J.L., & Hall, H. (2001). Achievement goal theory in sport: recent extensions and future directions. In R.N. Singer, H.A. Hausenblas & C.M. Janelle (eds), *Handbook of sport psychology* (pp. 417–443). New York: Wiley.

Duda, J.L., & Whitehead, J. (2016). Toward quality not quantity in sport motivation. In J. Lambert & J. Wallis (eds), *Becoming a sports coach* (pp. 110–121). Abingdon: Routledge.

Elliott, R. (2012). New Europe, new chances? The migration of professional footballers to Poland's Ekstraklasa. *International Review for the Sociology of Sport, 48*(6), 736–750.

Elliott, R. (2014). Football's Irish exodus: Examining the factors influencing Irish player migration to English professional leagues. *International Review for the Sociology of Sport, 51*(2), 147–161.

Erickson, K., Bruner, M.W., MacDonald, D.J., & Côté, J. (2008). Gaining insight into actual and preferred sources of coaching knowledge. *International Journal of Sport Sciences & Coaching, 3*, 527–538.

European Commission (2016). *Grassroots sport – shaping Europe*. Report to Commissioner Tibor Navracsics. Retrieved from http://ec.europa.eu/assets/eac/sport/library/policy_documents/hlg-grassroots-final_en.pdf.

Fairley, S., & Gammon, S. (2005). Something lived, something learned: nostalgia's expanding role in sport tourism. *Sport in Society, 8*(2), 182–197.

Fairs, J. (1987). The coaching process: the essence of coaching. *Sports Coach, 11*(1), 17–20.

Farstad, S. (2007). Protecting children's rights in sport: the use of minimum age. *Human Rights Law Commentary, 3*, 1–20.

Fasting, K., & Brackenridge, C. (2009). Coaches, sexual harassment and education. *Sport, Education and Society, 14*(1), 21–35.

Fasting, K., Brackenridge, C.H., & Sundgot-Borgen, J. (2000). *Female elite sport and sexual harassment*. Oslo: Norwegian Olympic Committee and Confederation of Sport.

Fasting K., Chroni S., & Knorre, N. (2014). The experiences of sexual harassment in sport and education among European female sports science students. *Sport, Education & Society, 19*, 115–130.

Fasting, K., Chroni, S., Hervik, S.E., & Knorre, N. (2011). Sexual harassment in sport toward females in three European countries. *International Review for the Sociology of Sport, 46*(1), 76–89.

Fee, C.E., Hadlock, C.J., & Pierce, J.R. (2006). Promotions in the internal and external labor market: evidence from professional football coaching careers. *The Journal of Business, 79*(2), 821–850.

Felton, L., & Jowett, S. (2013). Attachment and well-being: the mediating effects of psychological needs satisfaction within the coach-athlete and parent-athlete relational contexts. *Psychology of Sport and Exercise, 14*(1), 57–65.

Felton, L., & Jowett, S. (2015). On understanding the role of need thwarting in the association between athlete attachment and well/ill-being. *Scandinavian Journal of Medicine and Sports Sciences, 25*, 289–298.

Field, T. (2003). *Touch*. Cambridge, MA: MIT Press.

Fitzgerald, L.F., Gelfand, M J., & Drasgow, F. (1995). Measuring sexual harassment: theoretical and psychometric advances. *Basic and Applied Social Psychology, 17*, 425–445.

Fletcher, D., & Scott, M. (2010). Psychological stress in sports coaches: a review of concepts, research, and practice. *Journal of Sports Sciences, 28*(2), 127–137.

Fondacaro, K.M., Holt, J.C., & Powell, T.A. (1999). Psychological impact of childhood sexual abuse on male inmates: the importance of perception. *Child Abuse & Neglect, 23*(4), 361–369.

Foucault, M. (1977). *Discipline and punish: the birth of the prison*, trans. A. Sheridan. Harmondsworth: Peregrine.

Foucault, M. (1979). *Discipline and punish: the birth of the prison*. New York: Vintage Books.

Foucault, M. (1983). The subject and power. In H.L. Dreyfus & P. Rabinow (eds), *Michel Foucault: beyond structuralism and hermeneutics* (2nd edn) (pp. 58–72). Chicago, IL: University of Chicago Press.

Fraleigh, W. (1986). The sports contest and value priorities. *Journal of the Philosophy of Sport, 8*, 65–77.

Franken, R.E. (2007). *Human motivation* (6th edn). Belmont, CA: Thomas Wadsworth Publishing.

Frankena, W. (1973). *Ethics* (2nd edn). Englewood Cliffs, NJ: Prentice Hall.

Franks, I., Sinclair, G.D., Thomson, W., & Goodman, D. (1986). Analysis of the coaching process. *Sports Science Periodical on Research and Technology in Sport*, 1, 1–2 (January).

Fraser-Thomas, J., & Côté, J. (2009). Understanding adolescents' positive and negative developmental experiences in sport. *The Sport Psychologist, 23*, 3–23.

French, J.R.P. Jr., & Raven, B. (1959). The basis of social power. In D. Cartwright (ed.), *Studies in social power* (pp. 150–167). Ann Arbor, MI: University of Michigan Press.

Frey, M. (2007). College coaches' experiences with stress – 'problem solvers' have problems too. *The Sport Psychologist, 21*, 38–57.

Gallimore, R., & Tharp, R.G. (2004). What a coach can teach a teacher, 1975–2004: reflections and reanalysis of John Wooden's teaching practices. *The Sports Psychologist, 18*(2), 119–137.

Ganim, S. (2015, August 29). University of Illinois fires head football coach after player complaints. *CNN.* Retrieved from http://edition.cnn.com/2015/08/28/us/university-illinois-coach-fired/index.html.

Geirland, J. (1996, January, 9). Go with the flow. *Wired Magazine.* Retrieved from www.wired.com/1996/09/czik/.

Gervis, M., & Dunn, N. (2004). The emotional abuse of elite child athletes by their coaches. *Child Abuse Review, 13*(3), 215–223.

Ghaye, T. (2001). Reflection: principles and practices. *Faster, Higher, Stronger, 10*, 9–11.

Ghaye, T., & Lillyman, S. (2000). *Reflection: principles and practice for healthcare professionals.* Dinton: Quay Books.

Giatsis, S.G. (2000). The organization of chariot-racing in the great hippodrome of byzantine Constantinople. *The International Journal of the History of Sport, 17*(1), 36–68.

Gibbs, G. (1988). *Learning by doing: a guide to teaching and learning methods.* Oxford, UK: Oxford Brookes University, Further Education Unit.

Giddens, A. (1991). *Modernity and self-identity: self and society in the late modern age.* Cambridge: Polity Press.

Gilbert, W., & Trudel, P. (2001). Learning to coach through experience: reflection in model youth sport coaches. *Journal of Teaching in Physical Education, 2*(10), 16–34.

Gilbert, W., & Trudel, P. (2004). The role of the coach: how model youth team sport coaches frame their role. *The Sport Psychologist, 18*, 21–43.

Gilbert, W., Côté, J., & Mallett, C. (2006). Developmental pathways and activities of successful sport coaches. *International Journal of Sports Science and Coaching, 1*(1), 69–76.

Gilbourne, D., Marshall, P., & Knowles, Z.R. (2013). Reflective practice in sports coaching: thoughts on process, pedagogy and research. In R.L. Jones & K. Kingston (eds), *An introduction to sports coaching: connecting theory to practice* (pp. 3–11). Abingdon: Routledge.

Gilchrist, M., & Mallett, C.J. (2017). The theory (SDT) behind effective coaching. In R. Thelwell, C. Harwood & I. Greenlees (eds), *The psychology of sports coaching: research and practice* (pp. 38–53). Abingdon: Routledge.

Gillet, N., Vallerand, R.J., & Rosnet, E. (2009). Motivational clusters and performance in a real-life setting. *Motivation and Emotion, 33*, 49–62.

Glynn, C. (2008). *'Coaching female style: Tough but achievable': female coaches inform us about their journey to the top* (unpublished BSc thesis). University of Limerick, Ireland.

Gmelch, G., & San Antonio, P.M. (2001). Baseball wives: gender and the work of baseball. *Journal of Contemporary Ethnography, 30*(3), 335–356.

Goffman, E. (1959). *The presentation of self in everyday life.* Garden City, NY: Doubleday.

Goffman, E. (1969). *Where the action is.* London: Penguin Press.

Gogol, S. (2002). *Hard fought victories: women coaches making a difference*. Terre Haute, IN: Wish Publishing.

Goode, E., & Ben-Yehuda, N. (1994). *Moral panics: The social construction of deviance*. Malden, MA: Blackwell Publishers.

Gore, J.M., Griffiths, T., & Ladwig, J.G. (2004). Towards better teaching: productive pedagogy as a framework for teacher education. *Teaching and Teacher Education, 20*, 375–387.

Gould, J. (2009). *Learning theory and classroom practice in the lifelong learning sector*. Exeter: Learning Matters.

Gould, D., Greenleaf, C., Guinan, D., & Chung, Y. (2002). A survey of U.S. Olympic coaches: variables perceived to have influenced athlete performances and coach effectiveness. *The Sport Psychologist, 16*, 229–250.

Gleaves, T., & Lang, M. (2017). Kicking 'no touch' discourses into touch: athletes' parents' constructions of appropriate adult coach-child athlete physical contact. *Sport and Social Issues*. DOI: 10.1177/0193723517705543.

Griffiths, M. (2010). *Mentoring as a learning strategy with volunteer sports coaches* (unpublished PhD thesis). Loughborough University, Loughborough, UK.

Griffiths, M. (2011). Mentoring and professional learning. In K. Armour (ed.), *Introduction to sport pedagogy for teachers and coaches: effective learners in physical education and youth sport* (pp. 299–311). London: Routledge.

Griffiths, M. (2015). Training coaches as mentors. In F. Chambers (ed.), *Mentoring in physical education and sports coaching* (pp. 163–171). Abingdon: Routledge.

Griffiths, M., & Armour, K. (2012). Formalised mentoring as a professional learning strategy for volunteer sports coaches. *Mentoring & Tutoring, 20*(1), 151–173.

Gunz, H., & Peiperl, M. (2007). *Handbook of career studies*. Los Angeles, CA: SAGE.

Guttmann, A. (2004). *From ritual to record: the nature of modern sports*. New York, NY: Columbia University Press.

Haas, H. (2011). A culture of volunteering: charitable activities among British retirement migrants in Spain. *Ageing & Society, 22*(8), 1374–1400.

Halgin, D. (2009). *The effects of social identity, network connectivity, and prior performance on career progression and resilience: a study of NCAA basketball coaches* (unpublished doctoral dissertation). Boston College, Chestnut Hill, MA.

Hall, D.T. (1996). *The career is dead–long live the career: A relational approach to careers*. San Francisco, CA: JosseyBass.

Hallam, S., & Ireson, J. (1999). Pedagogy in the secondary school. In P. Mortimore (ed.), *Understanding pedagogy and its impact on learning* (pp. 68–97). London: Paul Chapman Publishing.

Hamilton, E.R. (2016). Picture this: multimodal representations of prospective teachers and teaching. *Teaching and Teacher Education, 55*, 33–44.

Hardman, A., & Jones, C. (eds) (2010). *The ethics of sports coaching*. Abingdon: Routledge.

Hardman, A., & Jones, C. (2013). Philosophy for coaches. In R.L. Jones & K. Kingston (eds), *An introduction to sports coaching: connecting theory to practice* (2nd edn) (pp. 99–110). Abingdon: Routledge.

Hardman, A.R., Bailey, J., & Lord, R. (2014). 'Is it OK for me to touch you?': discourse on the concept of care in the everyday coaching of trampoline gymnastics in the UK. In H. Piper & D. Garrett (eds), *Touch in sports coaching and physical education: fear, risk and moral panic* (pp. 151–166). Abingdon: Routledge.

Hardman, A., Jones, C., & Jones, R. (2010).Sports coaching, virtue ethics and emulation. *Physical Education and Sport Pedagogy, 15*(4), 345–359.

Hargreaves, J. (1994). *Sporting females: Critical issues in the history and sociology of women's sports*. Abingdon: Routledge.

Hargreaves, J. (2000). *Heroines of sport: The politics of difference and identity*. Abingdon: Routledge.

Hargreaves, J., & Vertinsky, P. (2006). *Physical culture, power and the body*. Abingdon: Routledge.

Hartill, M. (2009). The sexual abuse of boys in organized male sports. *Men and Masculinities, 12*(2), 225–249.

Hartill, M., & Lang, M. (2015). *Safeguarding, child protection and abuse in sport: international perspectives in research, policy and practice*. Abingdon: Routledge.

Harvey, S., & Jarrett, K. (2014). A review of the game-centred approaches to teaching and coaching literature since 2006. *Physical Education and Sport Pedagogy, 19*(3), 278–300.

Hawkins, K., & Blann, F.W. (1993). *Athlete/coach career development and transition*. Canberra: Australian Sports Commission.

Hobson, A.J., Ashby, P., Malderez, A., & Tomlinson, P. (2009). Mentoring beginning teachers: what we know and what we don't. *Teaching and Teacher Education, 24*, 207–216.

Hochschild, A.R. (1983). *The managed heart: commercialization of human feeling*. London: University of California Press, Ltd.

Hofman, A., Sinning, S., Shelton, C., Lindgren, E.C.M., & Barker-Ruchti, N. (2014). 'Football is like chess – you need to think a lot': women in men's sphere. National football coaches and their way to the top. *International Journal of Physical Education, 15*(4), 20–31.

Hollembeak, J., & Amorose, A.J. (2005). Perceived coaching behaviors and college athletes' intrinsic motivation: a test of self-determination theory. *Journal of Applied Sport Psychology, 17*, 20–36.

Horine, L., & Stotler, D. (2003). *Administration of physical education and sport programs*. Madison, WI: Brown & Benchmark.

Horn, T.S. (2008). Coaching effectiveness in the sport domain. In T.S. Horn (ed.), *Advances in sport psychology* (pp. 239–267). Champaign, IL: Human Kinetics.

Hovden, J. (2010). Female top leaders – prisoners of gender? The gendering of leadership discourses in Norwegian sports organizations. *International Journal of Sport Policy, 2*(2), 189–203.

Hoyle, E. (1982). Micro-politics of educational organisaions. *Educational Management Administration & Leadership, 10*, 87–98.

Hubball, H. Lambert, J., & Hayes, S. (2007). Theory to practice: using the games for understanding approach in the teaching of invasion games. *Physical and Health Education,* Autumn, 14–20.

Huber, J. (2013). *Applying educational psychology in coaching athletes.* Champaign, IL: Human Kinetics.

Hughson, J. (2012). Sport and identity – introduction. In J. Hughson, C. Palmer & F. Skillen (eds), *The role of sports in the formation of personal identities.* Lampeter: The Edwin Mellen Press.

Hums, M.A., Bower, G.G., & Grappendorf, H. (2007). *Women as leaders in sport: impact and influence.* Oxon Hill, MD: AAHPERD Publications.

Ibarra, H. (1999). Provisional selves: experimenting with image and identity in professional adaptation. *Administrative Science Quarterly, 44*, 764–791.

Ingham, A.G., Blissmer, B.J., & Davidson, K.W. (1999). The expendable prolympic self. *Sociology of Sport Journal, 16*(3), 236–268.

International Council for Coaching Excellence (ICCE) (2013). *The international sport coaching framework.* Version 1.1. Champaign, IL: Human Kinetics.

Irwin, G., Hanton, S., & Kerwin, D. (2004). Reflective practice and the origins of elite coaching knowledge. *Reflective Practice, 5,* 426–442.

Jacobs, F., Claringbould, I., & Knoppers, A. (2014). Becoming a 'good coach'. *Sport, Education and Society, 18*(8), 1–20.

Jacobs, F, Smits, F., & Knoppers, A. (online 2016). 'You don't realize what you see': the institutional context of emotional abuse in elite youth sport. *Sport in Society*, 126–143. DOI: 10.1080/17430437.2015.1124567.

Jenkins, R. (1996). *Social identity.* London: Routledge.

Jenkins, R. (2008). *Social identity.* (3rd edn). Abingdon: Routledge.

Johns, C. (2000). *Becoming a reflective practitioner: a reflective and holistic approach to clinical nursing, practice development and clinical supervision.* Oxford: Blackwell Science.

Johns, D.P., & Johns, J.S. (2000). Surveillance, subjectivism and technologies of power: an analysis of the discursive practice of high-performance sport. *International Review for the Sociology of Sport, 35*(2), 219–234.

Johnson, R.T. (2015). Training 'safe' bodies in an era of child panic in the United States: New technologies for disciplining the self. In H. Piper (ed.), *Touch in sports coaching and physical education: Fear, risk and moral panic* (pp. 76–92). Abingdon: Routledge.

Jonassen, D.H. (1991). Objectivism versus constructivism: do we need a new philosophical paradigm? *Educational Technology Research and Development, 39*(3), 5–14.

Jones, R.L. (2005). *Resource guide to sports coaching.* Unpublished document prepared for the Higher Education Academy Network for Hospitality, Leisure, Sport and Tourism. Retrieved from www.heacademy.ac.uk/system/files/sports_coaching.pdf.

Jones, R.L. (2006). Dilemmas, maintaining 'face' and paranoia: An average coaching life. *Qualitative Inquiry, 12*(5), 1012–1021.

Jones, R.L., & Turner, P. (2006). Teaching coaches to coach holistically: can problem-based learning (PBL) help? *Physical Education and Sport Pedagogy, 11*(2), 181–202.

Jones, R.L., Armour, K.M., & Potrac, P. (2002). Understanding coaching practice: a suggested framework for social analysis. *Quest, 5*(1), 34–48.

Jones, R.L., Armour, K.M., & Potrac, P. (2004). *Sports coaching cultures: from practice to theory*. London: Routledge.

Jones, R.L., Bailey, J., & Santos, S. (2013). Coaching, caring and the politics of touch: A visual exploration. *Sport, Education and Society, 18*(5), 648–662.

Jones, R.L., Bailey, J., Santos, S., & Edwards, C. (2012). Who is coaching? Developing the person of the coach. In D. Day (ed.), *Sports and coaching: pasts and futures* (pp.1–12). Crewe: MMU Press.

Jones, R.L., Morgan, K., & Harris, K. (2012). Developing coaching pedagogy: seeking a better integration of theory and practice. *Sport, Education and Society, 17*(3), 313–329.

Jones, R.L., Potrac, P., Cushion, C., & Ronglan, L.T. (eds) (2011). *The sociology of sports coaching*. London: Routledge.

Jowett, S. (2005). The coach-athlete partnership. *The Psychologist, 18,* 412–415.

Jowett, S. (2008). What makes coaches tick? The impact of coaches' intrinsic and extrinsic motives on their own satisfaction and that of their athletes. *Scandinavian Journal of Medicine & Science in Sports, 18,* 664–673.

Jowett, S. (2009). Validating the coach athlete relationship measures with the nomological network. *Measurement in Physical Education and Exercise Science, 13,* 34–51.

Jowett, S., & Chaundy, V. (2004). An investigation into the impact of coach leadership and coach – athlete relationship on group cohesion. *Group Dynamics: Theory, Research and Practice, 8,* 302–311.

Jowett, S., & Cockerill, I.M. (2003). Olympic Medallists' perspective of the athlete – coach relationship. *Psychology of Sport and Exercise, 4,* 313–331.

Jowett, S., & Meek, G.A. (2000). The coach–athlete relationship in married couples: an exploratory content analysis. *The Sport Psychologist, 14,* 157–175.

Jowett, S., & Ntoumanis, N. (2004). The coach–athlete relationship questionnaire (CART – Q): development and initial validation. *Scandinavian Journal of Medicine and Science in Sports, 14,* 245–257.

Jowett, S., & Poczwardowski A. (2007). Understanding the coach–athlete relationship. In S. Jowett & D. Lavallee (eds), *Social psychology in sport* (pp. 3–14). Champaign, IL: Human Kinetics.

Jowett, S., & Shanmugam, V. (2016). Relational coaching in sport: its psychological underpinnings and practical effectiveness. In R. Schinke, K.R. McGannon & B. Smith (eds), *Routledge international handbook of sport psychology* (pp. 471–484). Abingdon: Routledge.

Jowett, S., Shanmugam, V., & Caccoulis, S. (2012). Collective efficacy as a mediator of the link between interpersonal relationships and athlete satisfaction in team sports. *International Journal of Sport and Exercise Psychology, 10*, 66–78.

Kamphoff, C.S. (2010). Bargaining with patriarchy: former women coaches' experiences and their decision to leave collegiate coaching. *Research Quarterly for Exercise and Sport, 81*(3), 367–379.

Kane, M.J. (2016). A socio-cultural examination of a lack of women coaches in sport leadership positions. In N.M. LaVoi (ed.), *Women in sports coaching* (pp. 35–48). Abingdon: Routledge.

Kanter, R.M. (1977). *Men and women of the corporation*. New York: Basic Books.

Kavanagh, E., Knowles, Z., Brady, A., Rhind, D., Gervis, M., Miles, A., & Davison, R. (2016). The BASES expert statement on safeguarding in the sport and exercise sciences. *The Sport and Exercise Scientist, 49*, 20–21.

Kelchtermans, G. (2009a). Who I am in how I teach the message: self-understanding vulnerability, and reflection. *Teachers and Teaching: theory and practice, 15*(2), 257–272.

Kelchtermans, G. (2009b). Career stories as a gateway to understanding teacher development. In M. Bayer, U. Brinkkjaer, H. Plauborg & S. Rolls (eds), *Teachers' career trajectories and work lives* (pp. 29–47). London: Springer.

Kelchtermans, G., & Vandenberghe, R. (1994). Teachers' professional development: a biographical perspective. *Journal of Curriculum Studies, 26*(1), 45–62.

Kenkmann, A. (2009). *Teaching philosophy*. London: Continuum.

Kennard, J., & Carter, J.M. (1994). In the beginning: the ancient and medieval worlds. In D.M. Costa & S.R. Guthrie (eds), *Women and sport: interdisciplinary perspectives* (pp. 15–26). Champaign, IL: Human Kinetics.

Kerr, G. (2010). Physical and emotional abuse of elite child athletes: the case of forced physical exertion. In C.H. Brackenridge & D. Rhind (eds), *Elite child athlete welfare: international perspectives* (pp. 41–50). West London: Brunel University Press.

Kidman, L. (2001). *Developing decision makers: an empowerment approach to coaching*. Christchurch, NZ: Innovative Print Communications Ltd.

Kidman, L. (2005). *Athlete-centred coaching: developing inspired and inspiring people*. Christchurch, NZ: Innovative Print Communications, Ltd.

Kidman, L., & Hanrahan, S.J. (2011). *The coaching process: a practical guide to improving your coaching effectiveness* (3rd edn). Abingdon: Routledge.

Kilty, K. (2006). Women in coaching. *The Sport Psychologist, 20*, 222–234.

Kirk, D., Naught, J., Harahan, S., Macdonald, D., & Jobbing, I. (1996). *The sociocultural foundations of human movement*. Melbourne: Macmillan.

Knights, S., & Ruddock-Hudson, M. (2016). Experiences of occupational stress and social support in Australian Football League senior coaches. *International Journal of Sports Science & Coaching, 11*(2), 162–171.

Knights, S., Sherry, E., & Ruddock-Hudson, M. (2016). Investigating elite end-of-athletic career transition: a systematic review. *Journal of Applied Sport Psychology, 28*(3), 291–308.

Knoppers, A., & Anthonissen, A. (2008). Gendered managerial discourses in sport organizations: multiplicity and complexity. *Sex Roles, 58*, 93–103.

Knowles, M. (1984). *Andragogy in action. Applying modern principles of adult education*. San Francisco, CA: Jossey-Bass.

Knowles, Z., Borrie, A., & Telfer, H. (2005). Toward the reflective sports coach: issues of context, education and application. *Ergonomics, 48*(11–14), 1711–1720.

Knowles, M., Holton, E., & Swanson, R. (2011). *The adult learner: the definitive classic in adult education and human resource development* (7th edn). Oxford: Butterworth-Heinemann, Elsevier.

Knowles, Z., Gilbourne, D., Borrie, A., & Neville, A. (2001). Developing the reflective sports coach: a study exploring the processes of reflection within a higher education coaching programme. *Reflective Practice, 2*, 185–207.

Kohe, G.Z. (2014a). (Dis)located Olympic patriots: sporting connections, administrative communications and imperial ether in interwar New Zealand. *Sport in Society* DOI:10.1080/17430437.2014.990686

Kohe, G.Z. (2014b). Judging Jack: rethinking historical agency and the sport hero. *Sport History Review, 44*(2), 200–219.

Köhne, E., & Ewigleben, C. (2000). *Gladiators and Caesars*. London: British Museum Press.

Kondo, D.K. (1990). *Crafting selves: power, gender, and discourses of identity in a Japanese workplace*. Chicago, IL: University of Chicago Press.

Krane, V., & Barber, H. (2005). Identify tensions in lesbian intercollegiate coaches. *Research Quarterly for Exercise and Sport, 76*(1), 67–81.

Kretchmar, R.S. (2005). *Practical philosophy of sport and physical activity* (2nd edn). Leeds: Human Kinetics.

Kristjánsson, K. (2006). Emulation and the use of role models in moral education. *Journal of Moral Education, 35*(1), 37–49.

Lafrenière, M.A.K., Jowett, S., Vallerand, R.J., Donahue, E.G., & Lorimer, R. (2008). Passion in sport: on the quality of the coach–athlete relationship. *Journal of Sport & Exercise Psychology, 30*, 541–560.

Lang, M. (2009). *Swimming in the Panopticon: an ethnographic study of good practice and child protection in competitive youth swimming* (unpublished PhD thesis). Leeds: Leeds Metropolitan University.

Lang, M. (2010). Surveillance and conformity in competitive youth swimming. *Sport, Education and Society, 15*, 19–37.

Lang, M. (2015). Touchy subject: a Foucauldian analysis of coaches' perceptions of adult–child touch in youth swimming. *Sociology of Sport Journal, 32*, 4–21.

Lang, M., & Pinder, S. (2016). Telling (dangerous) stories: a narrative account of a youth coach's experience of an unfounded allegation of child abuse. *Qualitative Research in Sport, Exercise and Health, 9*(1), 99–110.

Lavallee, D. (2006). Career awareness, career planning and career transition needs among sports coaches. *Journal of Career Development, 33*, 66–79.

Lavallee, D., Kremer, J., Moran, A., & Williams, M. (2012). *Sport psychology: contemporary themes* (2nd edn). New York, NY: Palgrave Macmillan.

LaVoi, N.M. (2014). *The status of women in collegiate coaching: A report card, 2013–2014*. Minneapolis, MN: Tucker Center for Research on Girls & Women in Sport.

LaVoi, N.M., & Dutove, J.K. (2012). Barriers and supports for female coaches: an ecological model. *Sports Coaching Review, 1*(1), 17–37.

Lawler, S. (2008). *Identity: sociological perspectives*. Cambridge: Polity Press.

Leach, J., & Moon, B. (1999). *Learners and pedagogy*. London: Paul Chapman Publishers.

Leder, D. (1990). *The absent body*. Chicago, IL: The University of Chicago Press.

Lemert, C. (1997). *Social things: an introduction to the sociological life*. New York: Rowman & Littlefield.

Lemyre, F., Trudel, P., & Durand-Bush, N. (2007). How youth sport coaches learn to coach. *The Sport Psychologist, 21*, 191–209.

Leonard, D.C. (2002). *Learning theories: A to Z*. London: Greenwood Press.

Leskinen, E.A., Cortina, L.M., & Kabat, D.B. (2011). Gender harassment: broadening our understanding of sex-based harassment at work. *Law and Human Behavior, 35*, 25–39.

Light, R. (2006). Game sense: innovation or just good coaching? *Journal of Physical Education New Zealand, 39*, 8–20.

Light, R. (2008). Complex learning theory – its epistemology and its assumptions about learning: implications for physical education. *Journal of Teaching in Physical Education, 27*(1), 21–37.

Light, R.L., & Evans, J.R. (2010). The impact of game sense pedagogy on Australian rugby coaches' practice: a question of pedagogy. *Physical Education and Sport Pedagogy, 15*(2), 103–115.

Light, R., & Wallian, N. (2008). A constructivist approach to teaching swimming. *Quest, 60*(3), 387–404.

Light, R., Harvey, S., & Mouchet, A. (2014). Improving 'at-action' decision-making in team sports through a holistic coaching approach. *Sport, Education and Society, 19*(3), 258–275.

Locke, L.F. (1985). Research and the improvement of teaching: the professor as the problem. In G. Barrette, R. Feingold, R. Rees & M. Pieron (eds), *Myths, models and methods in sport pedagogy* (pp. 1–26). Champaign IL, Human Kinetics.

Loland, S. (2011). The normative aims of coaching. In A. Hardman & C.R. Jones (eds), *The ethics of sports coaching* (pp. 15–22). Abingdon: Routledge.

Lonsdale, C., Hodge, K., & Rose, E. (2009). Athlete burnout in elite sport: a self-determination perspective. *Journal of Sports Sciences, 27*(8), 785–795.

Lukes, S. (1974). *Power: a radical view*. London: Macmillan.

Lukes, S. (1993). Three distinctive views of power compared. In M. Hill (ed.), *The policy process: a reader* (pp. 50–58). London: Harvester Wheatsheaf.

Lundkvist, E., Gustafsson, H., Hjälm, S., & Hassmén, P. (2012). An interpretative phenomenological analysis of burnout and recovery in elite soccer coaches. *Qualitative Research in Sport, Exercise and Health, 4*(3), 400–419.

Lyle, J. (1999). The coaching process: an overview. In N. Cross & J. Lyle (eds), *The coaching process: principles and practice for sport* (pp. 3–24). Oxford: Butterworth-Heinemann.

Lyle, J. (2002). *Sports coaching concepts: a framework for coaches' behaviour.* Abingdon: Routledge.

Lyle, J. (2011). What is coaching and what is a coach? In I. Stafford (ed.), *Coaching children in sport* (pp. 5–16). Abingdon: Routledge.

Lyle, J., & Cushion, C. (2017). *Sports coaching concepts: a framework for coaches' behaviour* (2nd edn). Abingdon: Routledge.

Lynch, M., & Mallett, C. (2006). Becoming a successful high performance track and field coach. *Modern Athlete & Coach, 44*(2), 15–20.

Macdonald, D., & Tinning, R. (1995). Physical education teacher education and the trend to prolatarianization: a case study. *Journal of Teaching in Physical Education, 15*, 98–115.

Macdonald, D., Côté, J., Eys, M., & Deakin, J. (2011). The role of enjoyment and motivational climate in relation to the personal development of team sport athletes. *Kinesiology and Physical Education, 25*(1), 32–46.

MacIntyre, A.C. (1984). *After virtue.* London: Duckworth.

MacLean, J.C., & Chelladurai, P. (1995). Dimensions of coaching performance: development of a scale. *Journal of Sport Management, 9*(2), 194–207.

MacLean, M., & Pritchard, I. (2013). History for coaches. In R.L. Jones & K. Kingston (eds), *An introduction to sports coaching: connecting theory to practice* (2nd edn) (pp. 83–97). Abingdon: Routledge.

Mack, D.E. & Gammage, K.L. (1998). Attention to group factors: Coach considerations to building an effective team. *Avante, 4*(3), 118–129.

Mageau, G.A., & Vallerand, R.J. (2003). The coach–athlete relationship: a motivational model. *Journal of Sports Sciences, 21*, 883–904.

Mallett, C.J. (2007). Modelling the complexity of the coaching process: a commentary. *International Journal of Sports Science and Coaching, 2*(4), 419–421.

Mallett, C.J. (2010). Becoming a high-performance coach: pathways and communities. In J. Lyle & C. Cushion (eds), *Sports coaching: professionalism and practice* (pp. 119–134). Edinburgh: Churchill Livingstone.

Mallett, C.J., Rossi, T., Rynne, S., & Tinning, R. (2016). In pursuit of becoming a senior coach: the learning culture for Australian Football League coaches. *Physical Education and Sport Pedagogy, 21*, 24–39.

Mallett, C.J., Trudel, P., Lyle, J., & Rynne, S. (2009). Formal vs informal coach education. *International Journal of Sports Science and Coaching, 4*(3), 325–334.

Manza, J., Arum, R., & Haney, L. (2013). *The sociology project.* London: Pearson.

Marshall, K., & Mellon, M. (2011). Crowding out wisdom: the mechanisation of adult–child relationships. In L. Bondi, D. Carr, C. Clark & C. Clegg (eds), *Towards professional wisdom: practical deliberation in the people professions* (pp. 187–204). Farnham: Ashgate.

Maslach, C., & Jackson, S.E. (1981). The measurement of experienced burnout. *Journal of Occupational Behavior, 2*, 99–113.

Maslach, C., & Leiter, M.P. (2008). Early predictors of job burnout and engagement. *Journal of Applied Psychology, 93,* 498–512.

Maslach, C., & Schaufeli, W.B. (1993). Historical and conceptual development of burnout. In W.B. Schaufeli, C. Maslach & T. Marek (eds), *Professional burnout: recent developments in theory and research* (pp. 1–16). Washington, DC: Taylor & Francis.

Mathiesen, T. (1997). The viewer society: Michel Foucault's 'panopticon' revisited. *Theoretical Criminology, 1*(2), 215–234.

Matos, N., Winsley, R., & Williams, C. (2011). Prevalence of nonfunctional overreaching/overtraining in young English athletes. *Medicine and Science in Sport and Exercise, 43*(7), 1287–1294.

May, R. (1972). *Power and innocence.* New York: W.W. Norton

McAlinden, A. (2006). 'Setting 'em up': personal, familial and institutional grooming in the sexual abuse of children. *Social and Legal Studies, 15*(3), 339–362.

McCarthy, P.J., Jones, M.V., & Clark-Carter, D. (2008). Understanding enjoyment in youth sport: a developmental perspective. *Psychology of Sport and Exercise, 9,* 142–156.

McDonald, M.G., & Birrell, S. (1999). Reading sport critically: a methodology for interrogating power. *Sociology of Sport Journal, 16,* 283–300.

McGhee, M. (2009). Wisdom and virtue, or what do philosophers teach? In A. Kenkmann (ed.) *Teaching philosophy* (pp. 23–37). London: Continuum.

McGillivray, D., Fearn, R., & McIntosh, A. (2005). Caught up in and by the beautiful game. A case study of Scottish professional footballers. *Journal of Sport and Social Issues, 29,* 102–123.

McLean, K.N., & Mallett, C.J. (2012). What motivates the motivators? An examination of sports coaches. *Physical Education and Sport Pedagogy, 17*(1), 21–35.

McNamee, M. (2008). *Sport, virtues and vices: morality plays.* Abingdon: Routledge.

McNamee, M. (2011). Celebrating trust: virtues and rules in the ethical conduct of sports coaches. In A.R. Hardman & C. Jones (eds), *The ethics of sports coaching* (pp. 23–41). Abingdon: Routledge.

McPherson, L., Long, M., Nicholson, M., Cameron, N., Atkins, P., & Morris, M.E. (2017). Secrecy surrounding the physical abuse of child athletes in Australia. *Australian Social Work, 70*(1), 42–53.

McRobbie, A. (2002). Clubs to companies: Notes on the decline of political culture in speeded up creative worlds. *Cultural Studies, 16,* 516–531.

McWilliam, E., & Sachs, J. (2004). Towards the victimless school: power, professionalism and probity in teaching. *Educational Research for Policy and Practice, 3,* 17–30.

Mechikoff, R.A., & Estes, S. (1998). *A history and philosophy of sport and physical education: from ancient civilizations to the modern world.* London: McGraw-Hill.

Merriam, S.B., & Bierema, L.L. (2014). *Adult learning: bridging theory and practice.* San Francisco, CA: Jossey-Bass.

Mesquita, I., Isidro, S., & Rosado, A. (2010). Portuguese coaches' perceptions of and preferences for knowledge sources related to their professional background. *Journal of Sports Science Medicine, 9,* 480–489.

Messner, M.A. (2009). *It's all for the kids: gender, families, and youth sports.* Berkley, CA: University of California Press.

Midgley, M. (1996). *Utopias, dolphins and computers: Problems of philosophical plumbing.* Abingdon: Routledge.

Miller, A.L., & Nakazawa, A. (2015). Who safeguards the child in Japanese sports? In M. Lang & M. Hartill (eds), *Safeguarding, child protection and abuse in sport: international perspectives in research, policy and practice* (pp. 163–171). Abingdon: Routledge.

Mirsafian, H. (2016). Legal duties and legal liabilities of coaches toward athletes. *Physical Culture and Sport Studies and Research, 69*(1), 5–14.

Molnar, G., & Kelly, J. (2013). *Sport, exercise and social theory: an introduction.* Abingdon: Routledge.

Moran, D. (2000). *Introduction to phenomenology.* Abingdon: Routledge.

Morgan, K. (2008). Pedagogy for coaches. In R.L. Jones, M. Hughes & K. Kingston (eds), *An introduction to sports coaching: from science and theory to practice* (pp. 3–15). Abingdon: Routledge.

Mosston, M. (1966). *Teaching physical education.* Columbus, OH: Charles E. Merrill Publishing Co.

Mosston, M., & Ashworth, S. (2008). *Teaching physical education* (1st online ed.). Retrieved from www.spectrumofteachingstyles.org/pdfs/ebook/Teaching_Physical_Edu_1st_Online_old.pdf.

Nash, C., & Collins, D. (2006). Tacit knowledge in expert coaching: science or art? *Quest, 58,* 465–477.

Nash, C.S., & Sproule, J. (2009). Career development of expert coaches. *International Journal of Sports Sciences and Coaching, 4*(1), 121–138.

Nauright, J., & Parrish, C. (eds) (2012). *Sports around the world: history, culture and practice.* Santa Barbara, CA: ABC-CLIO.

Newmann, F.M. (1994). School-wide professional community: issues in restructuring schools. *Issues in Restructuring Schools,* 6, Spring. Retrieved from www.wcer.wisc.edu/archives/completed/cors/Issues_in_Restructuring_Schools/

Nicholls, J. (1984). Conceptions of ability and achievement motivation. In R. Ames & C. Ames (eds), *Research on motivation in education: student motivation* (pp. 39–73). New York: Academic Press.

Nicholls, J. (1989). *The competitive ethos and democratic education.* Cambridge, MA: Harvard University Press.

Norman, L. (2008). The UK coaching system is failing women coaches. *International Journal of Sports Science and Coaching, 3*(4), 447–464.

Norman, L. (2010). Feeling second best: elite women coaches' experiences. *Sociology of Sport Journal, 27*(1), 89–104.

Norman, L. (2011). Gendered homophobia in sport and coaching: Understanding the everyday experiences of lesbian coaches. *International Review for the Sociology of Sport, 47*(6), 705–723.

Norman, L. (2013). The challenges facing women coaches and the contributions they can make to the profession. *International Journal of Coaching Science*, 7(2), 3–23.

Ntoumanis, N. (2001). A self-determination approach to the understanding of motivation in physical education. *British Journal of Educational Psychology*, 71, 225–242.

Nyberg, D. (1981). *Power over power*. London: Cornell University Press.

Öhman, M., & Grundberg-Sandell, C. (2015). The pedagogical consequences of 'no touching' in physical education – the case of Sweden. In H. Piper (ed), *Touch in sports coaching and physical education: fear, risk and moral panic* (pp. 70–84). Abingdon: Routledge.

Oliver, J.L., & Lloyd, R.S. (2015). Physical training as a potential form of abuse. In M. Lang & M. Hartill (eds), *Safeguarding, child protection and abuse in sport: international perspectives in research, policy and practice* (pp. 163–171). Abingdon: Routledge.

Olusoga, P., Butt, J., Hays, K., & Maynard, I.W. (2009). Stress in elite sports coaching: identifying stressors. *Journal of Applied Sport Psychology*, 21(4), 442–459.

Olusoga, P., Butt, J., Maynard, I.W., & Hays, K. (2010). Stress and coping: a study of world class coaches. *Journal of Applied Sport Psychology*, 22(3), 274–293.

Olusoga, P., Maynard, I.W., Butt, J., & Hays, K. (2014). Coaching under pressure: mental skills training for sports coaches. *Sport & Exercise Psychology Review*, 10(3), 31–43.

Olusoga, P., Maynard, I.W., Hays, K., & Butt, J. (2012). Coaching under pressure: a study of successful British Olympic coaches. *Journal of Sports Sciences*, 30(3), 229–239.

Orlowski, J., Wicker, P., & Breuer, C. (2016). Determinants of labour migration of elite sport coaches. *European Journal of Sport Science*, 16(6), 711–718.

Ortiz, S.M. (2004). Leaving the private world of wives of professional athletes: a male sociologist's reflections. *Journal of Contemporary Ethnography*, 33(4), 466–487.

Ortiz, S.M. (2006). Using power: An exploration of control work in the sport marriage. *Sociological Perspectives*, 49(4), 527–557.

Owusu-Sekyere, F., & Gervis, M. (2014). Is creating mentally tough players a masquerade for emotional abuse? In D. Rhind & C. Brackenridge (eds), *Researching and enhancing athlete welfare* (pp. 44–48). London: Brunel University.

Parent, S., & Bannon, J. (2012). Sexual abuse in sport: what about boys? *Children and Youth Services Review*, 34, 354–359.

Park, R.J. (1994). A decade of the body: Researching and writing about the history of health fitness, exercise and sport, 1983–1993. *Journal of Sport History*, 21(1), 59–82.

Park, R.J. (2010). *Women, sport, society: further reflections, reaffirming Mary Wollstonecraft*. Abingdon: Routledge.

Park, R.J., & Vertinsky, P. (2013). *Women, sport and society: further reflections, reaffirming Mary Wollstonecraft*. Abingdon: Routledge.

Parker, P., Douglas, T.H., & Kram, K.E. (2008). Peer coaching: a relational process for accelerating career learning. *The Academy of Management Learning and Education, 7*(4), 487–503.

Partington, M., & Cushion, C.J. (2012). Performance during performance: using Goffman to understand the behaviours of elite youth football coaches during games. *Sports Coaching Review, 1*(2), 93–105.

Partington, N. (2016). Sports coaching and the law of negligence: implications for coaching practice. *Sports Coaching Review, 5*, 1–21.

Pearson, M., & Brady, B. (2013, 4 April). Rutgers coach fired after abusive video broadcast. *CNN*. Retrieved from http://edition.cnn.com/2013/04/03/sport/rutgers-video-attack/index.html.

Pensgaard, A.M., & Roberts, G.C. (2002). Elite athletes' experiences of the motivational climate: The coach matters. *Scandinavian Journal of Medicine & Science in Sports, 12*, 54–59.

Pfister, G., & Radtke, S. (2009). Sport, women and leadership: results of a project on executives in German sports organisations. *European Journal of Sport Science, 9*(4), 229–243.

Phillips, M. (2000). *From sidelines to centerfield: a history of sports coaching in Australia*. Sydney: University of New South Wales Press Ltd.

Pike, E., & Scott, A. (2014). Safeguarding, injuries and athlete choice. In M. Lang & M. Hartill (eds) *Safeguarding, child protection and abuse in sport: international perspectives on research, policy & practice* (pp. 172–180). Abingdon: Routledge.

Pike, E., & Scott, A. (2015). Safeguarding, injuries and athlete choice. In M. Lang & M. Hartill (eds), *Safeguarding, child protection and abuse in sport: international perspectives in research, policy and practice* (pp. 172–180). Abingdon: Routledge.

Pinheiro, C., Pimenta, N., Resende, R., & Malcolm, D. (2014). Gymnastics and child abuse: an analysis of former international Portuguese female artistic gymnasts. *Sport, Education and Society, 19*(4), 435–450.

Piper, H., & Stronach, I. (2008). *Don't touch! The educational story of a panic*. Abingdon: Routledge.

Piper, H., Duggan, J.R., & Rogers, S. (2013). Managerial discourse, child safeguarding, and the elimination of virtue from in loco parentis relationships: an example from music education. *Power and Education, 5*(3), 209–221.

Piper, H., Taylor, B., & Garratt, D. (2012). Sports coaching in risk society: no touch! No trust! *Sport, Education and Society, 17*, 331–345.

Potrac, P., & Jones, R.L. (2009). Power, conflict and co-operation: towards a micro-politics of coaching. *Quest, 61*, 223–236.

Potrac, P., & Marshall, P. (2011). Arlie Russell Hochschild: the managed heart, feeling rules and emotional labour: coaching as an emotional endeavour. In R.L. Jones, P. Potrac, C. Cushion & L.T. Ronglan (eds), *The sociology of sports coaching* (pp. 27–39). London: Routledge

Potrac, P., Gilbert, W., & Denison, J. (eds) (2013). *Routledge handbook of sports coaching*. Abingdon: Routledge.

Potrac, P., Jones, R.L., & Armour, K. (2002). 'It's all about getting respect': the coaching behaviours of an expert English soccer coach. *Sport, Education and Society, 7*(2), 183–202.

Potter, D. (2011). *The victor's crown: a history of ancient sport from Homer to Byzantium*. London: Quercus.

Purdy, L.G. (2006). *Coaching in the 'current': the climate of an elite men's rowing training programme* (unpublished doctoral thesis). University of Otago, New Zealand.

Purdy, L.G., & Glynn, C. (2008). *Coaching her way: women coaches reflect on their involvement in sport*. In A. MacPhail, M. O'Sullivan & D. Tannehill (eds), *Proceedings of the third Physical Activity and Youth Sport Forum: engaging young people in physical activity and sport*. University of Limerick, Ireland, 12–13 June.

Purdy, L.G., & Jones, R. (2011). Choppy waters: elite rowers' perceptions of coaching. *Sociology of Sport Journal, 28*(3), 329–346.

Purdy, L.G., & Jones, R.L. (2013). Changing personas and evolving identities: the contestation and re-negotiation of researcher roles in field work. *Sport, Education and Society, 18*(3), 292–310.

Purdy, L.G., & Potrac, P. (2014). Am I just not good enough? The creation, development and questioning of a high performance coaching identity. *Sport, Education and Society*. DOI: 10.1080/13573322.2014.941795.

Purdy, L.G., Kohe, G.Z., & Paulauskas, R. (2017). Coaches as sports workers: professional agency within the employment context of elite European basketball. *Sport, Education and Society*. http://dx.doi.org/10.1080/13573322.2017.1323201.

Purdy, L.G., Kohe, G.Z., & Paulauskas, R. (in review). Changing it up (again): Mid-season coach change and implications on elite basketball players' professional and career identities.

Purdy, L.G., Potrac, P., & Jones, R. (2008). Power, consent and resistance: an autoethnography of competitive rowing. *Sport, Education and Society, 13*(3), 319–336.

Rachlin, H. (1991). *Introduction to modern behaviourism* (3rd edn). New York: Freeman.

Reade, I., Rodgers, W., & Norman, L. (2009). The under-representation of women in coaching: a comparison of male and female Canadian coaches at low and high levels of coaching. *International Journal of Sports Science and Coaching, 4*(4), 505–520.

Reeve, J. (2009). Why teachers adopt a controlling motivating style toward students and how they can become more autonomy supportive. *Educational Psychologist, 44*, 159–175.

Reichert, E. (2006). Human rights: an examination of universalism and cultural relativism. *Journal of Comparative Social Welfare, 22*(1), 23–36.

Reid, P., & Harvey, S. (2014). We're delivering Game Sense … aren't we? *Sports Coaching Review, 3*(1), 80–92.

Rhind, D., & Jowett, S. (2010). Relationship maintenance strategies in the coach–athlete relationship: the development of the COMPASS model. *Journal of Applied Sport Psychology, 22*(1), 106–121.

Rhind, D., Jowett, S., & Yang, S. (2012). A comparison of athletes' perceptions of the coach– athlete relationship in team and individual sports. *Journal of Sport Behavior, 35*, 433–441.

Richards, N. (1992). *Humility*. Philadelphia, PA: Temple University Press.

Ritzer, G. (2016). *Introduction to sociology*. London: Sage.

Roberts, G.C. (1992). Motivation in sport and exercise: conceptual constraints and convergence. In G.C. Roberts (ed), *Motivation in sport and exercise* (pp. 3–29). Champaign, IL: Human Kinetics.

Roderick, M.J. (2006). *The work of professional football: A labour of love?* Abingdon: Routledge.

Roderick, M.J. (2012). An unpaid labor of love: professional footballers, family life and the problem of job relocation. *Journal of Sport and Social Issues, 36*(3), 317–338.

Ronglan, L.T. (2011). Social interaction in coaching. In R.L. Jones, P. Potrac, C. Cushion & L.T. Ronglan (eds), *The sociology of sports coaching* (pp. 151–165). Abingdon: Routledge.

Ronglan, L.T., & Aggerholm, K. (2014). 'Humour helps': elite sports coaching as a balancing act. *Sports Coaching Review, 3*(1), 33–45.

Ronglan, L.T., & Havang, Ø. (2011). Niklas Luhmann: coaching as communication. In R.L. Jones, P. Potrac, C. Cushion & L.T. Ronglan (eds), *A sociology of sports coaching* (pp. 79–93). Abingdon: Routledge.

Rose, N. (1989). Calculable minds and manageable individuals. *History of the Human Sciences, 1*(2), 179–200

Ryall, E. (2016). *Philosophy of sport: key questions*. London: Bloomsbury.

Ryan, R.M., & Deci, E.L. (2000). Intrinsic and extrinsic motivations: classic definitions and new directions. *Contemporary Educational Psychology, 25*, 54–67.

Ryan, R. M., & Deci, E. L. (2002). An overview of Self-determination Theory: an organismic-dialectical perspective. In E. L. Deci & R. M. Ryan (eds), *Handbook of self-determination research* (pp. 3–33). Rochester, NY: The University of Rochester Press.

Ryan, R.M., & Deci, E.L. (2007). Active human nature: self-determination theory and the promotion and maintenance of sport, exercise and health. In M.S. Hagger & N.L.D. Chatzisarantis (eds), *Intrinsic motivation and self-determination in exercise and sport* (pp. 1–19). Champaign, IL: Human Kinetics.

Ryan, S. (2016, 12 April). Illinois reaches settlements with Tim Beckman, former women's basketball players. *The Chicago Tribune*. Retrieved from www.chicagotribune.com/sports/college/ct-illinois-reaches-settlement-20160412-story.html.

Rylander, P. (2016). Coaches' bases of power and coaching effectiveness in team sports. *International Sport Coaching Journal, 3*(2), 128–144.

Rynne, S.B. (2008). The learning and mentoring of high performance coaches in Australian sport. *Coach, 24*(2), 76–79.

Rynne, S.B, Mallett, C., & Tinning, R. (2006). High performance sport coaching: institutes of sport as sites for learning. *International Journal of Sports Science and Coaching, 1*(3), 223–234.

Rynne, S.B., Mallett, C.J., & Tinning, R. (2010). Workplace learning of high performance sports coaches. *Sport Education and Society, 15*(3), 315–330.

Sandström, E., Linnér, L., & Stambulova, N.B. (2016). Career profiles of athlete–coach relationships: descriptions and interpretations. *International Journal of Sports Science & Coaching, 3*(3), 371–374.

Schempp, P., Manross, D., Tan, S., & Fincher, M. (1998). Subject expertise and teachers' knowledge. *Journal of Teaching in Physical Education, 17*, 342–356.

Schön, D.A. (1983). *The reflective practitioner: how professionals think in action.* New York: Basic Books.

Schrodt, B. (1981). Sports of the Byzantine Empire. *Journal of Sport History, 8*(3), 40–59.

Schuh, K.L., & Barab, S.A. (2007). Philosophical perspectives. In J.M. Spector, M.D. Merrill, J. van Merriënboer & M.P. Driscoll (eds), *Handbook of research on educational communications and technology* (pp. 67–84). (3rd edn). London: Taylor & Francis.

Schunk, D.H. (2004). *Learning theories: an educational perspective* (4th edn). Upper Saddle River, NJ: Pearson Prentice Hall.

Schunk, D.H. (2008). *Learning theories: an educational perspective* (5th edn). Harlow, Essex: Pearson.

Schunk, D.H. (2014). *Learning theories: An educational perspective* (6th edn). Harlow, Essex: Pearson.

Segas, M., Cunningham, G., & Pastore, D. (2006). Predicting head coaching intentions of male and female assistant coaches: an application of the theory of planned behaviour. *Sex Roles, 54*(9), 695–705.

Sennett, R.R. (1998). *The corrosion of character: the personal consequences of work in the new capitalism.* London: W.W. Norton.

Serpa, S. (1999). Relationship coach–athlete: outstanding trends in European research. *Journal of Human Performance Studies, 12*, 7–20.

Sherman, C., Crassini, B., Maschette, W., & Sands, R. (1997). Instructional sport psychology: a reconceptualisation of sports coaching as sports instruction. *International Journal of Sport Psychology, 28*(2), 103–125.

Sibson, R. (2010). I was banging my head against a brick wall: exclusionary power at the gendering of sport organizations. *Journal of Sport Management, 24*(4), 379–399.

Simon, R.L. (ed.) (2013). *The ethics of coaching sports: moral, social and legal issues.* Boulder, CO: Westview Press.

Sisley, B.L., Weiss, M.R., Barber, H., & Ebbeck, V. (1990). Developing competence and confidence in novice women coaches: a study of attitudes, motives, and perceptions of ability. *Journal of Physical Education, Recreation and Dance, 61*, 60–64.

Smith, R. (1986). Toward a cognitive-affective model of athletic burnout. *Journal of Sport Psychology, 8*, 36–50.

Smyth, J. (1991). *Teachers as collaborative learners*. Milton Keynes: Open University Press.

Snyder, E.E. (1991). Sociology of nostalgia: sports halls of fame and museums in America. *Sociology of Sport Journal, 8*(3), 228–238.

Spears, B. (1984). A perspective of the history of women's sport in Ancient Greece. *Journal of Sport History, 11*(2), 32–47.

sports coach UK (2011). *Sports coaching in the UK III: executive summary*. Retrieved from www.sportscoachuk.org/sites/default/files/Sports%20 Coaching%20in%20the%20UK%20III%20exc%20summ.pdf.

Stafford, A., Alexander, K., & Fry, D. (2015). Playing through pain: children and young people's experiences of physical aggression and violence in sport. *Child Abuse Review, 22*(4), 287–299.

Stafford, I. (2011). *Coaching children in sport*. Abingdon: Routledge.

Stambulova, N. (2010). Counseling athletes in career transitions: the five-step career planning strategy. *Journal of Sport Psychology in Action, 1,* 95–105.

Standage, M., Duda, J.L., & Ntoumanis, N. (2005). A test of self-determination theory in school physical education. *British Journal of Educational Psychology, 75*, 411–33.

Stebbings, J., & Taylor, I.M. (2017). Definitions and correlates of coach psychological well- and ill-being. In R. Thelwell, C. Harwook & I. Greenlees (eds), *The psychology of sports coaching: research and practice* (pp. 170–184). Abingdon: Routledge.

Stewart, B. (1989). The nature of sport under capitalism and its relationship to the capitalist labor process. *Sporting Traditions, 6*, 43–61.

Stirling, A.E. (2009). Definition and constituents of maltreatment in sport: establishing a conceptual framework for research practitioners. *British Journal of Sports Medicine, 43*(14), 1091–1099.

Stirling, A.E. (2013). Understanding the use of emotionally abusive coaching practices. *International Journal of Sport Science & Coaching, 8*(4), 625–639.

Stirling, A.E., & Kerr, G.A. (2008). Defining and categorizing emotional abuse in sport. *European Journal of Sport Science, 8*(4), 173–181.

Stirling, A.E., & Kerr, G.A. (2013). The perceived effects of elite athletes' experiences of emotional abuse in the coach–athlete relationship. *International Journal of Sport and Exercise Psychology, 11*, 1–14.

Strauss, A. (1962). Transformations of identity. In A.M. Rose (ed.), *Human behaviour and social processes: an interactionist approach* (pp. 63–85). London: Routledge; Kegan Paul.

Stringer K.J., & Kerpelman J.L. (2010). Career identity development in college students: decision making, parental support, and work experience. *Identity: An international Journal of Theory and Research, 10*, 181–200.

Telfer, J. (2010). Coaching practice and practice ethics. In J. Lyle & C. Cushion (eds), *Sports coaching: professionalization and practice* (pp. 209–220). Edinburgh: Churchill Livingstone Elsevier.

Tharp, R.G., & Gallimore, R. (1976). Basketball's John Wooden: what a coach can teach a teacher. *Psychology Today, 9*(8), 74–78.

The Canadian Press (2016, 25 October). Quebec minor hockey coach to sit out season for ordering push-ups after loss. *The Globe and Mail*. Retrieved from www.theglobeandmail.com/sports/hockey/quebec-minor-hockey-coach-to-sit-out-season-for-ordering-push-ups-after-loss/article32461580/.

Theberge, N. (1993). The construction of gender in sport: women, coaching and the naturalization of difference. *Social Problems, 40*(3), 301–313.

Thelwell, R.C., Weston, N.J.V., & Greenlees, I.A. (2010). Coping with stressors in elite sport: a coach perspective. *Journal of Sport Sciences, 26*, 905–918.

Theodosius, C. (2008). *Emotional labour in health care: the unmanaged heart of nursing*. London: Routledge.

Thomas, G. Morgan, K., & Mesquita, I. (2013). Examining the implementation of a Teaching Games for Understanding approach in junior rugby using a reflective practice design. *Sports Coaching Review, 2*(1), 49–60.

Thompson, A., Potrac, P., & Jones, R.L. (2015). 'I found out the hard way': micro-political workings in professional football. *Sport, Education and Society, 20*(8), 976–994.

Thorndike, E.L. (1932). *The fundamentals of learning*. Teachers College Bureau of Publications, New York: Columbia University.

Tinning, R., Kirk, D., & Evans, J. (1993). *Learning to teach physical education*. London: Prentice Hall.

Trudel, P., & Gilbert, W.D. (2006). Coaching and coach education. In D. Kirk, M. O'Sullivan & D. McDonald (eds), *Handbook of physical education* (pp. 516–539). London: SAGE.

Trudel, P., Gilbert, W., & Werthner, P. (2010). Coach education effectiveness. In J. Lyle, & C. Cushion (eds), *Sport coaching: professionalisation and practice* (pp. 135–152). London: Elsevier.

Tusting, K., & Barton, D. (2003a). *Models of adult learning: a literature review*. Leicester, UK: NIACE.

Tusting, K., & Barton, D. (2003b). *Research review: models of adult learning: a literature review*. Leicester, UK: NIACE. Retrieved from http://dera.ioe.ac.uk/22486/1/doc_2768.pdf.

Vallerand, R.J. (2007). Passion for sport in athletes. In S. Jowett & D. Lavallee (eds), *Social psychology in sport* (pp. 249–264). Champaign, IL: Human Kinetics.

Vallerand, R.J., & Rousseau, F.L. (2001). Intrinsic and extrinsic motivation in sport and exercise: a review using the hierarchical model of intrinsic and extrinsic motivation. In R.N. Singer, H.A. Hausenblas & C.M. Janelle (eds), *Handbook of Sport Psychology* (2nd edn) (pp. 389–416). New York: Wiley.

van Ours, J.C., & van Tuijl, M.A. (2016). In-season head-coach dismissals and the performance of professional football teams. *Economic Inquiry, 54*, 591–604.

Vanden Auweele, Y., Opdenacker, J., Vertommen, T., Boen, F., Van Niekerk, L., De Martelaer, K., & De Cuyper B. (2008). Unwanted sexual experiences in sport: perceptions and reported prevalence among

Flemish female student-athletes. *International Journal of Sport and Exercise Psychology, 6*, 354–365.

Vargas-Tonsing, T.M. (2007). Coaches' preferences for continuing coaching education. *International Journal of Sports Sciences and Coaching, 2*, 25–35.

Vinnai, G. (1976). *Football mania*. London: Ocean.

Wagstaff, C.R.D. (2017). *The organizational psychology of sport: key issues and practical applications*. Abingdon: Routledge.

Warburton, N. (2011). *A little history of philosophy*. New Haven, CT: Yale University Press.

Watkins, R. (1997). *Gladiators*. New York: Houghton Mifflin Company.

Wells, G. (1999). *Dialogic inquiry: towards a sociocultural practice and theory of education*. Cambridge: Cambridge University Press.

Welsh, S., Carr, J., MacQuarrie, B., & Huntley, A. (2006). 'I'm not thinking of it as sexual harassment': understanding harassment across race and citizenship. *Gender & Society, 20*, 87–107.

Wenger, E. (1998). *Communities of practice: learning, meaning and identity*. Cambridge: Cambridge University Press.

Wenger, E., McDermott, R.A., & Snyder, W. (2002). *Cultivating communities of practice: a guide to managing knowledge*. Cambridge, MA: Harvard University.

Werthner, P. (2005). Making the case: coaching as a viable career path for women. *Canadian Journal of Women in Coaching, 5*(3), 1–9.

Werthner, P., & Trudel, P. (2006). A new theoretical perspective for understanding how coaches learn to coach. *The Sport Psychologist, 20,* 198–212.

Wharton, L., & Rossi, T. (2015). How would you recognise an expert coach if you saw one? *International Journal of Sport Science and Coaching, 19*(2+3), 577–588.

Wiedemann, T. (1995). *Emperors and gladiators*. Abingdon: Routledge.

Wilensky, H.L. (1969). Work, careers and social integration. In T. Burns (ed), *Industrial man* (pp. 110–139). Middlesex: Penguin.

Willee, A. (1978). Directive and non-directive teaching methods. *Federation Internationale Education Physique Bulletin, 48*(4), 13–30.

Williams, J. (2014). *A contemporary history of women's sport, part one: Sporting women, 1850–1960*. Abingdon: Routledge.

Wiman, M., Salmoni, A.W., & Hall, C.R. (2010). An examination of the definition and development of expert coaching. *International Journal of Coaching Science, 4*(2), 37–60.

Wright, T., Trudel, P., & Culver, D. (2007). Learning how to coach: the different learning situations reported by youth ice hockey coaches. *Physical Education and Sport Pedagogy, 12*(2), 127–144.

Wright Mills, C.W. (1970). *The sociological imagination*. Harmondsworth: Penguin.

Yang, S.X., & Jowett, S. (2017). Understanding and enhancing coach–athlete relationships through the 3 + 1C model. In R. Thelwell, C. Harwood & I. Greenlees (eds), *The psychology of sports coaching: research and practice* (pp. 54–67). Abingdon: Routledge.

INDEX